"In her new book *Intentional Neuroplasticity*, Dr. Desautels captures the essential elements of Interpersonal Neurobiology and its application in the classroom and beyond. She presents a model of the human brain as a social organ of adaptation that becomes primed to learn and heal through empathy, attunement, and positive human interactions. Very much recommended!"

—**LOU COZOLINO, PH.D.**, Author of *The Social Neuroscience of Education* and *Attachment-Based Teaching*

"Dr. Desautels has interpreted vital learnings from decades of research in the neurobiology of trauma into friendly, engaging messages, and she shares an abundance of creative resources and ideas that are so relevant and so needed in classrooms today! This book is filled with real world stories, examples, and solutions *from* educators and *for* educators. The message is clear—to help soothe the unsettled nervous systems of my students, it starts with how I manage my nervous system. It begins with me!"

—**DR. JUDITH HOWARD**, Associate Professor in Trauma-Aware Education, Queensland University of Technology, Australia

"This book will undoubtedly transform the way in which you view the emotional state of our children in a school environment. The practical strategies provided in this book for how to support the emotional well-being of children are unparalleled. Lori Desautels beautifully distills our current understanding of neurobiology and provides teachers with the tools necessary to more compassionately engage with their students."

—**CHRISTINE M. CRAWFORD, MD, MPH**, Associate Medical Director, Research, Support and Education, National Alliance on Mental Illness (NAMI)

"Wow! Dr. Desautels digs deep into the impact of trauma-informed work throughout this whole book. From the thought-provoking graphics to applying the theory to practice, this is a paradigm-shifting book that all educators need to read. Every chapter connected how we as educators can utilize science to ensure that our students experience safe, stable, nurturing relationships and environments, which are the keys to successful classrooms and schools."

—**MATHEW PORTELL**, Founder of the Trauma Informed Educators Network

"In this day and age, where the ravages of trauma burn through our nervous systems and wreak havoc in our communities and schools, Dr. Lori Desautels offers a glimpse into a possibility of a different world—a world in which our nervous systems are regulated, and we can learn, heal, and grow together. By softening our bodies, sharing our stories, and letting the light come in, there is indeed much cause for hope. Many thanks to Dr. Desautels for this marvelous book that helps lead the way."

—**DR. ALBERT WONG**, Director of the Trauma Certificate Program, Somatopia

"This book is an absolute must-read for educators. It brilliantly ties in trauma responses, applied neuroscience, and connection into tangible strategies. Dr. Desautels brilliantly combines, not just the 'why' and the skills needed for educators, but also provides real easy-to-use strategies for any educator to start using immediately. One of the best books I've ever read that combines research of applied neuroscience with easy-to-use strategies."

—**NATHAN MAYNARD**, Best-Selling Author, Educational Leader, and Internationally-Leading Expert in Restorative Justice

"*Intentional Neuroplasticity* is a timely compendium that translates the neuroscience of psychological stress and trauma with accessible language and practical applications. Built on the framework of Adaptive Educational Neuroscience (AEN), Desautels spearheads a comprehensive and transdisciplinary approach to understanding and fostering relational connections among students, parents, educators, and administrators. This book transcends its audience and offers practical wisdom to address ruptured systems and souls in the movement towards collective healing and growth."

—**JULIET L. KING (ABD), ATR-BC, LPC, LMHC**, Associate Professor Art Therapy, The George Washington University; Adjunct Associate Professor Neurology, Indiana University School of Medicine

"This book has everything you need to go beyond trauma-informed and move to nervous system-responsive. The resources for educators to help stay regulated and to learn to co-regulate with students, rather than just manage behavior, are amazing. I have read dozens of books on trauma and the brain these last few years and this is definitely on my list of the top must reads."

—**JOE BRUMMER**, Author of *Building a Trauma-informed Restorative School: Skills and Approaches To Improve Culture and Behavior*

"I am blown away by the examples and evidence in *Intentional Neuroplasticity* of how nervous systems and physiological states impact behaviors. Dr. Desautels takes the complexity of the brain and applied neuroscience and makes it accessible for educators to truly help students. This book demonstrates that there is always more to behaviors than what we see at the surface and is a great resource for parents, educators, and beyond!"

—**BRAD WEINSTEIN**, Chief Innovation Officer, Behavior Flip,
Co-author of *Hacking School Discipline*

"Through this excellent book, Dr. Desautels offers thought-provoking questions and rich educator stories as an urgent invitation to move toward individual and collective awareness, growth, and most importantly transformation in our lives."

—**BROOKE KANDEL, PH.D.**, Dean and Professor, College of Education,
Butler University

"In powerful ways, Dr. Desautels links practice, research, and personal connections to support the unbridled potential in our educational systems. *Intentional Neuroplasticity* provides a wealth of tools, research, and personal experiences to support educators as they fine-tune their understanding of neuroscience behind connections, behaviors, and learning."

—**DR. CATHERINE HAGERMAN PANGAN**, Professor, College of Education,
Butler University

"Dr. Lori Desautels' previous book, *Connections Over Compliance*, is one of my favorites. The book addresses the roles of connection and neuroscience in the classroom. In her latest book, *Intentional Neuroplasticity*, Dr. Desautels proposes an approach to meet the challenges facing our schools and educators in these difficult times. Dr. Desautels suggests the idea of creating nests in our schools. Nests are safe emotional and physical environments for students and educators. As we learn in the book, brain and body safety are critical to success and prerequisites to learning. Dr. Desautels presents a roadmap to creating nests and helping students, teachers, and staff to thrive. The book provides clear strategies and tools to help build classroom nests, and help children feel safe, connected, and successful through meaningful connection and intentional neuroplasticity."

—**GUY STEPHENS**, Founder and Executive Director, Alliance Against Seclusion
and Restraint

"Lori has written an amazing book that is so relevant to the current issues we are dealing with in the classroom and in our schools today. I believe this book will serve as a valuable resource for educators to understand how to use the practical strategies and tools to create safe nurturing adult relationships that provide the outcomes we seek for all students."

—**JIM SPORLEDER**, National School Trauma Responsive Trainer, Principal (retired) Lincoln High School where the documentary "Paper Tigers" was filmed

"**A manual for empathic and trauma-informed teaching.** In her latest book, Desautels, an assistant professor in Indiana-based Butler University's College of Education, builds on her work in *Connections Over Compliance* (2020) to offer a framework to create an effective learning environment for students while also optimizing teachers' mental health. Drawing on applied educational neuroscience and polyvagal theory (which foregrounds the role of the vagus nerve on emotions and reactions to trauma), Desautels explains how to approach and maintain emotional regulation, help students achieve stability, and create a supportive environment that allows space for learning.

The book encourages teachers to coregulate with students, modeling such behaviors as deep breathing, taking breaks, and mindfulness, while also understanding that the methods they find most useful may not be the ones their students prefer. Desautels addresses the specific problems that the Covid-19 pandemic has brought to the learning experience but reminds readers that there's always been a need for welcoming approaches to teaching.

The book responds to common objections to coregulating practices, including claims that they coddle students or reward bad behavior. The book includes several 'Guest Reflections' by other teachers, which offer additional perspectives on trauma-informed teaching and provide concrete examples of implementing this book's highlighted techniques. Desautels acknowledges that her methods may require a fundamental shift in classroom management, but she persuasively presents the work as worthwhile. **A thoughtful look at addressing students' emotional needs in a classroom setting.**"

—*KIRKUS REVIEWS*

Intentional Neuroplasticity

Moving Our **NERVOUS SYSTEMS** and **EDUCATIONAL SYSTEM** Toward **POST-TRAUMATIC GROWTH**

Lori L. Desautels, Ph.D.

AUTHOR OF *Unwritten, Eyes Are Never Quiet* and *Connections Over Compliance*

Wyatt-MacKenzie Publishing

DEADWOOD, OREGON

Each chapter is paired with beautiful images —scan this QR code
to view and enjoy the art in vibrant color:

 Many charts and diagrams can also be downloaded;
watch for the QR code with download symbol.
(revelationsineducation.com/intentional-neuroplasticity)

PASSWORD: **BeIntentional**

Intentional Neuroplasticity

Moving Our Nervous Systems and Educational System
Toward Post-Traumatic Growth

Lori L. Desautels, Ph.D.

Cover illustration ©Regan Desautels
Chapter art ©Regan Desautels

ISBN: 978-1-954332-33-1
Library of Congress Control Number on file.

©2023 Lori L. Desautels, Ph.D. All rights reserved.

Edited by Alan K. Lipton
Additional illustrations provided by Wyatt Cleary.

Wyatt-MacKenzie Publishing
DEADWOOD, OREGON

Large quantity orders: wholesale@wyattmackenzie.com

Table of Contents

Foreword

A Paradigm Shift in Education

On September 21, 2019, I presented the keynote at the 2019 Educational Neuroscience Symposium at Butler University. The symposium was a highlight of an innovative program developed by Dr. Desautels to introduce neuroscience to educators. As a prelude to the symposia, Lori invited me to discuss Polyvagal Theory with her graduate students through an interactive zoom dialog. As a laboratory-oriented scientist, it was a challenge for me to translate concepts from the Polyvagal Theory into a language that mapped into the issues that educators faced in their classrooms. The discussion with her and her students introduced me to aspects of the unique portal she was developing to embed neuroscience into the training of her graduate students that would enrich and expand their perspective of the educational experience.

In retrospect, I have always been engaged in exploring the educational process. Of course, as a professor for more than five decades, teaching, mentorship, and lifelong learning have always been the focus of my personal experiences. However, my personal link with the educational process goes back to my childhood. My parents both had experiences as classroom teachers and my father later became a school administrator.

As my academic career developed, in 1985 I shifted institutions and moved from being a Professor of Psychology at the University of

Illinois Urbana-Champaign to a professor of human development at the University of Maryland College Park. Unlike my position at the University of Illinois, the department of human development at the University of Maryland was administratively within the College of Education and early childhood education resided within the department. Later at the University of Maryland, I would chair the department and direct the Institute for Child Study which contained the preschool.

Exposure to the teacher training curricula from the various departments within the college provided me with insight into how educators conceptualized the behavior of children. In general, behaviors of school-aged children were viewed as intentional and independent of age. The courses in the teacher training curricula treated child behavior as manipulatable through the traditional principles of learning such as rewards and punishments. Even in the realm of developmental disabilities, there was little acknowledgement of neurobiological contributions due to maturation or to the observed individual differences among students. For many faculty and their students, behavior modification procedures were the primary tools for managing atypical, less desirable, or disruptive behaviors. I quickly realized that the educational curricula within the entire College had a strong behavioral orientation, virtually devoid of an understanding of potential biological contributions to variations in behavior especially behaviors that disrupt classroom activity, which have often become pathologized (e.g., ADD, oppositional).

As I developed my courses, I distilled a modest goal of embedding two biologically based principles into teacher training curricula. First, I realized that although children were the target populations for teachers, teacher training did not provide a strong foundation for understanding the maturational trajectories of the brain and nervous system. Since the status of the brain and nervous system are important neuroanatomical foundations for learning, then an understanding of these structures, their relation to learning and behavior, and their developmental trajectory should be important to teachers and should influence teaching strategy and content. Second, there seemed to be a lack of interest in individual differences especially in terms of behavioral state regulation. Both these important biological variations were masked with assessments of productivity usually indexed by relatively simple outcome metrics of vocabulary, memorization of facts, and math skills.

As a department chair within a college of education, I approached this void by attempting to hire faculty with strong biological orientations and an interest in the nervous system. Although I was able to hire strong faculty in the cognitive sciences, I was not successful in recruiting faculty who were committed to a new educational neuroscience, an area that is successfully being pioneered by Dr. Desautels and highlighted by the current volume, *Intentional Neuroplasticity*.

While I was a faculty member in a college of education, there were several faculty members across departments who had an interest in how the nervous system's contribution to child behavior could be leveraged in developing educational strategies. However, their interests were not supported by their academic background or passion to develop a program through the lens of a classroom teacher. Lori is a personification of this vision, which ironically, while being firmly based on science, leads to the treatment of students and their parents as well as teachers and staff with greater compassion. Lori would have been the dream candidate for the program I had envisioned. Not only does she understand neuroscience principles, but by having a classroom teacher perspective, she can, as she has done in this volume, effectively communicate with educators. Without a colleague like Lori, my interests in the neurobiology of development and developmental disabilities motivated me to move in 2001 to the University Illinois College of Medicine where I created and directed the Brain-Body Center in the Department of Psychiatry.

We learn from Lori's work that the principles of neuroscience and especially the Polyvagal Theory fit our intuitions and explain the "gut" and "heartfelt" feelings that we as well as our students, colleagues, friends, and family have. By appreciating the nervous system as a dynamically adjusting platform of behaviors and feelings, we treat students as living organisms with an instinctual motivation to survive and to seek safety. Once we see this vision, our responsibilities shift to finding effective portals of engagement and connectedness that will calm the nervous system and mitigate defensive physiological states that become behaviorally expressed as aggression, opposition, anxiety, and even social withdrawal and depression.

My experiences within a college of education taught me specific lessons. Initially, I was informed about the differences in the objectives and missions between colleges of education and colleges of liberal arts and sciences. Colleges of education are professional schools with a focused agenda of producing classroom teachers (i.e., K-12). In contrast, colleges of liberal arts and sciences are focused on the accumulation of knowledge within a discipline. Graduation from these schools result in different and contrasting products. For example, the teaching objectives and strategies are quite different for a college professor within an arts and sciences department when compared to an elementary school teacher. The professor's primary teaching role is that of mentorship to a few select graduate students, who are being motivated to be passionately driven by their curiosity to discover new information that optimistically will lead to them becoming independent scholars. Many will continue their scholarship post-graduation and become professors themselves replicating the process with their graduate students. In contrast, the K-12 schoolteacher has a set of goals for the students and needs to be trained to deliver and evaluate a relatively fixed curriculum.

In 2019 when Lori invited me to participate in the Educational Neuroscience Symposium at Butler University, I was intrigued with the concept of moving neuroscience into the training of educators. However, based on my own experiences, I was cautious about the outcome of such a program. One of the lessons I learned was that coming from the classroom is helpful in developing and implementing teacher education. When I was a faculty member in a college of education, there was internal pressure from the Dean's office to hire faculty who had experience teaching K-12. Being a laboratory-focused scientist, I did not agree with this bias. However, as I have watched Lori's presentations and read *Intentional Neuroplasticity,* I now have a better appreciation of the importance of the teacher's viewpoint in integrating a Polyvagal-informed or a more general neuroscience perspective that can enhance the educational process and may seamlessly be integrated into educational systems.

When I talked at the 2019 Educational Neuroscience Symposium, I boldly challenged the attendees by asking two questions:

1. How would your classroom experience be if there were no behavioral state regulation difficulties in your classroom?

2. How much of your training was dedicated to understanding and developing techniques to mitigate behavioral state regulation problems?

The answers to these questions were obvious to the attendees. If behavioral state regulation difficulties were not a problem, then students would more efficiently and effectively learn. The classroom experiences for students would change, if there were an appreciation that their behaviors were not solely determined by intention. A neuroscience-informed educational model incorporates the profound and potent role that the physiological state has in mediating behavior. It also highlights the portals through which the physiological state can be monitored such as voice, facial expression, posture, and muscle tone. Teachers will learn that not only do their students broadcast whether their physiological states are calm and welcoming or reacting to threat, but that they themselves are part of the communication loop; either co-regulating and calming or disrupting and triggering physiological threat reactions that are broadcast as fear or anger and felt in our bodies. The products of this paradigm shift would lead to the defensive behaviors expressed in the classroom being managed in a more Polyvagal-informed and compassionate manner. The results would provide opportunities for children to benefit from being in a calmer physiological state that would support sociality, learning, enjoyment, and even physical health.

Intentional Neuroplasticity is packed with accessible information to answer these questions and to change classroom teaching. Through the work of Dr. Desautels, educators now have information to understand the potent role of the physiological state in mediating the behaviors of their students, colleagues, and themselves. This knowledge can shift the paradigm in education and lead to schools becoming more effective, welcoming, and enjoyable.

STEPHEN W. PORGES, PhD
Distinguished University Scientist
Founding Director, Traumatic Stress Research Consortium
Kinsey Institute
Indiana University Bloomington
Professor of Psychiatry, University of North Carolina at Chapel Hill

Prologue

When I was little, I was always observing and intensely curious about how people interacted with each other by moving through so many emotional states each day. I wondered how human beings could physically, emotionally, or verbally hurt one another, and yet hours, days, or weeks later, or within other relationships, feel a sense of compassion and collaboration with such steadfast loyalty. I also wondered how I could feel such strong anger or jealousy toward my closest friends one day, and then the next day, laugh, hug, and plan secret adventures with these same friends. Why can't some people rejoice when wonderful things happen for their friends or families? Why do we sometimes feel such resentment for those we care about? Why is there "felt" divisiveness and competition between people, among communities, and inside schools, districts, and organizations? What drives people to feel such strong, blistering anger toward someone and then deeply feel a sense of safety and connection with someone else?

At age ten, I did not know or understand that the human nervous system is not only neurologically wired to survive and protect, but also that human beings are neurologically wired for connection, prioritizing attachment above everything else. Without attachment, we cannot survive. We not only need one another, we also begin to restore and heal from embodied emotional pain when we feel seen and heard, metabolizing the challenging and traumatic experiences that can keep us locked into survival nervous system states of fight, flight, and shutdown. The physiology of the brain is impacted by trauma, but the physiology of relational connection can mitigate the felt brokenness and disconnect from our earlier or ongoing adversities and trauma. We are creatures of attachment, and our endorphins (our internal opiate chemicals) facilitate attachment.

This book explores the plasticity of our individual and collective nervous systems, and how our sensations, feelings, thoughts, perceptions, and behaviors can change structurally and functionally through our internal, environmental, and relational experiences with others. Just as our bodies digest the food we eat, they digest our lived experiences, too. Intergenerational trauma can be explained by how our families receive and digest past generational embodied experiences. Our perceptions of what feels threatening or unsafe might have evolved from a highly sensitized and activated nervous system, and that reactive state can eventually become our new normal. This sensitized nervous system developed during states of protection that continuously detect cues of threat from the environment and from the people around us—cues based upon past experiences and relationships. Ordinary moments can begin to feel unsafe and threatening if we become triggered or activated by fragments of experiences that remind us of those terrifying times, or by the accumulation of adversities that leave us feeling disconnected from the chronic unpredictability.

These pages are filled with stories, questions, applied research, and practices that have been germinating in my mind and heart for a lifetime, but this book has manifested in this time because of the brilliant and courageous educators and students whom I have had the privilege to sit beside and learn from each day as we move through the challenges and shifts that our schools, families, and communities have recently encountered and are encountering yet again as another school year is born. I am learning that growth and healing occur in the present time. We are learning how trauma impacts the developing brain and body as we now address how connection, resiliency, and growth are significant players in our healing and wholeness. Post-traumatic growth is present-time work.

Introduction

Paradigm shifts do not happen overnight, but they can
slowly and intentionally kindle a spark of hope when
individuals reach out to one another, planting seeds of
possibility through acts of kindness and grace.
It has always been this way, as our capacity for love is far
greater than the appendages of fear.
I am always curious about the plasticity
of my own nervous system.
Acknowledging the state of my nervous system
creates a starting point as I become aware of the
sensations of unrest, anxious wavering,
winds of panic, or worries that swirl like dried brown
leaves, blowing around my feet on a cold afternoon.

Introduction to Intentional Neuroplasticity

"You had the power all along, my dear."
L. FRANK BAUM (THE WONDERFUL WIZARD OF OZ)

This book has been growing in my mind and heart throughout my life. As a young girl, I thought about all the ingredients (or experiences) that shift, sort, flow, become stuck, grow, wither away, and germinate to create the "me" that I am always becoming. Throughout my personal and professional life as a teacher, counselor, college professor, mom, and all roles that I have been honored to hold, I've noticed moments of streamlined thoughts and encouraging feelings that serve me well throughout a day; and then suddenly, there is a shift. I unconsciously revert to older practiced thoughts and feelings that are automatically activated, in a surge of negative emotion. I find myself protecting and defending through my survival responses that rupture what was a former flow of pleasant and calming experiences. When this rupture occurs, negatively impacting moments, days, or longer periods of time, I am learning about the gift of awareness and the ability of my body and brain to refocus and begin again. It is so difficult. Reflecting on these embodied moments, it feels as if my brain has been constantly adjusting or changing to adapt to these constantly moving parts and conditions in ways that I often wasn't consciously aware of, but that I accepted anyway as I moved through challenging or joy-filled times. I remember the curiosity, apprehension, worry, or an overflowing sensation of anxiety when sensory experiences felt too much and too fast for my nervous system to process!

As I write these opening words, I am plagued by the felt enormity of our nation's challenges and the present systemic conditions and inequities that are fueling such pain, hurt, racism, poverty, and violence in a world that feels to be in a persistent state of alarm. I hesitate, remembering that these huge communal swings begin with the individual—with me. Paradigm shifts do not happen overnight, but they can slowly and intentionally kindle a spark of hope when individuals reach out to one another, planting seeds of possibility through acts of kindness and grace. Paradigm shifts begin with questions. Questions move us into broader and novel spaces where we begin to think about options that elude us when we are focused on the challenges and perceived problems. Questions are capable of installing emotional and nurturing resources that we were not aware of before a challenging time or crisis. This book is filled with questions that I hope will begin to tap into the agency we uphold while supporting our strengths and imaginations. Although we are wired with a negative brain bias, our capacity for love is far greater than the appendages of fear and negativity. I am always curious about the plasticity of my own nervous system. Acknowledging the state of my nervous system creates a starting point as I become aware of the sensations of unrest, anxious wavering, winds of panic, or worries that swirl like dried brown leaves, blowing around my feet on a cold afternoon.

Through our losses, celebrations, hardships, anxieties, worries, joys, and all lived experiences, our brains are in a lifelong process of change. At birth and even in utero, our brains are continually organizing, disorganizing, and reorganizing as they adapt to our external and internal worlds.[1] We inherit the nervous systems of our mothers, and generational trauma can pounce upon us before we take our first breath.

In 2021-22, the educational system is deeply experiencing the effects from a third academic year moving through a pandemic. Educators are working with children and youth who are carrying their unrest, fatigue, and mental and emotional exhaustion into classrooms and schools. The educator fatigue and burnout is palpable. Once again, I return to consider the plasticity of my own nervous system. While I am unable to control the thoughts, feelings, and behaviors of others, there is always plasticity in my responses.

I am keenly aware that **neuroplasticity** can be the latest and greatest buzzword for advertisements, motivational speakers, businesses, and even educationalists. However, neuroplasticity is not the latest cure or fix or strategy. It is the complex reorganization of the nervous system from the lowest levels of molecular activity to the breadth and depth of the entire brain and body connection as it interacts with the world around us.[2] I have never understood how educational practitioners are not deeply informed and encouraged to share this dynamic, miraculous superpower of human potentiality with children and youth in our schools. When children understand why they feel the way they do, or how feelings and thoughts impact their mood, motivation, and engagement, we empower and relieve these young nervous systems, preparing our children for a lifetime of possibility through the knowledge of brain and body architecture and plasticity. Just as trauma and adversity form painful implicit memories, experiences of warm, nurturing, safe relationships can provide a foundation of flourishing neural networks each time we revisit and experience our connections with others. These connections buffer and protect the felt adversity and trauma while planting seeds of developmental growth and possibility. The more we reach out to others who provide us with a sense of felt safety, the more we activate and strengthen these neural networks in our brains.

Psychiatrist and author Dr. Norman Doidge defines neuroplasticity in this way: "Neuroplasticity is the property of the brain that enables it to change its own structure and functioning in response to activity and mental experience."[3] Neuroscientist Eric Kandel also demonstrated how all learning can turn on genes that change neural structure, while hundreds of studies followed demonstrating that mental activity is not only the product of the brain, but also the shaper of it.[4] We are learning that the brain is *not* where all the action resides! Our brains evolved millions of years after our bodies, and our brain and body are in constant communication, adapting to one another. Like the brain, the body contains neurons: our gut alone holds approximately 100 million neurons.[5] It is through the deep, fluid conversations between our bodies and brains that healing, resiliency, and growth can occur. This is the neuroplasticity of our nervous systems. Working together, our brains and bodies become partners in growth and healing. Indeed, the word "heal" comes from the Old English *haelan*, meaning "to make whole."[6]

Dr. Lara Boyd, a neuroscientist from the University of British Columbia, writes her definition of neuroplasticity. "Neuroplasticity is supported by chemical, structural, and functional changes in the brain, and these are happening across the whole brain. They can occur in isolation from one another, but most often they take place in concert. Together they support learning. And they're taking place all the time."[7] How does this occur? Learning something new causes the brain to develop connections between brain cells, called neurons. With added connections, the neurons can send and receive more messages. These connections help to strengthen the regions that we are activating, and the brain responds more readily. With practice, we become more efficient or skilled, whether we are learning a new behavior, playing a sport, learning academic content, or acquiring a different feeling, thought, perception, or belief.

Just 50 years ago, the idea that the adult brain could change was heretical. Researchers accepted that the young infant brain is malleable, but believed that it gradually hardens, becoming fixed and static, and that by five or six years of age, we are who we are forever.[8] Today we are learning how wrong the early research was. Our nervous systems evolved to change, enabling us to adapt to the environment and new experiences, based on past experiences. Neuroplasticity is an intrinsic and fundamental property of all nervous systems.[9]

In our schools, the focus has traditionally explored the behaviors of students as the fixed target of focus and change. We are currently exploring and paying attention to the plasticity of the brain and nervous system, while learning how adversity and trauma impact the developing nervous system to affect behaviors and the way we approach discipline and engagement. In the western parts of the world, we tend to be cognitive heavy; we think, reason, talk, lecture, and problem solve with words and logistics. Also, much like older, outdated medical models that fail to enlist the intelligence of the whole patient in his or her own care, schools unintentionally delete the intelligence of our bodies, which hold and carry the sensations, feelings, and patterns of perceptions that impact our behaviors and overall well-being. Hippocrates saw the body as the foundation of healing, with the expectation that physicians and patients would collaborate to help the body activate its own healing.[10] With the growing body of research in relational and affective neuroscience, our schools can benefit and serve the *whole* student as we prioritize the nervous system by addressing the embodied experiences, generational and historical trauma, and the stories they hold. Our bodies "keep the score" by holding onto adversities and trauma we have encountered, and our minds sometimes hide the score of those adversities and trauma.[11]

This book is about growth through exploring mindsets, practices, and perspectives that cultivate and lean into radical well-being. This book embraces the framework of Applied Educational Neuroscience, which addresses the brain and nervous system development through an educator's lens as we explore these four pillars: educator brain and body state, attachment/touch points, co-regulation, and teaching students and staff about their own neuroanatomy and nervous systems. These four pillars support a relational and nervous system-aligned discipline lens that addresses behaviors originating from nervous system function, the restorative power of relationships, and how our experiences begin to shape our sensations, feelings, and thoughts. As one young student said, "So I am not a bad kid? My brain is protecting me when I feel angry?"

I am a teacher, not a neuroscientist, yet I know that the translations and applications from the affective, developmental, social, and relational neuroscience research are critical to educational practitioners now more than ever. We are moving through a third pandemic school year with emotional and social challenges adding to the existing individual and community adversities that are challenging the emotional and mental health of our youth. No one could have been prepared for the felt emotional and social losses, challenging behaviors, and dysregulation that are impacting the well-being of our students during the past few years. Our collective nervous systems feel the tension and unrest. In some ways, maybe COVID-19 has kicked us off the pathway of least resistance, forcing us to jump off the hamster wheel and examine where we have been and what needs to change. Questioning and wondering may feel unfamiliar and therefore uncomfortable to our nervous systems.

Every class, assignment, relationship, environment, and experience that people encounter shapes the human brain and nervous system. Understanding how the brain processes sensory information into social, emotional, and cognitive learning allows us to teach for *transfer,* and this is a long-term goal for schools, organizations, and the overall well-being of our children and youth. Our brains and nervous systems build an internal model of the outside world. Why? We create our models or internal maps of our experiences so that we can make predictions to help keep us safe and connected to one another. Predictions help us survive and prepare for what comes next. Our brains prioritize safety. How we learn to sense, feel, behave, and live is predicated upon what we have already learned and experienced. Lived experiences are a part of our generational history and assist us in forming our perceptions, patterns of feelings, thoughts, and belief systems. We unconsciously associate personal meanings to the patterns of our lived experiences, and these can become the roadways (neural recipes) for how we live life! The more we activate and travel these nervous system roadways, the stronger and more efficient they become. We call these our habits. They become easily accessible but difficult to change.

- Is the anger that once served our survival still serving survival or a shift towards growth?
- Is the worry and anxiety that once served our survival still serving our survival or a shift toward growth?
- If we spend time feeling gratitude each day, can we begin to reframe difficult or challenging experiences?

If we practice any thought, feeling, perception, behavior, or skill with patterned repetition, these thoughts, feelings, perceptions, and skills create neural roadways in our brains that are easily available and fast! The neurons that fire together wire together, strengthening circuits (roadways) in the brain. We can also weaken connections between neurons, because neurons that fire apart wire apart. This can occur when we intentionally become aware of the habits we desire to lessen or diminish, whether these habits are thoughts, feelings, perceptions, or behaviors.

Throughout this book, we will explore practices that provide opportunities to build and grow resilience. Resilience is both a process and an outcome. We will focus on the process of resilience, as it involves engaging in behaviors and thoughts that support our well-being. This shift will impact the way we feel and how we sense our world as we move through difficult times. Resilience is about awareness and acknowledging the states of our ever-changing nervous systems. Maybe the outcome of resilience is increased awareness?

I cannot think of anything more critical to explore and communicate to our youth than the plasticity of our nervous system. Our brains and bodies are dynamic, in constant communication, and responsive to change in all moments. Our nervous systems know the way home, finding us a safe and balanced state—if we are listening. In other words, when we tap into how our bodies are experiencing a condition, relationship, event, conversation, place, smell, sound, or any piece of sensory information, this recognition of our state function can be an emotional buffer or protective factor for our psychological well-being.

Why is this important, especially now?

During the pandemic, we felt and maybe are still feeling the heaviness of the lived experiences from chronic unpredictability, isolation, and overwhelming emotions in this unprecedented time for educators, parents, and students in our schools and communities. Childhood anxiety has reached an all-time high, as many students during the past few years lost the emotional protection and safety that schools often provide. These emotional protective factors can help guard against mental illness, and include but are not limited to athletics, social gatherings, graduations, after-school programs, and many forms of connection within the school community. Families struggled with the complexities of online learning, even as parents and caregivers struggled with getting to work, the challenges of childcare, and the stress of planning for a now-uncertain future. Anxiety rates in children and teens have skyrocketed, as emergency room visits for pediatric mental health concerns rose by over 70%.[12]

More than six million children in the U.S. have a diagnosis of anxiety or depression, according to the most recent data by the Centers for Disease Control and Prevention. Suicide is now the second leading cause of death among 15- to 19-year-olds, the agency said. During the first pandemic year, mental health insurance claims for teens approximately doubled by spring, as did self-harm and substance abuse claims. During March 2020, overdose claims for teens jumped 119%. From February to March 2021, emergency room visits related to suicide attempts by teens rose by 31%, compared with February 2019. Younger children have suffered as well. Some 29% of parents of kids between ages 5 and 12 reported mental and behavioral problems among their children due to the pandemic, according to a report by the Kaiser Family Foundation.[13]

So here we are! This book is a disrupter to the "what is" with a focus on "now what."

As I have shared, there are varied definitions of neuroplasticity, and this term can become a catch-all, greatly misunderstand and inaccurately generalized. We will be exploring neuroplasticity through an educational and parenting lens, contrasting the differences between intentional neuroplasticity and neuroplasticity by default. We will explore the connections to post-traumatic growth through the Polyvagal Theory as our nervous systems impact our social, emotional, and physiological health.

As someone who is working within the field of education, or sitting beside children and youth in a caregiving, teaching, or mentoring capacity, you may be wondering how this content will apply to and enrich your classroom, school, organization, practice, or community presence, leadership, or parenting. Human beings are built to wobble but not break! We have degrees of control over our own nervous system engineering through our awareness of thoughts, feelings, perceptions, and behavior. Like Dorothy from *The Wizard of Oz*, we hold a power of transformation that we may not recognize as our own. I want our children and youth to know their power, their strong unique voice, to celebrate their authenticity and identity, because in the developing years, experiences are sticky. The brain is experience-dependent, and the plasticity of the nervous system is much greater in early childhood and throughout young adulthood.

In our fast-paced and reactive world, feeling stressed or out of sorts can often cause us to activate autopilot inside our thoughts and behaviors. We ourselves become reactive instead of proactive, responding with behaviors and ways of thinking that only increase our tightness, tension, and urge to protect ourselves. Awareness of where we are in our nervous system can move us from protection toward growth. When our children and youth experience our autonomic recognition and observe us caring for ourselves, this produces a co-regulatory moment and starting point. Growth is not linear. It may be sporadic, circular, zigzag, or all the above. As we become aware of the power and magnificence of our own nervous systems, judgment and labels begin to fall away.

Resilience is also defined as the ability to flexibly adapt to challenging life experiences.[14] Resilience is not something you have or will never have; rather, it is a set of practices that can be explored, questioned, and learned. Resilience is not about optimism. It is the awareness and focused attention on our capacity to grow through challenges. Just as the phoenix rises from the ashes, we have the capacity to rise again.[15]

Intentional Plasticity: A Personal Story

Every morning for the past several months, between 6:30 and 6:45 a.m., I hear the comforting "ding" of a text message arriving on my phone. Opening the message, I see images of sunrises from the South Florida beaches as the waves wash ashore bringing in a fresh new day. Some mornings these images show storms brewing in the Atlantic Ocean, rapidly approaching the quiet and empty beachline, but the images are about so much more than a sunrise. They signal a young man cultivating an *incremental change* in his life through intention and awareness! Our oldest son has struggled with anxiety and depression through his early, adolescent, and young adult years. His reactions to life experiences have traditionally been to retreat, avoid conflict, shut down, and shrink away, hoping the carried shame becomes invisible. Then, a few months ago, he developed a routine and ritual of walking four to five miles to the beach and back home, seven days a week, hoping this routine would set the day ahead and, at some point, ease some of the angst, worry, and anxiety that plague his brain and body when he awakens each morning. As I write these words, I am still amazed that, 157 days later, there is a visceral intentional advocacy bubbling from within Andrew. He is learning how to listen to his nervous system even with initial resistance, and this has become a predictable and comforting part of his daily emotional hygiene. For many, this may seem like an ordinary habit, but through the context of our son's lived experiences and history, this rhythmic sensory ritual has become the bedrock of transformation as his brain and body, in all their complexity, are integrating this inherent capacity to self-organize.

As we will explore in the following chapters, intentional plasticity occurs when we feel supported, seen, and felt by another. We are social individuals, and attachment is the carrier of our development. Ultimately the changes are ours to create, but as we explore cultures of awareness that drive elevated emotions and clear intentions, we need one another. It is through intentionality and the emotional support of others that, much like the neuronal synapses occurring in our brains (those tiny connections through which neurons communicate and which can change through experience), the social synapses between people are able to call forth what we see in one another, as the nervous system is social and has the miraculous ability to adapt and change in all moments.

"There's not a human being in this world who does not settle down a bit when they've been heard, seen, and felt! This is discipline. This develops the purpose our children and youth desire ... but can't see or feel ... just yet!"
LORI DESAUTELS

Awareness

Awareness is a cortex function allowing us to think, evaluate, reason, regulate, wonder, and become curious while we pay attention to our past patterns of survival, and also to those patterns of thought, feeling, or behavior that served us well whenever we leaned into resiliency. As I thought about resiliency during the past few years, I came up with the image and passage below to show how developing an inner knowing and trust can guide us, and even transform our entry into new ways of being through our future, ever-changing, lived experiences.

Meet "***Awareness***"

Awareness is with all of us in all moments but sometimes we become so busy "doing" that we do not see ***Awareness***!

When we are born, ***Awareness*** is born, but it takes a little while for us to know this as we begin developing a relationship.

Awareness opens our *eyes, hearts,* and *minds* and sometimes this hurts! ***Awareness*** makes their home with us, but we often miss the opportunity to befriend them. ***Awareness*** is always with us but to befriend ***Awareness*** we must explore with them and always learn. We will learn to trust Awareness and lean into their sensations and feelings, but this is a journey!

Without ***Awareness*** we cannot feel and sense all the experiences around us!

Without ***Awareness*** we cannot feel with others!

Without ***Awareness*** we can become close-minded, divisive, and hurtful!

Without ***Awareness*** we cannot learn deeply about our passions, strengths, pains, and purpose!

BUT ... with **Awareness** , we can feel our hearts beat, our long deep breaths, wet tears, our warm laughter, and all of the sensations that can lead us into the seas of calm as we join up with others who are still wondering and wandering without **Awareness** .

Awareness never leaves us, although we sometimes try to live without **Awareness** !

With **Awareness** we can sense safety and danger!

With **Awareness** we can sense all of our sensations, move-ments, thoughts, breaths, and those around us. Sometimes we know when others have lost **Awareness** , but we know **Awareness** is there for all, it is just that others have not called out, held them tightly, and listened to the soft whispers of their **Awareness** .

Sometimess **Awareness** is bold. Sometimes **Awareness** needs to be jostled awake. Sometimes as we grow older, we unintentionally push **Awareness** away and they become buried in all our "doing" in life. Sometimes we need other people or experiences to help awaken **Awareness** .

BUT...**Awareness** can lead us into new paths, new journeys and new discoveries! **Awareness** loves the present moment! **Awareness** knows that the present moment is magical and can give us the gift of a shift in perception and so much more...

"Our bodies are the social and emotional organs that we often attribute to the brain."
AMANDA BLAKE

Chapter 1

Our nervous systems are as unique as thumbprints. Each of us carries around an individualized backpack that holds our distinctive maps of the world. Those maps have been unconsciously created to help us interpret and survive, as we are constantly detecting the "temperature" of a safe or threatening environment, relationship, or experience.

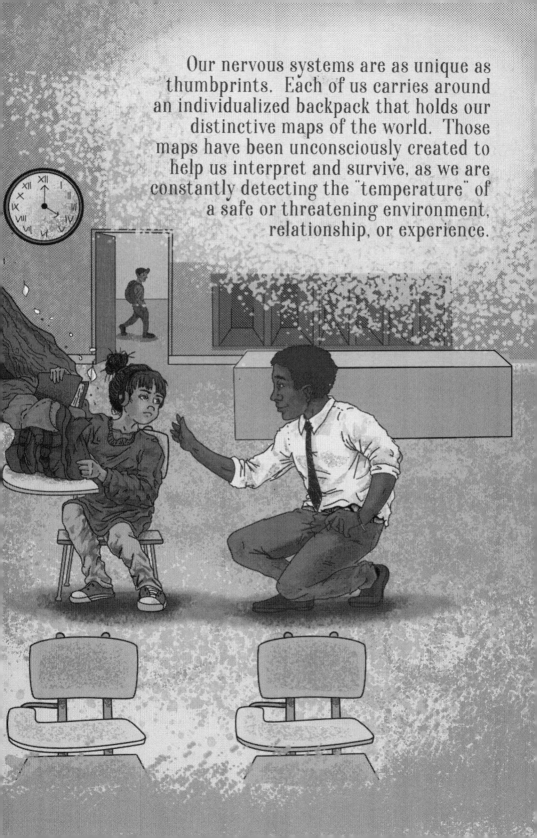

Living Inside the Gap

"Who are you?" said the Caterpillar. This was not an encouraging opening
for a conversation. Alice replied, rather shyly, "I-I hardly know, sir,
just at present—at least I know who I was when I got up this morning,
but I think I must have been changed several times since then."
LEWIS CARROLL (ALICE'S ADVENTURES IN WONDERLAND)

Our Nervous Systems, Plasticity, and Hope

Our children and youth are leading the educational system into
transformation. Their behaviors are crying out for connection and co-
regulation as their bodies crave felt safety. Our traditional educational
conventions are not addressing their developmental needs that are
impacting how they feel, learn, behave, and flourish through young
adulthood.

The start of the 2021 and 2022 school years have been so challenging for students, educators, and parents. Many children and
youth across the nation and world are carrying **broken belongings**
into schools: a term for felt detachment from human connection,
as described in Long and Fecser's *Conflict in the Classroom*.[16] The pandemic has created conditions of relative isolation and a significant
amount of chronic unpredictability within schools, homes, and our
communities, as we are directly experiencing this felt disconnection
simultaneously through dysregulated and contagious behaviors by
staff and students. These behaviors are signaling heightened patterns

of stress activation. Because people are emotionally contagious, we unconsciously pick up on the sensations and emotions of one another. The pandemic has added to the felt disconnection, which contributes to the social losses that our students currently bring into schools. Long and Fecser share, "Disconnected students are developmentally stuck because of the absence of nurturing adult relationships. They are not ready emotionally for school, and the school is not ready for them."[17] The pandemic has aggravated this felt social loss for many students. When a teacher and a disconnected student exchange words during ongoing conflicts, these students can sap the teacher's energy and can become a major contributor to professional stress.[18]

Our schools are being challenged to return to some type of normalcy, with policy leaders focusing on *learning loss* as we move through a third academic year inside a global pandemic. The developing nervous system of our children and youth requires felt safety before it learns, and many of our governmental leaders are uninformed and far removed from the current research on brain and nervous system development. Adults are also feeling the emotional and social fatigue from the mounting behavioral challenges in schools and the push to close learning gaps while sitting beside students and helping them adjust to the **social loss** that they are experiencing. This social loss is observed through verbal and physical aggression that significantly increased in schools across the world this past year. Our students are struggling to tolerate differences in one another with increased agitation and anger. Failing grades, incomplete assignments, and the chronic challenge to stay attentive and focused on tasks, assignments, and lectures through a seven-hour school day are also problematic, contributing to the overwhelming feelings of disconnect and anxiety impacting students' developing nervous systems, and therefore their behaviors.

As a species, humans are fortunate that our bodies and brains are equipped with plasticity of the nervous system, our ability to change or adjust with every experience. Moheb Costandi from MIT writes, "The brain is not only capable of change, but it does so continuously throughout life in response to everything we do and every experience we have."[19] Our brains and bodies are malleable in adjusting to environments, people, thoughts, and experiences by creating nervous system states of safety or perceived threat. **Neuroplasticity by default** can be defined as the automatic responses, routines, and reactions that we produce without intention or awareness, and this kind of plasticity has been at work while students were virtual, hybrid, or moving back and forth between remote and in-person school scenarios. In other words, our nervous systems adjusted to some independence during those less-structured virtual school days, when students could grab food, turn off the camera, take care of siblings, or contend with the ongoing distractions of being at home. These conditions have made returning to schools full-time an arduous task. While schools attempt a return to normalcy, plasticity of the nervous system is present and active as we begin again to address and readjust to the emotional and social needs of our staff, students, and families and the pain-based behaviors we are unconsciously transporting into our schools during and following a global crisis.

Belzer Middle School

Two mornings or afternoons a week, I am co-teaching in seventh-grade classrooms in a large Indianapolis middle school. As I walk down hallway B, there are times when the felt tension from staff and students permeates the air! Educators are questioning and wondering how we begin to reclaim environments of safety and connection for sustainable learning to occur. In this time, we are called not only to reclaim environments, but also to re-envision school cultures and environments that speak to the strengths, lived experiences, development, generational trauma, and hardships of students and staff—and all this while acknowledging the toxic levels of stress that have disrupted learning environments through the growing adversities and trauma in our children's and youths' lives. Could this *disruption* of how we have traditionally approached school, learning, and discipline protocols lead to an awareness and recognition of what our educational system can improve upon?

How Our Brains and Bodies Process the Plasticity of Experiences

Educator and author Zaretta Hammond says, "When we begin to address deep culture, and not just the heroes and holidays of surface culture, at the core of culturally responsive teaching, culture acts as our brain's software. But we need to understand how the brain uses culture to make sense of the world, and when we begin to hold this understanding in our teaching and leadership practices, we can more easily build on the brain's natural systems to activate its unique ability to grow itself."[20] We interpret the world through our cultural lens, experiences, relationships, and belief systems, forming our deep embedded values.[21] It is through the plasticity of individual and systemic changes that we can begin to create environments that minimize social threats, with an emphasis on a deeply caring social community. Are our schools positioned or can they be positioned to meet these conditions in this time, creating the social communities that our students need for emotional, social, and cognitive development?

Our brains grow through challenge with moderate, controllable, and predictable states of stress, but we need to feel an active part of the learning with relevant conscious processing of the information. This can only occur when we feel safe and connected in our environments.[22]

For the past several years, my work in the schools has focused upon how the impact of individual, familial, community, and systemic trauma and adversity influence the developing nervous system, and therefore the behaviors, thought processes, and learning of children and youth. Our brains are experience dependent and responsive. Our nervous systems can support safety and connection if we sense safety and connection. With growing awareness and recent research, I have learned that what we call trauma is an invisible epidemic, and that no one escapes or is immune to the life adversities that cultivate pain, abandonment, loss, and despair.

All life experiences shape key regions in the brain which organize and integrate incoming sensory information from the world and from within our bodies.[23] The brain and body begin to make sense of the world based on the interpretation and perception of those experiences. We predict experiences based on past experiences as the nervous system sorts, separates, and then stores our personal inter-pretations of the events. Dr. Bruce Perry explains, "Starting in the womb, the developing brain begins to store parts of our life experi-ences, and fetal brain development can be influenced by a host of factors including mother's stress; drug, alcohol, diet, and patterns of activities."[24]

Developmental neuroplasticity begins occurring before birth. Nervous systems are built over time. Our brains are constructed from the bottom up, and this basic architecture is an ongoing process that lasts well into adulthood. Developmental neuroplasticity occurs throughout our lives, but the first three years and early adolescence calibrate to the most significant time of brain change and growth.

The Developing Brain and Nervous System

Simpler neural connections and skills form first, followed by more complex neural circuits and skills. In the first few years of life, more than one million new neural connections form every second.[25] After this period of rapid proliferation, neuronal connections are pruned away, allowing the brain to become more efficient and specialized as development continues.

The developing brain is made up from billions of connections among individual neurons across different areas of the brain. These connections enable super-fast communication among neurons that specialize in different kinds of brain functions. The early years are the most active period for establishing neural connections, which are based upon an infant's and child's experiences. Because this dynamic process never stops, it is impossible to determine what percentage of brain development occurs by a certain age. More importantly, the early-forming connections provide either a strong or weak foundation for the connections that form later.

Our nervous systems are as unique as thumbprints. Each of us carries around an individualized backpack that holds our distinctive perceptual maps of the world. Those maps have been unconsciously created to help us interpret and survive, as we are constantly detecting the "temperature" of a safe or threatening environment, relationship, or experience.

Through three decades of teaching, the seemingly irrational student behaviors that I have observed are clearly understandable when we look beneath the behavior of our children and youth. Behaviors are signals, observable indicators that the nervous system is dysregulated and picking up on cues of danger or threat, even when none exist. Our nervous systems are designed to protect us, and trauma can be defined as the eternally present past. Behaviors are clues and roadmaps to a destination where we may not have traveled.

To access the frontal cortex of the brain where learning, attention, working memory, and emotional regulation occur, human beings require conditions of felt safety and a sense of belonging. When we produce these developmental conditions, we begin cultivating and reclaiming autonomic nervous system states of competency, autonomy, connection, safety, and motivation.

Connections and Belonging

Let's return to the impact and definition of those broken belongings that our students often carry into our schools and communities. Theologian Martin Marty argues that the core problem is the loss of our "tribes," which he also terms as broken belongings.[26] From earliest times, biological parents were often too young and overwhelmed to care for their own child, and because life spans were short, many children were orphaned and cared for by several members of the tribe to carry on the culture.[27] Today, our schools are the new tribes for many of our youth and children who come to school for safety and connection. As the pandemic has lingered, conditions of relative isolation and a significant amount of chronic unpredictability within communities and home environments have impacted the emotional and mental health of our children and adolescents, who are cut off from their tribes. Again, we can observe this felt disconnection through staff and student behaviors, which signal fatigue, anxiety, and burnout from trauma-altered stress-response systems.

In the words of Sylvia Ashton-Warner, "The two worst enemies of teaching are the students' interest in each other, and their desire for expulsion of energy."[28] In the 2021-22 school year, the nationwide and destructive TikTok challenges went viral in many of our secondary schools, encouraging destruction of school property, aggression, and violence. These behaviors are actions that reveal how even **distorted belongings** feel more comforting to students than feeling isolated and alone. The highly irrational middle school and high school TikTok challenges might have been driven by the developmental need for attachment to others, at the cost of an adolescent's need for authenticity. Authenticity can be defined as a condition of staying connected to our gut feelings, choices, and unique values and voice. There are two survival needs that humans inherit. Attachment and authenticity are foundational to nervous system development. Human beings are the least developed at birth of all mammals, so our attachment needs are critical to ongoing nervous system development. Initiating authenticity can be defined as knowing how you feel, while paying attention and listening to your gut instincts and making choices from this *felt* perspective. During development, if our attachment to caregivers, peers, or any significant relationship feels threatened, we often suppress what we want to say, what we feel, or how we respond, so that our connections to the group stay intact. Dr. Gabor Maté states, "This is the tragic conflict of development."[29] Our sense of belonging is so strong that we might vandalize or act in hurtful or destructive ways if we feel that we have lost or are losing connection to that individual or group where our sense of connection is felt and fed!

For educators and parents, our challenge is to share an empathic presence and response, exploring and tapping into our own nervous system states, reaching for a calm, balanced state before we approach our children and youth about group-influenced destructive behaviors. When we model and share our calm state, the conversations, questions, and consequences can be heard and digested as we move toward preventive and sustainable problem solving and planning.

Returning to the words of Sylvia Ashton-Warner's observation about the two worst enemies of teaching—students' interest in each other and desire for expulsion of energy—now more than ever, we must call educators to connect with these so-called enemies, deeply listening and validating students' authenticity and their sensory needs we might have unintentionally neglected, because this connection, listening, and validation will generate states of belonging and safety. Author Martha Straus writes, "A major developmental task of adolescence is, indisputably, establishing a coherent identity narrative—the 'story of me' that has both chronological linearity and attendant emotional awareness."[30] Early and ongoing relationships determine the degree to which a youth has the social milieu that will be able to seed the development of an integrated identity.[31] The story of our nervous systems needs to be held by a safe, trusted other, because a self without a co-written identity story is a very lonely place.[32] When we meet our students where they are developmentally, we are providing an accessible and emotionally available space that feels secure and safe.

Development, Nervous Systems, Behavior, and Neuroplasticity

Our nervous systems and physiological states create and produce the behaviors we observe, question, discuss, punish, suspend, seclude, and attend to each day in schools. As educators who sit with 30 to 180-plus nervous systems every day, we have traditionally paid attention to observable behaviors, assessing them as appropriate, disrespectful, inappropriate, oppositional, aggressive, and manipulative, alongside a variety of other labels and classifications.

The Polyvagal Theory, along with the growing developmental and relational neuroscience research, purports that education requires **state regulation**, so that we can access and integrate the cognitive and mental tasks our students need to succeed in school, coupled with working toward a growing self-awareness to safely navigate life experiences.[33]

Many individuals in the western part of the world have been conditioned, parented, and schooled through the lens of behaviorism.[34] Conventionally, our school systems and structures have embedded behaviorism along with contingency programs that address and focus upon compliance and control.[35] Many of these contingency behavioral regulations and handbooks mirror zero tolerance policies from the 1990s and early 2000s, often designed by racially privileged school leaders and groups who have both unintentionally and intentionally increased racial inequities and disparities for our children and youth of color, students from other cultures, and special education populations. It is true that most discipline protocols are implicit on the level of the educator, but some of the policies, rulings, and guidelines are more explicit. This is specifically true in the case of Black students, intentionally criminalized by our school systems during the era of mass incarcerations in the 1990s and early 2000s.[36]

Many educators have grown up with a law-and-order mentality focused on accountability solely through the lens of observable behaviors. In the United States today, we implement corporal punishment in 19 states.[37] But we have a significant disconnect. Our most struggling youth and children are flooded with behaviors from nervous systems that have been reprogrammed through the plasticity of living in survival states much of the time; and survival is prioritized and activated to protect ourselves, even at moments when danger or threat is not present. This often occurs through the plasticity of learned patterns of highly sensitized stress responses based on past experiences.

The pandemic has added layers of adversity and trauma to the lives of our children, families, and communities. Children remain the poorest age group in America, with children of color and young children suffering the highest poverty levels.[38]

• Nearly 1 in 6 (more than 11.9 million) were poor in 2018.

• Nearly 73 percent of poor children were children of color.

"If you look at the prevalence of kids who have school adjustment difficulties and mental health problems, it was too high before the pandemic—and it's going to be higher now," says Roger Weissberg, Ph.D., a distinguished professor emeritus of psychology at the University of Illinois at Chicago and chief knowledge officer of the Collaborative for Academic, Social, and Emotional Learning (CASEL).[39]

As we move through this collective crisis and the after effects, schools will benefit from exploring behaviors through the lens of physiological states. Neuroscience, through the understanding of the Polyvagal Theory, has significantly impacted and shifted the ways in which many schools and districts are now beginning to address observable behaviors from our children and youth who are carrying in chronic dysregulation and trauma. Our schools will feel the repercussions from this pandemic in years and generations to come, with approximately 20-plus million children and youth who were home due to school closures during this time; and many students disappeared from their classrooms altogether.[40] The pandemic has been an unconscious and felt threat to our nervous systems, shutting down accessibility to the cortex (the thinking and cognitive part of the brain).

Our physiological states are inherently social, affecting everything we feel, sense, do, and experience within our internal and external environments. The brain and body development of children and youth is constantly being shaped by experiences with others, and the perceptions of those experiences and environments. The chronic behavioral challenges that we face in our schools are often communicating states of threat and need for protection and connection. As I have shared, behaviors are only the indicators for how our brains and bodies are experiencing their internal and external environments. In moments of heightened conflict, educators are often unprepared to read our students' nervous systems, as our survival responses mirror those of our students when emotional temperatures rise and conflicts intensify.

In trauma-altered stress response states, our thinking shuts down, our emotions become hot, and our hearing changes! Scientist and author Dr. Stephen Porges describes this neurobiological change in what and how we hear when our nervous system detects threat or danger:

> When we feel unsafe, low frequencies represent predator-like sounds. Children who come from dangerous and toxic environments often have delayed language, and this can be the result of how our hearing changes when our nervous systems are in a threat and protect response. In a survival response, we do not hear the endings of words because the ear muscles are expanding and protecting us, so our ability to hear clear conversation, redirection, consequences, and the endings of words are limited as we are only able to respond to the beginning of words and tones of voice.[41]

Our **prosody** (tone of voice) can unintentionally reactivate and exacerbate threat detection in our nervous systems, escalating a cycle of protective and defensive behaviors that leads to repetitive discipline referrals, suspensions, restraints, and sometimes seclusion.[42] We unintentionally disconnect from our students by sending them away when they need us the most, putting them in time out, and withdrawing from them. We are implicitly teaching our children and youth that we are not available when they are most upset. Their survival behaviors are signaling an urgent call for protection and connection in that moment, but this is challenging when the adult nervous system is moving into threat-and-protect states of functioning.

From the research of Dr. Nicholas Long, "Those who work with troubled youth do not begin the day by saying, 'I'd better schedule some time this afternoon to be sarcastic to J, to yell at Sam, to threaten Sylvia, and to suspend Seymour.' Yet, school staff frequently find themselves in counteraggressive struggles with their students."[43] How do we explain adult counteraggression when our intentions are to help students, not fight them? Is counteraggression a function of personal inadequacies, a lack of self-control, a derivative of early child-rearing experiences? Or is counteraggression a biological instinct that all humans possess? When our survival feels at risk, our own nervous systems detect threat and danger and, like our students, we, too, can unconsciously move into the nervous system pathways of dissociation, or mobilize energy to fight or flee.

Our working models or perceptual maps of the world originate from our lived experiences, environments, and past generational adversities. We often project these lived experiences into the world, and when we do, children and youth feel the infectious tension, edginess, and irritation from many adult nervous systems generating a collective, transmissible fear and apprehension within our communities. Human beings desire felt safety and predictability, but sometimes adults, just like children, ask for understanding and clarity in the most unloving ways. Whether at the gas station, grocery, airport, or school event, we are often experiencing a fight-flight survival response from adult nervous systems. When nervous systems are living in heightened stress response states, we cannot parent, teach, lead, or learn well. *We cannot live well!*

Our children and adolescents are picking up on the emotional weariness of the adults in the community. Children are moving through an incredibly rapid time of brain development, and the experiences they encounter are often filtered through an adult lens. Because the brain is always making associations and predictions, young children and adolescents will feel the tension, restlessness, and depressed affect from caregivers and the adults around them, and they will begin creating their own deficient narratives about the world and the people that care for them. Often, these children keep these scary or unsafe narratives to themselves. When we are absorbed in persistent, sensitized stress responses, we tend to read nonverbal communication with an intensified negative bias and perceive threat or danger where none exists. Young children especially pick up on the nonverbal communication around them as their verbal language skills are still developing. They subconsciously read and interpret tones of voice, facial expressions, gestures, and postures from adults around them. Our nonverbal communication can produce an emotional tone that will always override our spoken words and conversations.

The last two books I have authored and co-authored, *Connections Over Compliance* and *Eyes Are Never Quiet*, go into much detail about how trauma and adversity impact the developing nervous systems of children and youth. This book will travel into the reparative and healing possibilities and the mindsets and practices that human beings require, as our nervous systems know the way home. But post-traumatic growth is not a fix, solution, or mindset that is glamorous, attainable, and looks the same for all. It is an individual journey of experiences that will be very different for each of us.

In summary, our children are hurting; however, what these statistics do not show is that our children and youth are also resilient. We are creatures of habit hardwired for survival, but we also are recognizing that our complex and malleable nervous systems change constantly with our thoughts, feelings, perceptions, and behaviors from encountered experiences.

Incremental change can lead to transformational change. This is true for both individuals and systems. We know that, for most of us, the unknown causes tremendous anxiety, dread, and apprehension. When we can purposefully create cultures, environments, and experiences that feel safe, predictable, and relational, we are better able to move through our experiences with a more flexible nervous system. Awareness of how our bodies and brains are intimately connected— streaming communication through an intricate highway of sensory and motor information from body to brain and brain to body— reinforces a new lens for a greater understanding of how our nervous systems hold the adversities, traumas, and states of growth and well-being in our lives.

In the western part of the world, we do not often listen to what our bodies are communicating. We often ignore what our nervous system is sharing from our internal organs, and therefore we may be missing instances of connection with our bodies that move us toward healing. Therapist and author Deb Dana writes, "The autonomic nervous system shapes the way you experience your life. Beliefs, behaviors, and body responses are embedded in the nervous system. Physiology and psychology are interconnected."[44] Some of the most critical work that we can integrate into our teaching and leadership practices is helping our students recognize and acknowledge the language of their nervous systems. By recognizing our autonomic states through sensation, we are creating space for resiliency and shifting from nervous systems functioning in protection to nervous systems moving toward growth. Autonomic awareness is a significant protective factor for psychological well-being. Our emotional health is tied to our physiological health. When we are aware of how our bodies and brains are experiencing, interpreting, and perceiving the world, we can begin to recognize our stories of adversity that live inside our autonomic pathways.[45]

Crisis -> Plasticity -> Opportunity

I am hopeful, because *in a crisis, we tap into the kind of courage that can create opportunities*, and this is where the intentional awareness of neuroplasticity becomes so relevant during stressful times: such as the one in which we currently live!

Neuroplasticity is our human superpower. As stated in the Introduction, there is growing research on plasticity, but one of the key principles of neuroplasticity shared by Dr. Bruce Perry is termed specificity.[46] Dr. Perry states, "In order to change any part of the brain, that specific part of the brain must be activated."[47] One of the remarkable properties of the brain and nervous system is its capacity to change and adapt to our individual worlds. Brain cells and brain networks work together in use-dependent ways, and with awareness, intention, and practice, we can strengthen those connections between neurons, leading to improved performance and well-being. Neuroplasticity is how our nervous systems produce and create feelings, thoughts, and behaviors through a process of structural and therefore functional change. How? Every time we think a thought and generate a feeling, we install neurological hardware that impacts our well-being in all moments.[48]

Our neural roadways or networks fire, and those connections between neurons signal the emotional limbic brain, which signals hormones, which enter the receptor sites on cells. In turn, those messages or emotional signals are signals to the genes that create new proteins; and proteins are the expressions of life, contributing to our well-being.[49] Author and speaker Joe Dispenza, D.C., states that with a clear intention and elevated emotion, we don't need to wait for a changing condition to bring us peace or hopefulness; we can begin to find moments or "glimmers" of conditions, such as pieces of experiences or thoughts that feel safe and hopeful, which can begin a new stream of improved thoughts, feelings, and behaviors.[50] Cultivating an elevated emotion and a clear intention often requires one another's support, and this is why co-regulation is so important as we move through the emotional and cognitive changes in our lives.

This takes repetition and is a process! These small moments that we notice each day can accumulate to become *thought routines* that begin to reframe a difficult day or challenging experiences.

The concept that the brain is "self-changing," meaning that it organizes, disorganizes, and reorganizes based upon experiences, prompts the revelation that the architecture of each brain is unique.[51] Adolescent brain psychiatrist and author Dr. Dan Siegel asserts that, because humans have the power to direct their own attention (focal attention), they thus have the power to shape and reshape the firing patterns and architecture of the brain, impacting the developmental processes of parenting, education, and psychotherapy.[52] Just as we are able to focus upon different muscle groups through physical exercise, we are also capable of stimulating the firing patterns of targeted neuron connections in certain areas of the brain by intentionally focusing so that we can strengthen and integrate those neural circuits.[53]

Defining plasticity is tricky, with both positive and negative implications in how our attention and experiences create neural networks. Author Martha Straus writes, "If an individual has no options for corrective experiences, his brain will continue to stimulate and develop neural networks that perpetuate old patterns. The brain exposed to psychological trauma, for example, responds to internal and external cues by structuring itself around those firings. However, if a trauma survivor develops the capacity to focus attention on the formation of new neural networks, theoretically, his brain can then restructure to experience that same trauma very differently."[54]

The Power of Awareness and Reframing

How can we consistently support ourselves—as well as our students—during these times of unpredictability and heightened emotional states? We can begin by becoming aware of and paying attention to our feelings and sensations. We can validate where we are in this moment by modeling this awareness for our children and youth. Following awareness and felt validation, we can choose an improved perspective or thought. We might begin reframing a thought or perspective, accompanied by a short regulatory practice, as that small action step begins to weaken the brain architecture of **synapses**, those specific connections between neurons that no longer serve us. Not only can we strengthen circuits between brain areas by getting these areas to fire at the same time and produce new feelings, thoughts, and behaviors, but we can also weaken connections because, as we shared previously, neurons that fire apart wire apart! Can we begin to weaken links of pain-based thoughts and feelings by replacing these habits of thoughts, feelings, and behaviors with practices that generate social and emotional well-being?

These reframing practices will require honest feedback and support from one another. We will need to be intentional and patient. Through careful, mindful effort, we can leave behind judgment or guilt, because awareness and recognition of our autonomic states begin to move our brains and bodies into conditions that feel hopeful and collaborative. Relational neuroscience increasingly assures us that we are continually shaping one another's embodied brains, and that the safety provided by deep listening to one another offers tremendous support.[55]

Education requires that we're able to regulate our own state. We serve our students better when we prepare our nervous systems for the mental and cognitive tasks needed for learning and academic growth, as well as social and emotional development at any age. Dr. Arielle Schwartz writes, "The human body is also equipped with an innate physiological resilience system, which is our autonomic nervous system."[56] There is more wisdom in your body than in your deepest philosophy. When we learn to partner with our autonomic nervous system, we can begin to reshape this system through listening to our sensations, the language of our bodies, with much appreciation.

Our nervous system drives all that we sense, feel, think, and are! It holds our past, and when experiences of trauma occur in our lives, our nervous system reorganizes and prioritizes protection. This automatic survival reaction is built into our biology and, when activated for long periods of time to produce an overactivation of stress hormones, this can create a chronic disruption of regulation in our brains and bodies. As mentioned earlier, this is neuroplasticity by default.

We are creatures of habit. Our thoughts produce biochemical reactions in the brain, sending signals to the body, and our bodies begin to feel in similar ways to how we were thinking. We can unconsciously think thoughts that produce feelings, and we can feel our way into similar thoughts that create a continuous cycle of habits of thoughts and feelings.[57] Without intention, our feelings, thoughts, and routines automatically recycle, producing the same behaviors and choices. Therefore, my brain activity and biology stay the same. As I stated in the Introduction, this work begins with me. When I am thinking the same thoughts, generating the same feelings, performing the same routines and actions, and swimming in the same emotions, my nervous system chemistry stays stagnant and, in some ways, I am living in the past. That state of sameness can feel comfortable and effortless, a state of knowing who you are, but it also can feel miserable and helpless. Dispenza states, "Your personality is made up of how you think, act, and how you feel. It is your present reality."[58] But if we want to change how we think, feel, and experience our lives, we must be willing to explore, question, and wonder what is serving us well in this time, and what is still serving our survival responses that we no longer need. Understanding how our nervous systems function in response to our environments and experiences is critical for children, youth, and adults to explore.

Our brains contain about 86 to 100 billion neurons. The synapses connecting those neurons are where our cells exchange information. If learning makes new connections, then remembering that learning will strengthen those connections.[59] As our brains create these structural changes, our thoughts produce **neurotransmitters**, a mixture of neurochemicals that create emotions. Dopamine and serotonin are two examples of neurotransmitters that may be familiar. When we think about something pleasurable, anticipate a vacation or a weekend gathering, or visualize a calming place with the sights, sounds, tastes, and people we love, we can stimulate the production of these neurotransmitters. Our thoughts produce how we feel, and those feelings produce related thoughts, and as this occurs, our neurons keep firing along the same pathways, strengthening the relationship between the cells so that their signal becomes stronger with repeated activation. If we repeat enough times what we have learned, we literally reinforce communities of neurons that begin to remember well the thoughts, feelings, or behaviors that we have consciously or subconsciously practiced and rehearsed. Neuroscientist Dr. Lara Boyd refers to these brain changes when she defines neuroplasticity as the chemical, structural, and functional changes that occur with learning.[60] When we are thinking the same thoughts and producing the same feelings, our brains are firing and activating the same neural circuits in the same patterns and sequences. This is what Dispenza refers to as **neuro-rigidity**.[61] He defines this concept as thinking inside the box, which means unintentionally creating a finite signature of automatic programs.[62]

Many of us have spent weeks, months, or longer trying to change habits of thoughts, feelings, or behaviors that we found next to impossible to change. The New Year brings promises and resolutions, yet by February, many of us are back to our patterned ways of being, behaving, and feeling. This is not because we lack will power, but because our nervous systems need patterned repetitive experiences over time. When we begin to think differently, feel differently, and choose novel behaviors, our brains and nervous systems may feel threatened and move to survival states. Therefore, we often relinquish new habits that feel uncomfortable and unfamiliar. Once we understand that the biological and chemical changes in our nervous system are causing this discomfort, we feel more powerful and confident as we move through these rivers of change. Most of us have been so conditioned to run from the unknown that we do not really question this fear. Dispenza states, "If you told me that you did not like being in that void of the unknown because it feels disorienting and you can't see what lies ahead, I'd say that's actually great, because the best way to predict your future is to create your future."[63]

To think outside the box generates neuroplasticity. When our brains change, our minds change, because our mind is the brain in action. As we use our brains, they grow and change through the use-dependent principle of neuroplasticity. Our brains prune away connections or synapses that we no longer use or need, while sprouting connections when we learn something new. Our brains are organized to reflect everything we know, and we use this historical information to predict new experiences. Therefore, change can feel very difficult as we keep records of the trillions and trillions of neurons that have connected with one another throughout our lives. The complex networks of neurons that have fired throughout our days on earth have formed memories of our past experiences, and if we do not create intentional changes or shifts, we become individuals and communities who are living in the past.

Neuroplasticity Practices

Recent research reveals that skills, behaviors, and thought patterns begin generating automaticity following 66 days of practice, on average, but that we also need continued support during these incremental moments of change because our nervous systems are social, and we rely on connection with others as we move through changes in our lives![64]

As we move through each chapter, I will share plasticity practices, questions, and examples of exercises that we can integrate into our homes, classrooms, and schools throughout the day, cultivating reflection by attending to the midbrain areas where the root circuitry of our emotional lives reside.[65] Following is an example practice of how our thoughts and feelings can slowly change, producing a modified perspective with intention and awareness. Recognizing and validating how we feel and sensing the conditions around us constitute our initial step of connecting with one another as we borrow each other's neural pathways in collaboration and reflection. Once we sit with our nervous systems and listen to those sensations and feelings, we have an opportunity to reframe how we feel, letting us move through a challenging time or situation with more self-compassion and broader understanding. Reframing our worn out and old "thought" stories (what we say and think to ourselves in dysregulation) allows us to see options as we identify patterns of thought that no longer serve us. Our windows of tolerance will also widen as we stretch into a bit of discomfort from this reframing practice. We must recognize that it will take time, practice, and a deep dive into our own biases, lived experiences, cultures, and misunderstandings, because under stressful conditions, we fall back into our old ways of judging, thinking, feeling and being.

Reframing Perspectives Through Plasticity

On our own or with our colleagues, we begin to reframe by recognizing and identifying how our personal thought patterns generate beliefs and perceptions that become distorted because of the subjectivity of our experiences. We know that reflection is critical in altering our thought processes, which become stagnant as the negative brain bias keeps us swimming in survival. Our nervous systems prioritize survival above all else, so the negative or implicit biases come to life when we question, wonder, and begin to plan for new ways of seeing a problematic situation or a long-held perspective that is no longer serving us. It helps to be curious and playful, as our nervous systems appreciate novelty but will often resist change. Plasticity practices begin with adults. The following chart is a guide for educators as we explore our struggles and options while beginning to reframe our experiences. This practice may later become helpful as we work with our children and youth when they feel stuck and plagued by helpless or powerless feelings. Dr. Arielle Schwartz says these powerful words: "All experiences are meant to come and go like waves in the ocean. They rise up, crest, and release. Similarly, we can think of our emotions as 'energy in motion.' They are meant to surge, be fully felt, and then subside."[66] Plasticity allows us to explore our strengths and handle conflicts with increased clarity and equanimity. Change takes awareness, intention, practice, and time. Regulation is never the goal. Recognizing when we are dysregulated as we listen to our nervous systems begins our journey toward growth. We do not have to believe everything we think! When we write down some of our troubling thoughts and create an "autopsy" of these thoughts, we may observe patterns of thinking (and therefore feeling) that are not valid for the present moment. Patterns of thought originate from our brain's need to predict experiences based on past experiences, and our recycled thoughts are possibly not true for us in this time. No one teaches us how to assess the thoughts that can reveal our direction when we generate feelings of growth or protection. We can learn to ask ourselves, "Is this thought moving me forward with a focus on growth, or is it moving me backward with a focus on protection?"

Please use this table of reframing suggestions, or create your own suggestions to share with your colleagues.

Plasticity Practices for Adults

MY WORLD What I say to myself (worries, shame, guilt, anxiety-provoking thoughts and feelings)	PRESENT MOMENT What is occurring without my interfering (thoughts, feelings, and perceptions)
1. This student is pushing all my buttons, and I have no control! I am helpless to do anything.	This student is having a hard time, and I am observing a very dysregulated nervous system and a brain in pain! I can remember to not personalize this behavior, as this is not about me. I can find some of my own calm to share with her, validating her feelings. I know that with some time and space, we can talk through this. In all moments, we can repair after a rupture. There is time!
2. I am feeling so disrespected by these students. How am I supposed to teach 30 students when I cannot get anyone's attention, and everyone is clowning around and acting up? This feels hopeless and unending!	In this moment, the only person or thing I can control is myself! My students are showing how they feel through their dysregulated nervous systems. I can ONLY control my own nervous system. I can take some deep breaths, grab some water, and start over by sharing my calm, emotionally available presence with these students. Maybe we can stop what we're doing and read a book together, watch a video and guess the ending, or draw or doodle while listening to music for a few minutes.

3. I cannot get up and do this every day! I have no support, and I do not deserve to be treated like this! I feel as if I am breaking or falling apart!	What I do know is that my body (nervous system) is speaking to me! If I listen deeply, I can find even the smallest amount of energy I need and reach out to a friend so that I can have some help reframing this day, minute, or moment. I can set up a meeting and talk through my challenges with an administrator. I can journal my thoughts and feelings or even write a letter to myself with some encouraging words and images. Difficult challenges always lead to growth!
4. I am feeling pulled in so many directions that I feel unsuccessful at everything I am attempting! I feel as if I am failing my administration, my family, and everything I touch right now! I am on a gerbil wheel, and I am not sure how to get off!	I know that these feelings and thoughts are more than likely coming from past experiences that my brain remembers, in order to protect me. In reality, many teachers and educators are feeling this exact way in this time! I am doing the best I can in all moments, and through these frazzled or scattered sensations, my body is telling me, "Rest a bit, take a deep breath, and find something soothing today." What are a few practices that would feel good to me this afternoon or this evening?
5. I feel as if there is so much out of my control, and I am worrying about everything!	Right in this moment, I captured a thought pattern! This is great news! I have acknowledged how I am feeling, and this is the most important step! Maybe I could find a distraction such as a walk, a deep breath, and two gratitudes for this recognition! I know that at every moment, I can begin again! My body is always working *for* me and never *against* me! Right now it's trying to find the way home to a balanced grounded presence, and it is normal to fluctuate between autonomic states, feeling everything!

Plasticity Practices for Students

Our breath is powerful in that it can change the entire physiology of our bodies and our brains. Throughout history, great healers have known that the breath can enhance people's physical, mental, emotional, and spiritual well-being. Physicians and authors Richard Brown and Patricia Gerbarg share, "The human body has the power to heal itself from the cellular level up. We regenerate our body tissues every day. Before the advent of synthetic medications, shamans, monks, priests, and tribal leaders learned how to turn on the body's natural abilities to prevent and cure illness."[67] Research reveals that, by changing the patterns of breathing, we can mitigate our stress response systems, finding balance while lessening anxiety and quieting the agitated mind.[68] When our children and youth begin using their breath to create calm states of focus and relaxation, they will carry this powerful ability into adulthood, knowing the physiological, emotional, and mental benefits while becoming proficient at young ages in one of the greatest superpowers of humanity—our breath.

The following exercises can help students begin to develop their self-regulation skills.

1. With apps on our phones or small pulse oximeter devices, we are able to measure our heart rate at any time. Ask students to write down their heart rate as they enter the classroom. This can be done individually, or we can share this practice in our morning meeting. We then take ten deep breaths with a long, slow outbreath as our heart rates begin to fall. We can observe our body changing with these deep belly breaths as we prime and prepare the brain and nervous system for learning. Another example is to have students run in place or do ten jumping jacks, measure their heart rate, and then follow up the physical activity with long slow breaths. Sometimes it can be difficult to stretch out that long exhale, so we ask students and staff to breathe in through their nose, and with lips pursed creating the letter O shape, we breathe out, creating a whistling sound through our pursed lips. This exhale allows for a long, slow outbreath that activates

the parasympathetic nervous system, slowing down our heart rate and respiration while lowering blood pressure. In the Resource Section of the book, you will find over 100 Focused Attention Practices integrating breath, movement, rhythm, and sensory regulatory practices.

2. Choosing a movement or physical activity, students can begin to see and feel their strength increase through various physical exercises that are fun and engaging. "Frog squats" are challenging, but we begin with one or two and then see if we can build up to 30 repetitions. In this exercise, we begin by squatting with our feet about 12 inches apart, knees bent and hands on the floor. As we inhale, we stretch out our legs and, on the exhale, we squat down again. This is a rhythmic activity that uses controlled breath, movement, and strength while building endurance and mental stamina. Students are not competing against one another but challenging the focus of their own bodies by adding an additional squat every couple of days or week. I encourage students to do what feels comfortable when they begin. This practice is excellent for all ages and produces a stimulation of blood flow throughout the entire body. What other simple physical exercises could you create with rhythmic repetitions that are engaging?

3. In this practice, we write our first names with our eyes closed or with our nondominant hand. With repetition and concentration, we can track how we improve the shape and spacing of the letters as we practice for a few minutes each day or week. We might begin to add our middle and last names, checking the spacing and lines as we improve.

4. We all have routines throughout the day. These might include how we get up in the morning, fall asleep at night, prepare for school, or observing the activities, thoughts, and behaviors that occur without intention or awareness. Choose one small routine and change the order of how we traditionally prepare for an experience. As a class,

we can also change up a routine at school and share one practice that we are willing to track and change up at home or school. Make a list with students of all the possibilities. Then, individually and collectively, begin to shift how we approach, transition, or end a day. Below are a few simple examples of plasticity practices to utilize as a group for one week.

a. Open every door we approach with the opposite hand for one week. Does it feel easier or more natural towards the end of the week?

b. Put away our phones 10 minutes before we fall sleep. What are the changes between the first few days and day seven?

c. Three times a day, pause to take three deep breaths, especially when we begin to notice worry, anxiousness, or irritation. How difficult is remembering to intentionally breathe?

d. Drink two or three additional glasses of water throughout the day, and share the ways in which you might feel more focused or energetic. Why is this routine critical to how we feel and learn? (As a class, research the many benefits of drinking water.)

e. Each morning or evening, spend two or three moments writing down things that went well. Even on our worst days, we can find something that went well!

f. Fall asleep to music or recorded sounds, or spend a few minutes before bed with a focused attention practice from the Resource Section of this book.

g. Text someone each day for one week to share something that you appreciate about him or her.

The scientific evidence is clear: Early experiences literally shape the architecture of the developing brain.[69] But what the public is often not aware of is that our brains are connected to all the systems in our bodies, and early experiences affect all of our biological systems, for better or worse, beginning in utero and throughout all the crucial years that follow.

This wider message relays a critical understanding for adult nervous systems. Dr. Jack Shonkoff says, "We all need to start paying closer attention to the science that explains how excessive adversity can undermine lifelong health as well as early learning. This knowledge can help us better understand why people of color in the United States are at greater risk of developing chronic medical conditions and aging prematurely than white people."[70]

Residential segregation—one of many converging consequences of systemic racism, personal discrimination, and poverty—results in significant inequities in exposure to air pollution, other environmental toxins, and neighborhood violence, as well as a lack of or unequal access to healthy food, stable housing, and equitable education and health care.[71] Dr. Shonkoff continues, "Black-white differences in preterm birth have been well-documented and linked to stress associated with discrimination, independent of socioeconomic status. Black children are three times more likely than white children to lose their mother by age ten."[72] Developmental and social neurosciences are sharing that preventing or alleviating the effects of adverse experiences and exposures in early childhood might be as important for long-term health as the conditions in which we live as adults and the health and medical care we receive.[73]

How can the impacts of adversity due to racism in early childhood affect a lifetime of health? One answer lies in the sensitivity of young, developing nervous systems to the physiological effects of a stressful environment.

As we have shared, toxic levels of stress from acute or chronic challenges activate our stress response systems inside our bodies. Blood pressure, respiration, and heart rate increase, elevating our stress hormones. The immune system activates an inflammatory response to prepare for wound healing and fighting infection, and metabolic systems prepare for mobilization of our fight-flight response.[74] If the stressor can be lessened, then our nervous systems return to a baseline of state functioning. But if the level of adversity remains high for long periods of time (from chronic discrimination or poverty), continuous activation of the stress response can wear down the nervous system, leading to toxic stress and the potential for many health challenges and diseases later in life.[75]

Many of our students of color or different cultures walk into our schools carrying in nervous systems that have been impacted by a young life filled with the adversities and discriminations discussed above. Students from historically marginalized groups often receive messages from society that can limit their beliefs about who they are. The following questions from author and graduate student Ivan Hernandez can begin to shift the way that students think about their backgrounds, adversities, and identities. These questions can initiate awareness and insight if we tap into group discussions with our students at the beginning or end of class.

1. What unique strengths have I developed from my life experiences, and how does this make me an asset to society?[76]

2. How can I use these strengths to help me succeed?[77]

3. What do most people misunderstand about me?

4. What have I traditionally viewed as a weakness or challenge in my life that, with a renewed perspective and practiced thought, could lead to a strength or an asset in my life?

5. Who are the people in my life that see my strengths and the powerful identity I embrace? How often do I reach out to these people who support my dreams and plans?

Guest Reflections

Each chapter in this book ends with stories from educators describing their journeys through personal and professional adversities and addressing the ongoing acknowledgment of how we have the capacity to move through states of pain and felt chaos, and move into growth. I have asked these educators to share stories about the intentional plasticity of our nervous systems, those moments when our awareness is awakened and our intentions come to life.

Thank you to Jenn Haak not only for sharing your story, but also for helping me conclude Chapter 1 by sharing your growing mindset and practices as you sit beside your students, while acknowledging and addressing your own nervous system states through the lens of the Applied Educational Neuroscience framework.[78] It is my hope that these shared journeys from educators and parents will be inspirational and thought provoking as we begin to explore resiliency through the lens of plasticity.

Guest Reflection from Jenn Haak, Elementary School Counselor and Doctoral Student, Salt Lake City, Utah

---

Intentional Neuroplasticity: The Power of the System

> *"You do not rise to the level of your goals.*
> *You fall to the level of your systems."*
> JAMES CLEAR

Hope is embedded in our very cells. The nature of our plastic brain's ability to grow and change illustrates potential for light to shine into each and every broken system. People change people. Changed people change systems. Changed systems offer an integrated web of safety, protection, inspiration, and opportunity to flourish. When we harness the power of intentional neuroplasticity, we can influence change at every level.

It can be both too hard and too easy to start with a goal like "I want to improve public education." Clear's quote regarding falling to the level of our systems encourages us to evaluate our current practices critically and create more effective and sustainable systems. Applied Educational Neuroscience (AEN) provides a framework for evaluating and creating innovative educational systems that foster positive outcomes for students and staff while valuing each individual's dignity and humanity. Each AEN pillar is grounded in neuroscience and compassion, valuing our innate human need for attachment and safety.

AEN holds enormous power for innovating education throughout the world as it provides a neuroscientific blueprint for unlocking the core of each district, school, and classroom: human connection. As educators begin to implement this brain-aligned framework into their arenas, they can consider the suggestions below to create a thoughtful 30,000-foot perspective before they jump in.

Go upstream: Review the practices, policies, and procedures currently in place that are contributing to the status quo. Are they effective? Equitable? Trauma-sensitive? Brain-aligned? If not, draft an alternative and share it with stakeholders for feedback. Collaborate to implement an improved system.

Dig deeper: Explore to discover the root of the issue. Center the root of the issue as the focus of your brainstorming. If you spend your energy focusing on the branches rather than the roots, the solutions you create will be temporary.

Influence foundational practices: For educators, this is Tier 1 intervention[79], the broadest level (whole-group instruction, classroom culture, group agreements). Consider what Tier 1 strategies can be implemented for students *and* staff. What routines, procedures, rituals, and traditions can you create that are rooted in regulating nervous system states and building meaningful relationships? Who has access? Is there a cost to that access of belonging, or is there a culture of unconditional belonging?

Practice and be patient: **Myelination** (the process of proteins insulating neural pathways allowing them to become faster and protected) takes time and repetition. The brain learns through patterned, repetitive experiences. Take a deep breath. Start slow. Let yourself be human.

Educator Brain State: Sustainable Self-Compassion and Boundaries

"Boundaries are the distance at which I can love you and me simultaneously."
PRENTIS HEMPHILL

Rachel Remen states: "The expectation that we can be immersed in suffering and loss daily and not be touched by it is as unrealistic as expecting to be able to walk through water without getting wet."[80]

As educators, we are immersed each day in the highs and lows of our students. We soar with them in victory, and we weep with them in sorrow. In order to give them our best, we must first give ourselves the space *we* need to heal. I frequently tell the teachers I work with (and myself), "You are your most valuable tool." Supporting your own regulation is one of the bravest, toughest, and most impactful things you can do for your students and for yourself.

I experienced a terrifying panic attack at work one day when I felt the weight of high-risk suicide assessments on me without policies of support. I realized that the demands of my job were outweighing the abilities of my coping skills. I had a sobering thought: "If something doesn't change, I need to quit. This is killing me."

As challenging as that experience was, it forced me to evaluate my self-care practices and get serious about incorporating active self-compassion throughout the day. Through incorporating these routines, I have experienced more peace, less anxiety, better quality sleep, greater joy in my marriage, and higher satisfaction at work.

My morning routine now consists of waking up without immediately checking social media, meditating with a Loving-Kindness guided audio from the Calm app[81], doing a short yoga practice or gentle stretches, journaling, and reading a daily devotional. On my drive to work, I listen to something that inspires me, like a podcast or audiobook. Throughout the day, I try to walk outside and get some fresh air at least once, even if it's just around the parking lot at school. Most evenings I try to get some kind of exercise or movement. Before bed, I record three things I'm grateful for, as cultivating a gratitude practice is shown to help those of us who tend to forbid joy.[82] I limit screen time past 9 p.m. and read something I genuinely enjoy before falling asleep.

These practices have all become part of my daily routine, and I notice the difference in my brain and body state after doing them. Witnessing the power of intentional neuroplasticity firsthand in my own routines and procedures has inspired me to incorporate healing practices I can share with my students and colleagues as well. Positive change starts with the adults in the building. (Counselor, heal thyself!)

Here are some strategies to support your nervous system states:

Intentional pause: Before I enter a classroom to teach, I pause outside the door to take at least one deep breath, relax my shoulders, and visualize leaving stress at the door.

Check your tone: I notice the sound of my own voice; if it sounds harsh or scary to me, it absolutely sounds that way to a child. I will set a visual timer for 2-5 minutes before we come back together as a group. During that time, I offer choices to the students to regulate: get a drink of water, go to the bathroom, draw, put your head down for a rest, breathe deeply, lie on the floor, etc. This practice normalizes the need to take a break, and honors the humanity and brain states of everyone in the room.

Name and model: "I'm starting to feel frustrated because I have explained the directions four times and folks are still talking. My face feels hot and my hands feel shaky. I'm going to get a drink from my water bottle and take a deep breath. If you're also feeling frustrated, you can take some deep breaths with me. I'm going to set the timer for two minutes, and then let's try again."

Tune into your sensations: Know and continue to learn your triggers. Notice and attend to the needs of my own body. The use of hand warmers, a heated or weighted blanket, drinking water, eating snacks, dimming the lights, or turning on lamps, and diffusing essential oils can all support sensory needs and promote regulation.

Give yourself the gift of time: As a counselor, I used to schedule my lessons, groups, and individual sessions back-to-back without any buffer time. I found myself physically reacting to stories I heard all day without giving myself time to process anything. I frequently shook slightly, my teeth chattered, I would become freezing cold, get headaches, stomachaches, and lose my appetite. Filling every minute of time was not helpful for me, nor for the people I was trying to help. I started to add 5-15 minutes of time between interventions so that I could tend to my basic needs, and the results have been startling. I feel empowered to sit lovingly beside students and colleagues, offering my full humanity and presence, when I take the time to care for myself throughout the day. For me, this looks like drinking water, using the bathroom (often a neglected need within schools!), chatting with colleagues, taking a quick walk around the parking lot, drinking coffee or tea, or simply staring out the window while I listen to a song.

Bolster your systems: Lovingly and (to the best of your ability) without judgment, notice what systems you have in place for compassionate, sustainable self-care, especially throughout the workday. If you fall into bed at night exhausted, spent, crabby, and dreading the next day, your systems are not serving you. What can be taken off your plate to reduce stress? What can be added to foster joy? Reach out to a safe person to help you if you need an accountability partner. Schedule therapy at least monthly to release the pressure valve that naturally builds when caring for others and holding their stories. You deserve to be cared for, too!

Co-Regulation: The Power of Sharing Our Calm

When little people are overwhelmed by big emotions,
it's our job to share our calm, not join their chaos.
L.R. KNOST

Many of us who grew up in unpredictable environments learned to fear anger. We learned to manage and manipulate our environments as a survival mechanism. For some students, chaos feels familiar to them; put them in a silent reading situation, and they will make noise the entire time in order to feel familiar. For some students, yelling feels normal; when you lower your voice and speak calmly, this is an unfamiliar behavior that may trigger their sympathetic nervous system response. They may yell and curse because that's what feels familiar. Through patterned, repetitive experiences in calm environments, these students will begin to form new neural pathways that allow them to access their prefrontal cortexes instead of being stuck in their fight or flight response.

Other students have internalized that their worth relies on being small, quiet, happy, and cute. These students do not ruffle feathers, are compliant and pleasing, and are terrified to make a mistake or disappoint you. Show them it's OK to be messy, normalize feeling angry, allow them to make a mistake and be a kid. Little by little, as they experience a predictable and supportive environment, those neural pathways will form that allow them to finally relax and release the weight of the world off their tiny shoulders.

Adults can co-regulate with students[83] (and other adults!) through sharing their regulated nervous system with someone who is dysregulated, offering validation, and giving unconditional support and acceptance. Due to the brain's ability to change through repetitive experiences, students are able to build new pathways by learning to identify when they start to feel escalated, and experiencing co-regulation with a trusted adult. What a beautiful and humbling picture of the capacity for healing and the potential for their future successes in and out of the classroom.

Here are some co-regulation strategies:

Encourage your students to notice their sensations: Including a "sensation wall" with sensation words helps students build their sensation vocabulary and competency. Consider that students raised without an attentive caregiver could have difficulty with sensory processing; including sensations in your routines and procedures allows these systems to develop over time.

Give choices where both options are acceptable: Choice is an antidote for restraint, which is one of the conditions unable to be tolerated by the brain (along with isolation and chronic unpredictability).[84] When offering choices, ensure that both options are acceptable and positive for the student. If you offer a sarcastic choice and the student chooses that option, you may end up in a difficult power struggle.

One afternoon, a boy who was struggling to attend to the lesson began rolling around on the carpet in the classroom. The teacher put her hands on her hips and asked him, "Do you want to come into the classroom or just flop around on the floor all day?" The student replied, "I'm good here," making the class laugh and the teacher exasperated. (Haven't we all been here at some point?)

An alternative response could have been something along the lines of "Would you rather go get a drink of water or take a one-minute stretch break before joining us for the lesson?" Here, both options are acceptable, and the child isn't shamed for expressing an unmet need. The teacher could follow up with the student later, once regulated, and check in to see at what point the student felt like they needed a break, and what could be done in the future instead of rolling around on the floor (asking for help, repeating instructions, having a non-verbal sign to indicate the student doesn't understand, etc.).

Be a thermometer, not a temperature: Be intentional about modeling the tone, language, and culture you want to exist in your environment. When you witness the opposite of what you hope to cultivate, meet it with what you hope to instill in your students. For example, when students get loud and hostile toward each other, you can try addressing them with gentleness and kindness. Emotions are contagious by nature. If you are intentional about radiating calm towards your students, they'll pick up on it. Eventually, they may radiate it back toward you and each other.

Get on their level: If a student is lying on the ground, sometimes I will lie down next to them. I'll model taking a few deep breaths before asking them any questions or telling them anything. When I sense that they are comfortable with my presence, I'll lean toward them and whisper a question, such as, "Would you like to come to my office for a little while?" or "Would you like a hug?" Almost always, I'll get a head nod as a response. However, I always want to be careful that my physical presence doesn't intrude their perception of safety; if a student is clearly in a sympathetic response (fight-flight), I won't approach them in this way because their nervous system could view it as a threat to survival.

Offer non-verbal responses as options: Sometimes students are dys-regulated to the point that they cannot verbally respond. When a student is in this state, I will offer choices and non-verbal response options. For example, I'll say, "Point to me if you want to come to my office, and point to your classroom if you want to go back there." Another example could be physically offering two tools for regulation, such as putty in one hand and a Rubik's cube in the other. Insisting that a student verbalize their response to you can sometimes lead to a power struggle. Allowing them the opportunity to express themselves nonverbally honors where they are, while still offering support.

Identify and respond to the need hidden beneath the behavior: Ask questions to identify the root of the issue, and offer solutions that address the root. During a lesson, a student kept repeating, "Do we *have* to do this?!" At first, I was offended; I had put together what I thought was a fun and engaging game. Once the other students began the game, I walked over to this student, got on his level, and whisper-asked him, "What's making you not want to participate?" He wouldn't make eye contact with me, but whispered back, "I don't get it." I offered to explain it to him to the side and play the first round together. He nodded, and we spent a few minutes playing the game together until he felt confident enough to join his classmates.

Use silence: It can be overwhelming for students (and adults) to be surrounded by people offering lots of options, even with a helpful intent. I use silence as a co-regulation tool when I sense that someone is overwhelmed by a crowd or situation. I'll sit or stand beside them and model taking slow, deep breaths. When I sense a shift in the individual and feel they may be ready to process or relocate, I'll offer two options (if someone is coming out of a shut-down, immobilized state, the simpler the options the better). For example, "Would you like to draw in my office or walk around outside?" provides two regulatory options. If they are not ready to talk, process, or take any other action,

I offer for them to come to my office, assuring that they won't have to say anything if they don't want to. If that's the case, I'll follow up with that student later in the week to see if they would like to process whatever happened at that point. Forcing anyone to talk about a difficulty before they are ready can cause more harm than good; respecting another's silence honors where they are in the process and creates a safe environment if they choose to share in the future.

Make your body as unthreatening as you can: Most of communication is non-verbal; allow your tone, body language, posture, and facial expression to send the message that you are there to support, not hurt. Posture your body slightly away from the person in crisis (squaring up with them can signal threat), open your palms and keep your hands within their line of sight, use a gentle voice, allow the path to their exit to remain open (don't stand in front of the door).

Answer questions with information: Remember, students will look defiant over stupid every time. When you hear a student exclaim, "Oh my God, what are we even doing?!" answer them informationally, preferably close to them and in a gentle voice. When students are living in constant adversity and unpredictability, it's possible that a tiny ear muscle swells making it difficult to attend and hear.

Fall back to your Multi-Language Learner (MLL) teaching strategies:[85] Visuals, repeating directions, cueing nonverbally, offering explicit directions simply and clearly will support all learners (including adults), especially those who have experienced or are experiencing significant adversity. Individuals who have experienced significant adversity are not always operating in their prefrontal cortex, but rather their amygdala or brainstem; they may need modifications and accommodations in order to access what you're trying to teach or share.

Meet them where they are: Keep in mind that their sense of time may be different than yours. They may not be able to daydream, plan, reflect, reason, etc. This goes for parents and families as well.

Example: In a recent family engagement training, the question, "What are your hopes and dreams for your student?" was suggested to start family conferences. The intention is honorable: get to know the family on a deeper level, explore their strengths, allow them the space to be the expert on their child. However, if the family is in deep struggle, pain, trauma, and survival-brain, this question can be difficult. They may not be able to access their prefrontal cortex to dream, reflect, and imagine; use of those skills is shut off in favor of survival, safety, and attending to the most immediate needs. Their sense of time is right here, right now, let's get through this moment. Perhaps an alternative to this question could be, "What would you say are the most important needs of your child right now?"

Attachment Touch Points: The Power of Language, Presence, and Being Known

"Remember: Everyone in the classroom has a story that leads to misbehavior or defiance. Nine times out of ten, the story behind the misbehavior won't make you angry. It'll break your heart."

ANNETTE BREAUX

Empathy and kindness need to be taught, practiced, modeled, and reinforced just like learning math and reading. Neural pathways for empathy resemble those for other skills. If empathy is not modeled and practiced at a young age, those pathways will not develop spontaneously. Educators can harness the power of young people's neuroplasticity and foster their empathetic growth through validation, active listening, and co-regulation. Through embedding these practices within routines, procedures, and classroom culture, we are also developing family privilege. For the students who come to school to be loved, we especially need to be intentional about building their experiences of receiving empathy and kindness. Our brains learn from patterned, repetitive experiences, and this includes empathy, kindness, compassion, and humility.

I have a third-grade student this year who comes from a household of about fifteen people. She describes her home environment as disconnected, with each member wrapped up in their own world, older siblings absorbed in their phones, and parents fighting constantly. She tends to isolate from her peers, hide outside at recess when her classmates line up at the whistle, and falls asleep constantly. Applied Educational Neuroscience helped me to recognize the question I need to ask: *What experiences does this child need?*

She needs to be seen. She needs to be valued. To be known. And to know that she is loved. In our counseling sessions, she shares that no one notices her other than to tell her what chores to do. I asked, "Who listens to you?" She answered, "No one." Slightly scared of the answer, I asked, "Who loves you?" Her answer surprised me. She looked at me. "You do." "Who else?" I wondered aloud to her. She shook her head.

In Spanish, there are two different words that mean "know." *Saber* is to know facts, dates, and information. *Conocer* is to know a person or a place, to have a relationship. What our students (and colleagues!) need is to be *conocer*-level known. To be seen, known, and valued is to matter. We know that the sense of mattering within a community, environment, relationship, and school leads to positive outcomes academically, behaviorally, personally, mentally, emotionally, and in the future.

Here are some attachment touch point strategies:

Allow Multi-Language Learners to emote in the language of their choice: If you choose to include a reflection of any kind, either verbal or written, allow them to choose the language of expression. Even if you don't understand them, it will be more beneficial for them to release those thoughts, emotions, and sensations in the way that's most closely connected to their heart, culture, and upbringing. Individuals can experience greater catharsis (emotional release) when emoting in their native language.

One fifth grader wrote a word in Arabic on the white board in my office as she was leaving a friendship group. She comes from a family that values toughness and is very skilled at having the last word and appearing powerful. During one group, she kept making hurtful comments directed towards the other group members. I asked the group to share what kind of culture they wanted to create within this group (kind, vulnerable, open). I reiterated that in order to create a safe space, we each have to commit to using that kind of language; I spoke directly to the student making hurtful comments and said that I would not let anyone say those things to her either, and so encouraged her not to say them to anyone else. She rolled her eyes and let out an exasperated sigh but altered the language she chose towards others for the remainder of the group.

As she was leaving, she wrote a word in Arabic (her home language) on my white board. To be honest, I assumed it was a bad word directed towards me for redirecting her several times throughout the group. I was touched to learn that the word meant relief, similar to the sensation of a weight being lifted off one's chest. What struck me was wondering if she had not experienced being in a "safe" environment with guardrails surrounding language and treatment of others. Perhaps that experience reached deeper into her development and connected with her innate need for attachment.

Greet warmly: Instead of "Did you have a good weekend?" ask "How was your weekend?" Notice when a student was absent, and when they come back say, "We missed you! How are you feeling?"

Family Photos: Allow students (and staff!) to bring in pictures of their loved ones, including pets, neighbors, characters. Expand the definition of family to include those who make you feel loved, inspired, and valued. Hang the pictures up on the wall and add to it throughout the year.

Shared calendar: Create a calendar where students can add their special events. Encourage each other to attend and support at dance recitals, sports games, theater performances, and more. Each of us exists outside the walls of the classroom!

Polyvagal Theory: An Example from the Field

"I'm not here to be right. I'm here to get it right."
BRENÉ BROWN

Internally, I felt like a car running out of gas. I could almost hear the *whir* come to a stop inside me as I felt something like a primitive autopilot kick on. This was not the first time this student had kicked and punched me, but it would be the last.

I had come to dread the sound of my name being called on the walkie talkie. *Your assistance is needed.* If I were regulated, this would have been the time for me to offer my peace and co-regulate with the seven-year-old child. However, due to the chronic unpredictability, lack of administrative support, and constant physical assault experienced daily, I had not been regulated at work for weeks.

I knew I had to keep my voice calm as I responded to the incident; the class was already evacuated to the hallway, they would be attuned to my presence, my tone, and my perception of their classmate. Although this was a routine occurrence for them, the fear in their eyes broke my heart. *They are afraid to come to school because we can't keep their classmate from assaulting them.* Cue shame gremlins whispering, *"You are not good enough at your job."*

This child and I had been working together for months to try and build her ability to regulate and form positive relationships with other students and staff. Thankfully, on those occasions, she came with me when she saw me in her classroom. Usually, we would walk to my classroom, co-regulate, and then reflect on different choices to make in the future. None of that would happen today.

I could tell something was different by the look in her eye. She wasn't "there." In place of the spark of recognition, safety, and connection I usually found in her gaze, there was something primitive. Her gaze looked at me and said to her body: *danger.*

What I know now is that her neuroception was interpreting cues from her environment, assessing for safety, and responding based on our basic human need for survival. Her sympathetic response was activated, preparing her body for fight and flight.

What I knew at that moment was: *oh, shit.*

She ran towards me, stomped on my foot, and took off down the hallway. Unfortunately, classes were just starting to transition to and from specials, and the hallways were filled with terrified children (many had witnessed or received physical harm from this child in the past).

Cue shutting down.

My visceral thought was: *protect the kids.* I evacuated the hallways and ran interference when the student ran towards other children swinging. She then turned toward the only other target available: me.

Three of us ended up in urgent care, one (me) was transferred to the hospital after having lost consciousness. I had a concussion, strained hip, bruised ribs, and a spinal injury.

As I reflected on the incident in the coming weeks and months, I wondered, *"Why couldn't I move away from her as she was hitting, punching, kicking, biting, and jumping on me?"* It was like I was in a daze (even before I was concussed). I felt like I was outside of my body looking in. I didn't feel anything as I was getting hurt; I just felt numb. I felt nothing.

Learning about the Polyvagal Theory has illuminated this experience in a way that has brought more healing than anything else. My autonomic nervous system correctly perceived danger in my environment and responded by preparing my body for injury. My heart rate slowed, my sense of time shifted, chemicals were released automatically to protect me from feeling the pain of my injuries. I thought there was something wrong with me for my inability to respond more clearly or feel any pain while it was happening. In actuality, my brain and body were doing exactly what they've evolved to do to protect me and to try to keep me safe. I ended up taking a medical leave. I never saw the student again.

People, even friends and family who have heard my stories from working in elementary schools for years, have a hard time believing that such a young child could cause such extensive injuries. What the Polyvagal Theory offers is insight into how deeply ingrained is our need for survival. Her young life had been fraught with abuse, neglect, and trauma; her autonomic nervous system was hypervigilant and wired for protection at any cost. She was a kiddo who lived in her sympathetic brain state. If I met her now, equipped with the knowledge of Applied Educational Neuroscience and the Polyvagal Theory, I could support her accessing her prefrontal cortex and building new neural pathways through providing predictable, relationship-based, sensory-integrated routines and procedures. Slowly but surely, her autonomic nervous system could have experienced feeling *felt*, perceived safety, and begun to trust that adults could be safe.

I didn't get to have the repair conversation that I can have now; I had to take time away to recover mentally and physically. I still think of her often, that look in her eyes, and use the insight gained from that experience to advocate for asking the question *"What experiences does this child need"?* when addressing "difficult" behaviors.

Jenn Haak, School Counselor

"Fear defeats more people than any one thing in the world."
RALPH WALDO EMERSON

Chapter 2

The story of our sympathetic autonomic states is one of searching for our home.

It Begins With Me

"There is more wisdom in your body than in your deepest philosophy."
FRIEDRICH NIETZSCHE

The Science of the Nervous System

Trauma and adversities are extremely challenging in the lives of so many adults, youth, and children. We cannot be talked out of a trauma or lectured about the sometimes-terrifying embodied experiences we have lived through. As I write about the significant possibilities following adverse experiences, through intentional neuroplasticity, I am most aware of this vulnerable notion and hold deep respect for individuals who have experienced horrifying conditions, painful relationships, and experiences I cannot imagine. Ten years ago, our family went through significant adversity and trauma, because when one family member is hurting, the entire family system is impacted in so many ways. For days, pieces of weeks, and months at a time, we scrambled to find some peace and felt safety. At that time, I was not sure how to move through each day, and there were moments when a deep sea of fog suffocated my thinking and perceptions, leaving a residue of tension that became my normal, as I felt to be recycling survival states in all moments. Out of respect, I am unable to share specifics, but the words in this book, embody my personal experiences and those of so many.

The Science of the Nervous System

Post-traumatic growth through intentional plasticity is a process or journey from autonomic states of protection to autonomic states of growth. We are learning that the greatest growth signal for human beings is love, and that our nervous systems require a sense of felt safety to begin recalibrating survival states through regulatory practices and hundreds of moments of connection. We will be discussing and sharing this recalibration throughout these chapters. It can feel overwhelming to work through the adversity and trauma that are often held in the tissues of the nervous system, and by no means will merely changing our thoughts magically change our lives and our world. Trauma lives in brains and bodies, creating a fundamental reorganization of how the brain manages perceptions. In many ways, we become stuck in the past when our present experiences mirror embodied information that often has no coherent narrative. Trauma changes not only how we think, but also our capacity to think, while our bodies, still holding our sensations and feelings, need to gradually learn that the danger has passed.[86] Our bodies can feel the sadness that our brains cannot express. This post-traumatic growth journey is a process, and it can take us five steps forward and eight steps backward on many days.

Emotions and reason work together, and this partnership is what places value on our experiences. Dr. Bessel Vander Kolk writes, "When our survival is at stake, our reasoning or rational brain is not accessible, and our emotional brain is severed and functions relatively independent from our reasoning brain. When the alarm bell of the emotional brain keeps signaling that we are in danger, no amount of insight will silence it."[87]

Our brains and nervous systems organize to protect us, reflecting everything we know in our environment to keep us safe. All the experiences, conditions, and information to which we have been exposed are stored in our nervous system. At an unconscious level, we have memorized these experiences, places, relationships, and environments without intentional awareness, predicting new experiences based on our past experiences! These are often the embodied, procedural, and emotional memories that we hold in our brains and bodies. When we tune into our nervous system, we hear three different stories reflecting our ever-changing autonomic states. When we feel safe, connected, curious, and hopeful, we are functioning with more clarity and purpose, and this can elevate our emotions. In this calm and safe state, our nervous systems reflect what the Polyvagal Theory shares as the "social engagement system."

Within seconds, minutes, or hours, we feel or sense a shift in sensations, thoughts, and feelings as our external or internal environments change, producing a condition or experience that alters how we think, feel, and respond. If I receive a text or call that my child is sick, read an unkind e-mail, feel a migraine approaching, or hear upsetting news, my nervous system (brain and body) reacts with thoughts, feelings, and responses that are familiar to me, although they may not be pleasant. My body and brain no longer feel safe, focused, and connected, as my nervous system mobilizes its energy to fight, run, or possibly shut down. Familiar embodied and historical memories remind us to unconsciously reproduce the same reactions toward those experiences or conditions. This is not a conscious act or practice, unless we begin to become curious and question our perceptions, beliefs, thoughts, and feelings that engineer those fast automatic perceptions. When I begin to experience dysregulation, through worry, agitation, irritation, or anger, the story of my nervous system is searching for its balanced sense of "home." This searching is a fight-flight survival response. If our nervous system is shutting down, leading us to feel disconnected, numb, untethered, or lost, we begin to retreat and pull away from ourselves, others and the world. In this immobilized or shut-down state, we feel overwhelmed and alone, because belonging is a biological need shared by humans and most mammals. When we experience a lost connection, our nervous system tells us stories that reverberate hopelessness. Traditionally, this shut-down or immobilized state has been referred to as freeze. Through the lens of the Polyvagal Theory, this is a reptilian response initiated by the dorsal vagal system, which strips us of conscious awareness as we begin to retreat and shut down. In the absence of cues of safety, this circuit evolved to adaptably respond to immense terror and threat and is our most primitive response to stress.[88] Recognizing and becoming aware of our reactions to our external and internal environments is a hope-filled step, as we inch away from feeling emotionally overwhelmed or a loss of control. When we become aware and begin to question how our patterned and held nervous system stories are shaping our thoughts, beliefs, and emotions, we may discover that what once served our survival is no longer serving us at the present moment. We may also discover encouraging feelings about this growing awareness and gentle gratitude for the new perspective it brings.

Author and speaker Joe Dispenza, D.C., says, "Your identity becomes defined by everything outside of you because you identify with all of the elements that make up your external world. Thus, you are observing your reality with a mind that is equal to it. You may not think that your environment and your thoughts are that rigidly similar and your reality is so easily reproduced, but when you consider your brain is a complete record of your past, and your mind is the product of consciousness, in one sense, you might always be thinking in the past."[89] When we think and react from past memories (often unconscious and embodied), we can only create past experiences, and in some ways we are living in the past! Our brains and bodies are always in communication. If we keep firing the same neural networks through similar thoughts, beliefs, and perspectives, we strengthen those neural networks and they become our brain's hardware. In other words, we begin to hardwire our nervous systems to align with our experiences and conditions, because when clusters of neurons have fired so many times in the same patterns, they express as our habits of thought, feeling, behavior, and perspective. This becomes our mental and emotional signature as our thought processes become equal to our environments, and as our environments or conditions mirror our thoughts and therefore our feelings.[90] Trauma and adversity occur on a continuum, and they are personal: we can never know how another individual experiences a condition, relationship, or event.

Following is an event that I initially hesitated to include here because it is not on the scale of the horrific traumas through which so many people are trying to move through: neglect, abuse, poverty, and the debilitating effects of domestic or environmental violence and systemic racism. It is, however, a personal realization about how a traumatizing experience can shift our cognition, perception, and ways of being in the blink of an eye, and how we can find ourselves not who we were before that experience.

Eighteen months ago on a warm fall evening, I was walking our rescue dog Nellie, a 40-pound puggle. As we turned a corner, my eyes caught a glimpse of an enormous black Great Dane barking, growling, and struggling to get away from its owner who was half the size of her massive dog. Suddenly, Nellie and I stopped, as my heart thumped at an unfamiliar speed inside my chest. Nellie froze at my feet, not moving and starting to tremble as she picked up on my fear and terror. Within a few seconds, the Great Dane broke away from its owner, snarling, and began attacking Nellie. Screaming, I stupidly held tighter to the leash, battling my shock, and prepared to battle the Great Dane for Nellie's survival. There was no logic accessible in that moment. Suddenly, Nellie's collar snapped and she broke free, running off through the neighborhood streets and darting cars, while the growing darkness hid her small frame and frantic pace. The Great Dane ran after Nellie for a block or two but could not keep up. I don't remember much else, other than my crying, stumbling, shaking, and panting as I ran down the side streets with wet yoga pants, trying to keep up with her, as we were a little over a half mile from home. As I approached our driveway, I saw Nellie lying in our yard fervently licking herself as the bloodstained fur caught my jangled attention. Sobbing, I knelt beside her, murmuring softly, and waiting until I could see what injuries she had.

Nellie survived the physical attack and injuries, but the emotional trauma for both of us is visceral. Even writing this narrative reactivates it for me. There has never been a time since that evening when the sound of a jingling collar, a deep bark, the sight of that infamous overgrown side yard where we encountered the Great Dane, or the approach of any large dog does not activate those sensations in my body. The same is true for Nellie. On our walks, she is cautious, hair standing up on her back, assuming a posture and making a low whining sound that we'd never heard from her before the attack. I instantly know that she's activated or triggered, and a jolt of adrenaline speeds up my heart, and all attention is focused on what I now understand as the survival response. Thinking about these moments brings back a fragmented sensory memory as my hands tingle and I feel a lumpy sensation in my throat—even sitting at this computer with no Great Dane threat! My mind knows this, but my body keeps a survival account through held experiences and the sensations that initiate a threat-and-protect response inside my nervous system.

My healing and growth begin with the awareness of how these dog walks feel in my body today. What am I noticing? What feels comforting or soothing to my nervous system in moments when my body perceives threat even though I am inside a safe environment? I begin to intentionally breathe deeply with an extended outbreath. I find that talking to myself as we walk feels comforting, reminding my nervous system that this is now. I also carry my phone on long walks so that, during these activated moments, I can reach out and connect with someone I trust.

As we think different thoughts, our brain circuits fire in specific patterns and sequences to produce mindsets that equate with those thoughts.[91] As those activated neuron networks fire, the brain produces specific chemicals that match those thoughts so that we begin feeling the way we are thinking, which activate more thoughts matching those chemicals, speeding up the neurochemical assembly line, strengthening the chemical signature of an emotional response that becomes our state of being around these thoughts. We begin to unconsciously memorize this state of being, identifying with what we think and feel equating this with who we are.

For many of our students, the environment is not trustworthy. By asking them to soften their defenses, we may be traumatizing them in our classrooms and schools.

LORI DESAUTELS

Early Brain Development and the Impact of Adversity and Trauma (A Review)

We are no different than our children and students. We carry in our own lives experiences that have created patterns of thoughts, feelings, beliefs, and perceptions that can be so difficult to change. In this section, I want to review (from my previous book, *Connections Over Compliance*) how trauma and adversity live in the nervous system and can impact how we perceive and walk through our lives, not only as children, but also as adults.

Our early years hold great plasticity, and without awareness and intention, we may be swimming in early or childhood survival states and living in our past. During early development, when our caregivers read our signals of hunger, thirst, discomfort, or distress, they may or may not meet our needs in predictable and consistent ways through attention and attunement. Psychiatrist Bruce Perry writes, "In the case of responsive parenting, pleasure and human interactions become inextricably woven together ... This interconnection, the association of pleasure with human interaction, is the critical neurobiological glue that bonds and creates healthy relationships."[92] When any of us—our students or we, their teachers—walk into classrooms without this "glue" from embodied attachment experiences, we struggle within relationships and may have created a memory template of adult intervention that reads as one of hostility rather than protection. How do these memory templates form?

The brain organizes from the bottom up, as our **brainstem** controls autonomic functions like digestion, respiration, breathing, and heart rate. The brainstem also collects sensory input from our external (surrounding) and internal (body) environments, which is initially registered through signals that are tracking previous experiences to determine safety and threat within our environments.[93] Our sensory input begins to organize through prior stored sensory experiences, and this bottom-up hierarchy is designed for our survival. Perry says, "All sensory experiences are processed from the bottom up, and our brains are organized to sense, feel, and act before we think."[94] The brainstem is the only part of our brain fully developed at birth. The rest of the developing brain is waiting for experiences to assist in its growth and maturation, and because the brainstem is also the area that initiates our stress response systems, this area must be organized, regulated, and integrated for children and adolescents to feel safe and calm.[95] Often, in chronic states of stress, the only parts of the brain left functioning are the lower regions where our survival responses live, and where we sense danger, which activates and elevates our heart rates, respiration, and blood pressure. Perry states:

> Our life experiences shape the way key systems in our brain organize and function. Starting in the womb, the developing brain begins to store parts of our life experiences, including our attachment dynamics. Fetal brain development can be influenced by a host of factors before birth, but without human connection, our stress response systems are altered, and we may begin developing a broken and distorted sense of belonging.[96]

Children, youth, and adults experiencing developmental and relational trauma can begin to feel so threatened by the sensations in their bodies that they rapidly move into a fight-flight survival state, and the higher parts of the brain begin moving offline. Stress chemicals shut down the prefrontal cortex (thinking brain), and cognition clearly becomes a challenge. Children and youth may begin to feel threatened and unsafe, compromising their sense of connection, which can prohibit rewarding experiences from emotional or relational interaction with others.[97] Without awareness, connection, or some form of healthy intervention, adults carrying past trauma into everyday life may also begin living in a prolonged, highly sensitized stress response where they are scanning environments, people, and experiences from threat and protective states.

Broken attachments can create poor impulse control and vulnerable conscience development. Children and youth impaired by damaged attachments are often unable to manage or make sense of their feelings and sensations. There is a "felt abandonment" from these children and youth that can be observed as a deep emotional void within interpersonal relationships through superficiality, distrust, hostile dependence, and the need to control all situations.[98]

Toxic stress can be defined as excessive or prolonged activation of stress response systems in the body and brain which may result in damaging effects on behavior, cognition, and overall physiological health across the lifespan.[99] This type of stress can be activated when any child, youth, or adult is exposed to ongoing, and therefore, elevated levels of adversity and uncertainty. This can include a wide variety of noxious experiences along a continuum: chronic neglect, physical abuse, ongoing emotional abuse, exposure to violence in the community, social rejection and humiliation, and many other negative adversities and experiences that increase levels of anxiety impacting the neurological systems in our bodies—such as our immune, digestive, cardiovascular, and perceptual systems—affecting adult health and well-being.[100]

Adversity and trauma impact the developing brain, but there is more. Perry states, "We need to understand that along with childhood adversities, there is the timing, severity, and patterns of stress activation along with the emotional buffers that serve as protective factors during adversity and times of trauma... Our history of relational health, our connectedness to family, community, and culture, is more predictive of our mental health than our history of adversity."[101] This is hopeful. This awareness leads us down the path of resilient possibilities.

Every day, educators across the country are seeing the consequences and personally feeling the effects of chronically activated stress response systems from adults and students expressing this anxiety, fear, and angst through negative behaviors. The students' behaviors, to the outside world, often look aggressive, disruptive, apathetic, shut down, and unmotivated, but the physiology of their nervous systems tells a different story. These children and youth are often functioning from survival states, and they experience the world through a frenzied and dangerous perception producing feelings of isolation, aggression, anxiety, or immobilization from the adversities and trauma that land inside their nervous systems. Trauma is never a singular event. Trauma lives in the nervous system and produces a chronic disruption of felt safety.[102]

Polyvagal Theory for Adults

Why is it so hard to change? Imagine if your mother or caregiver lived with tremendous guilt and possibly shame that caused them to question relationships and current experiences as they suffered through their own conflicted thinking and perceptions from past experiences. As children, we unconsciously observe behavior patterns of others, taking in information around us like digital recorders. We begin to observe and identify with the emotional patterns, practiced thoughts, and feelings from those around us. Our own thoughts and feelings about our lives and ourselves tend to be distorted from the observations and interactions with our caregivers, and we unconsciously begin to memorize maps of other people's guilt and suffering as our own! We therefore have conditioned our bodies and brains to hold onto the feelings of guilt and suffering without much conscious thought.[103]

In this section, we are going to explore how our bodies hold the unconscious mind through the language of sensations and feelings. Joe Dispenza, D.C., writes:

> Psychologists tell us that by the time we're in our mid-30s, generally our identity or personality will be completely formed. This means that for those of us over 35, we have memorized a select set of behaviors, attitudes, beliefs, emotional reactions, habits, skills, associative memories, conditioned responses, and perceptions that are now subconsciously programmed within us. Those programs are running us because the body has become the unconscious mind. This means that we will think the same thoughts, feel the same feelings, react in identical ways, behave in the same manner, believe in the same dogmas, and perceive reality the same ways.[104]

It is as if we live most days on autopilot, because the moment we have a thought, feeling or reaction, our nervous system simply reacts, and we live unconsciously! Becoming aware of our thoughts, feelings, and behavioral patterns moves us into a new understanding of how our nervous system is continually communicating to us.

Until fairly recently, the psychological, neuroscience, and traumatology fields in the western part of the world rarely recognized the bidirectional communication between our brains and bodies. Today, the continual and fluid dance between our bodies and brains leads us toward an emotional/sensory environment for addressing adversity, trauma, and the resiliency that is possible. In 1994, Dr. Stephen Porges introduced the Polyvagal Theory, which provides a refined understanding of the biology of survival and felt safety.[105] Being able to feel safe with others is one of the most critical aspects of post-traumatic growth. Our nervous systems are built to help us belong and connect to one another even when we are by ourselves. We might be watching a game show or a Netflix movie, listening to music, or engaged with a podcast, and our nervous systems respond to the emotions, tones, facial expressions, and movements of others. Dr. Bessel Van Der Kolk says, "Most of our energy is devoted to connecting with others."[106] We will be sharing the plasticity of co-regulation and connection in the following chapter.

Hierarchical Nervous System States

I want to take a deeper dive into the nervous system states, as these were briefly mentioned at the beginning of the chapter. The human nervous system has evolved over time to respond to the needs, strengths, and environments of our ancestors. What kept them alive was a vigilant system that prioritized safety while redirecting energy when there was danger. If a predator appeared, the body would focus its attention on getting oxygen and blood to the muscles and away from the internal organs so that we could fight or flee. After the threat was gone, we could then rest and recuperate. Through the process of evolution, human beings inherited three building block states that became our autonomic hierarchy: the 500-million-year-old brainstem; the 400-million-year-old sympathetic system; and the 200-million-year-old ventral vagal hierarchy.[107] Through the lens of Dr. Stephen Porges' Polyvagal Theory, we recognize that these older pathways are still in place, and that we still utilize them in present day situations every time we encounter stressful conditions. By understanding how these nervous system pathways developed, when they engage, and how they impact our bodies and minds, we can better understand how we interact within our environments and why we feel and experience the world in the ways that we do. Through the Polyvagal lens, we will also explore how we can learn the language of our nervous systems to improve our relationships while creating safe, productive spaces for emotional well-being, learning, growing, and living life with a renewed awareness.

Our nervous system (which includes our brain and body) is constantly scanning for cues in the environment to determine whether or not we are safe. Safety can begin with the absence of predators or scary situations, but our focus will emphasize that safety must also include the presence of connection, security, friendly faces, and places; this is known as **relational safety**. This constant scanning of our environments is our autonomic intuition at work, an unconscious action of which we're unaware. We call this safety radar **neuroception**.[108] Our neuroception detects safety and danger. It operates differently from perception, which includes conscious awareness and reflection. Neuroception is an automatic and constant scanning and gathering of information from our outside world, inside world, and our relational world.[109] This information is interpreted by our brainstem and body as either safe or not safe. It's like our radar or "Spidey sense" checking to see if we need to be on high alert. From there, our vagal nerves are engaged to automatically respond based on their initial interpretation. Again, neuroception is an automatic process, and it has an automatic default setting to detect danger, safety, unfamiliarity, or anything that alerts our nervous system. Humans have a natural negativity bias that has benefited us in the past. It is better to assume that something is dangerous and to be prepared, rather than to ignore possible danger and be hurt or killed!

Vagus Nerve Pathway

Nerves are made from bundles of neurons, which are significant players in our nervous system. Specifically, the vagus nerve is a cranial nerve (pathway of nerves) that originates from the brainstem and branches off into many locations within the body.[110] It is so widely integrated throughout the body that it is considered the "wandering nerve" (vagus means wandering). The vagal pathways innervate and interact with a wide range of muscles and organs: the heart, the lungs, facial muscles, ear muscles, and many organs in our digestive system.[111] The brain and the body are in constant communication with each other. What is interesting to note is that approximately 80% of the nerve fibers are sending information from the body to the brain, and only 20% of those nerve fibers are sending information from the brain to the body—meaning that the vagal pathways are majorly interested in receiving cues from our body to determine how safe we feel.[112] We are constantly using our body's "gut feeling" to determine how comfortable we are. This wandering nerve has evolved over time to adapt to our evolutionary history and respond to our ancestors' needs and survival tactics.

Hierarchical Nervous System States

The autonomic nervous system is divided into three systems or states of functioning and survival. Each part of our nervous system has a unique set of protective actions:

- The **dorsal vagal system** assists us in immobilizing or collapsing when our bodies and brains meet significant threats. This is a reflexive survival response.

- The **sympathetic system** mobilizes us to fight or run when we perceive danger. This higher-level survival response on the autonomic hierarchy prompts us to action beyond simply shutting down.

- The ventral vagal system creates a cohesive and rhythmic partnership between our brains and bodies when it is activated. The ventral vagal system provides the neural platform to support social connection and prosocial behaviors creating felt safety in our internal and external environments.

As we learn about these autonomic states, we find a direct relationship to brain structure and function. The prefrontal cortex is aligned with the ventral vagal system, allowing an oxygenated blood flow to access the reasoning, safety, and emotional regulation skills we need. The limbic system holding the **amygdala** is a part of our survival fight-flight response attending to emotional disruptions—think of it as a smoke alarm. The brainstem (reptilian brain) is activated in dorsal shut-down, collapsed, and immobilized states. Our brains and bodies are always working together, and the brain structures and nervous system are not schematic, but blend and integrate in a variety of ways. For this description, I have simplified so that we can correlate the two.

As you are imagining the dorsal vagal system, the word "dorsal" means toward your "back" (think of a dorsal fin), and "ventral" means toward your "belly." The dorsal vagal nerve is the most ancient nerve pathway, approximately 500 million years old.[113] We share this pathway with our older, reptilian ancestors. Think of what a reptile might do if it were threatened.

A great analogy of our dorsal vagal pathway and function is how a turtle generally responds to threats. When it perceives danger, the turtle shuts itself down and hides in its shell. This reaction allows it to conserve energy and make itself less noticeable to its predators. Because the dorsal vagal pathway is so old, we share it with other mammals as well. Have you ever seen a mouse that's been caught by a cat and appears to be dead? Its eyes are closed, its posture is limp, its mouth is agape—even if it hasn't been harmed. This is a survival tactic called **death feigning**. The mouse perceives such a high level of danger that pretending to be dead makes more sense than risking flight from or fighting against a threat too big to escape or conquer. By collapsing and death feigning, the mouse conserves its energy for survival because predators will assume that an already-dead animal is diseased and will turn away. The interest is gone. The dorsal vagal pathway is responsible for this immobilization response.

Next along the evolutionary story is the development of the sympathetic system. This pathway for our fight-flight response has been around for about 400 million years. As can be inferred, the sympathetic pathway is the part of our nervous system that *sympathizes* when our brain and body feel like we need to mobilize energy in response to a challenge. It engages our body by increasing our heart rate, decreasing our digestion, increasing pupil size, and activating respiration, so that our body can either run away or attack. The sympathetic nervous system is our mobilization response, and the vagal brake is likened to a regulator providing access to a continuum of energized responses, as there is a significant accessibility of function within the sympathetic system. Our sympathetic pathways prepare or energize us for protection—or even excitement or play. The sympathetic pathways can merge with the ventral experiences because we have a vast range of emotions and sensations, so our range of ventral (social engagement) experience is also huge! In contrast, the vagal pathway (both the dorsal and ventral vagal) is a part of the contrasting **parasympathetic** organization of the nervous system. So when you think of a sympathetic response, imagine that your body is responding by ramping up, whereas a parasympathetic response is like putting on the brakes. How does the ventral vagal pathway differ from the dorsal vagal pathway? This is where the ventral vagal brake accesses a wide range of emotions and sensations and is a regulator for our nervous system. When the brake is on, we slow down, yet we can be joyful, content, passionate, or playful because the vagal brake allows us accessibility to sympathetic energy!

The ventral vagal system is the newest pathway and is specifically something only humans and social mammals can access. This pathway was developed about 200 million years ago. The ventral vagal is the pathway of connection; its location is more anterior, closer to your front or belly. It touches and interacts with the heart and is known to be the "brake" on the heart. You might think, "Why would I want to slow down my heart? I want my heart to beat, especially if I am in danger." And yes, this is true. We want our hearts to beat so that we can push oxygen to our body and get rid of the waste products that our organs and muscles produce. And when we encounter danger, we need to ramp up the blood supply to better fuel our muscles for defense. But we can't live in this heightened state forever! When we are in a fight-flight state, our body is prioritizing a mobilization of quick energy while putting other functions like digestion, healing, or growing on the back burner. We hope that the danger is short-lived so that we can go about our other responsibilities and our bodies can return to homeostasis. It takes a lot of energy to defend ourselves—

and that isn't sustainable! So, to bring us back down, we also require a "brake" to slow our heart rate and breathing. The ventral vagal pathway does that when it is activated. Once we stop experiencing stress that we perceive as a threat, our ventral vagal system can slow our heart rate and breathing pace.

The question then is, "How is this pathway different from the slowing down of the dorsal vagal pathway if they are both a part of the parasympathetic nervous system?" The major difference is the environment and purpose of these pathways. The dorsal vagal pathway engages when an organism is in danger, and its nervous system collapses into immobility because of extreme risk and fear. The ventral vagal pathway, on the other hand, is a regulating response that allows us to connect with others and feel safe, because that pathway has access to the higher executive functions of our prefrontal cortex. This ventral pathway is only accessible when we are *not* in danger—when we feel safe, curious, and connected in our environment. This pathway feels enjoyable to our nervous system. When our ventral vagal pathway is engaged, we can "do life and do school." We aren't feeling threatened, so we can attend to the tasks of learning, teaching, parenting, problem-solving, cooperating, and decision-making that we are expected to do every day. When our ventral vagal system is engaged, we are able to experience felt safety and focus our attention on prosocial behavior. Our priority is no longer survival, but connection, safety, and possibly curiosity. The ventral vagal pathway stimulates the heart to reduce its rate and innervates other muscles and organs, allowing us to interact more positively as we connect with one another. As an analogy, think of a car entering a garage. Your foot can't always be on the accelerator, increasing the speed, because we need to slow down to park in that garage. We also need to slow down when we are completing a task, problem-solving, or creating a pause before we act or speak in an irrational way. It is hard on the nervous system when we are always on high alert, elevated in the fight-flight protective system, when our sympathetic nervous system is always engaged. To productively interact with others, take care of ourselves, and complete the tasks expected of us throughout the day, we need to be in a head and body space that is conducive to letting us focus our attention appropriately.

I would like for you to imagine how you feel when your needs are met. How do you feel and sense the world when you aren't stressed, and you feel approachable and curious?

1. What sensations, emotions, and thoughts feel delicious, exhilarating, inspiring, or comforting?

2. What body language are you displaying when you are confident, safe, and content?

3. How do you interact with others when you aren't being activated by the other stressors in your life?

4. What body language cultivates safety and connection in your everyday life?

As we explore the Polyvagal Theory and the three hierarchical states, we find that the newest system, the ventral vagal pathway, creates what Dr. Stephen Porges calls a biological face-heart connection that humans and social mammals can access. In other words, our faces offer cues about how we are feeling.[114] Since humans, as social mammals, have this special ventral vagal pathway, does that mean we utilize it in all moments of the day? Unfortunately, no. To engage and interact as society expects, it is preferred that we have accessibility to the higher executive functioning skills found in our prefrontal cortex (which occurs when our ventral vagal system is engaged). That's where learning happens. That's where we are when we feel calm, hopeful, curious, and social. However, our neuroception is still actively engaged, even when we are feeling comfortable; if it notices something awry, our nervous system responds and shifts to a more protective response. This switch is automatic, not a conscious choice. Our nervous system has a bias toward perceived dangerous stimuli because it's wired to keep us safe, and therefore doesn't leave us time to ask, "What was that? Should I be worried? How should I respond? Should I beat my heart faster so I can have more blood running through my system in case I need to run or fight?" If we took the time to think through these conscious decisions, it might be too late to answer those questions, which is why we have a protective system that directs our body and mind to keep us safe in the face of danger. It is automatic, unconscious, and overriding. This system was evolutionarily adapted over millennia to respond to predators and ensure our ancestors' cooperation in mutual survival. We should be grateful that our bodies and brains have been programmed to do what is necessary for our survival! The main structure that we can thank for our autonomic nervous system's hierarchy of protection is our vagus nerve.

Our brains and bodies are always on a quest for safety. Safety is experienced when the cues for safety outweigh the cues for threat or danger. We experience a felt sense of relational trust around us, and we can focus our energy on healing and higher-order functioning. This is when our ventral vagal system is engaged and allows us to be social, calm, and ready to learn. But when our autonomic nervous system is scanning the environment and notices an activating stimulus, it will automatically switch gears to prioritize survival. That survival might mean engaging the sympathetic nervous system when there's a chance that fighting or fleeing may keep us safe, or that survival might mean engaging the dorsal vagal system and shutting down in the face of immense danger, because disconnecting may save our lives. As we explore our plasticity through the lens of Polyvagal Theory, I hope to fill your knowledge base with a deeper understanding of how our stories of connection, protection, and disconnection drive our thoughts, feelings, perceptions, and behaviors in all moments. Together, we will explore ways to experience felt safety in our personal and professional lives. The nervous system has plasticity, and together, we can promote truly equitable learning and healing spaces in our schools, homes, and communities.

When we feel safe, we can learn. When we feel safe, we can teach well. When we feel safe, we parent well and live well. Take a moment to reflect on these statements, and then consider these questions:

• What does safety look like to you?

- What does it feel like?

- What can you hear and see when you feel safe?

- What do you need to feel safe in a classroom, inside a relationship, or within any environment?

- What cues your body to feel safe?

As I have shared, when our brains and bodies feel safe, connected, and secure, we are able to attend to relationships, ask for and receive support from others, and uphold responsibilities and tasks as we cultivate the connection, curiosity, and creativity that begin to shift our perceptions, and therefore shift the state of our nervous systems. In this autonomic ventral vagal state, our attention is in the present moment. When we feel safe, we can put our energy into higher-order tasks with clarity in our learning, creating sustained attention, stronger working memory, and deeper listening. Our goal in our classrooms, schools, and organizations is to foster rich learning environments where adults and students experience felt safety. Yet we still aren't able to fully reach everyone, because feeling safe is more than just the removal of a threat or telling someone there is nothing to worry about. *Feeling* safe and *being* safe are two different experiences.

The education field is moving to more trauma-responsive practices in an effort to accommodate for the adversities and diversity in classrooms, but we have a ways to go. The hope is to be more aware of the emotional worlds that students and adults are carrying into classrooms. When we provide space to share our stories while validating one another's experience, we open up a deeper journey toward growth for our staff and students. With the integration of the Polyvagal Theory, we are creating more awareness of the inner emotional maps that hold our lived experiences residing in our nervous systems. How can we begin to support our own nervous systems for optimal learning and emotional well-being that leads to growth, embracing our superpower of plasticity? Education requires brain and body state regulation. A regulated nervous system is prepared for cognitive and mental tasks. A regulated nervous system is ready to parent with all the challenges we encounter. A regulated nervous system is ready to lead. But we cannot always find calm regulation; acknowledging when we are dysregulated is critical in our journey toward well-being.

Polyvagal Theory provides our autonomic nervous systems with stories! These stories help us to learn about ourselves, the world, and the relationships in our lives founded in the emotions, thoughts, sensations, perceptions, and behaviors held in our nervous systems.

In conclusion, when we are functioning from our ventral vagal system, our prefrontal cortex is activated, and we feel at home in our nervous system. This is our story of connection. Ventral vagal autonomic states allow connection with others so that we are able to experience a rhythm of reciprocity, knowing that relationships rupture and repair and that this is a balanced, healthy rhythm. What helps each of us to find our way home? In other words, what feels comforting? What soothes us? What assists us in experiencing a connection to ourselves that is grounding and revitalizing? Each nervous system state holds a large range of emotion, and our ventral, sympathetic, and dorsal states can blend with one another. When I experience ventral vagal activation, I am able to be in a flow with my work. I am more creative, more compassionate, and can overlook the experiences or people that may have felt unkind or triggering when I am dysregulated. There are sensory practices, strategies, places, and people that can help our nervous systems return to a balanced state. Therapist and author Deb Dana refers to these places, people, and practices as **anchors**.[115] Anchors hold us steady and can lead us onto our pathways of safety in difficult times. When we are aware of our anchors, we can integrate them into our day to be accessible and familiar if we encounter a crisis or challenge. By understanding our anchors, we begin to create a framework for processing and addressing a difficult condition or event. Our autonomic nervous system shapes the way we experience life, and our nervous system stories are continually changing and evolving. Plasticity is our nervous system's ability to reshape itself as new patterns of thoughts, feelings, perceptions, and behaviors evolve.

The story of our sympathetic autonomic states is one of searching for our home. We are often frantically trying to find our way to our nervous system's balanced state, which we liken in this chapter to "home." As we shared, this system activates midbrain regions and can set off an emotional survival alarm as our nervous system automatically mobilizes us to fight or flee. This system protects us as it works to circulate blood and regulate body temperature while providing us with the energy we need for adapting to the environment or experiences. In sympathetic states, I may feel jumpy, anxious, worried, irritable, antsy, or just overly energetic.

The story of our dorsal system is one of homelessness. We feel forever lost when we have entered this survival state where our nervous system is conserving energy just to stay alive. This state feels unfamiliar, much like unchartered waters that we have never navigated. For me, when I enter dorsal, I want to sleep. I have no energy to talk, and I want to be left alone. There is a sense of numb heaviness when I am experiencing this type of survival response in a difficult situation or period of time.

When we recognize the stories of our nervous system, we begin to reclaim the power and autonomy to listen and tune into what our body is communicating. This is resiliency! Being aware of the states of our nervous system builds flexibility and as I have shared, the goal in post-traumatic growth is not about being regulated, but about recognizing when we are dysregulated. Author and therapist Deb Dana says, "Be curious about your story."[116] Recognizing our cues of safety, threat, or danger strengthens pathways of awareness, and that awareness may soon interrupt the patterns of thoughts, feelings, and behaviors that bind us to the reflexes of survival. We are works in progress. Our nervous system is always listening and learning as we ebb and flow with the thoughts, feelings, and perceptions that we feed it. The goal of embracing neuroplasticity is to stretch our system by attending to the moment-by-moment awareness as we sculpt new ways of being!

Following is the Polyvagal chart of the hierarchy of autonomic states that we discussed in this chapter. Notice the wide range of emotion and how the states can blend and lean into one another as we move through our experiences each day. We are integrating these charts as check-ins and opportunities for staff and students to share their nervous system states throughout a day, class period, morning, or afternoon. We could even track these changing states for a week at a time, noticing patterns or gaps where we observe chaos or rigidity in the flow. When we recognize where our bodies and brains have landed as we experience the world around us, we can create environments, experiences, conditions, and relationships for aligning to what we need. The practices below will help to bring awareness and intentionality to our ever-changing nervous system. These practices can be used at the opening of staff meetings, during morning meetings with students, and within our own families. You can find the practices following the charts.

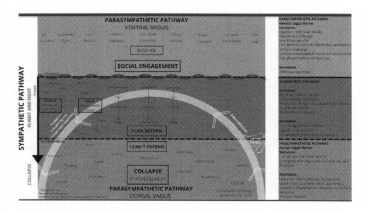

Download these charts:

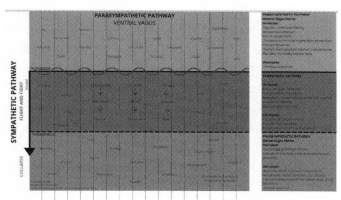

Adapted from the original version www.traumaprevention.com

Sensory and Regulatory Practices for Awareness and Growth: Anchors

In this practice, I ask staff and students to identify the people, places, experiences, and things that help them to feel safe, connected, and calmer.

1. What people anchor you? Who do you trust? Who can you call upon any time of the day or night?

2. What places anchor you? Do you have a special room, piece of furniture, walking path, vacation spot, or any space that seems to melt away your anxiety, tension, or angst?

3. What times of the day anchor you? Are you a morning person? Do you prefer midday? Is evening or late night your rejuvenating time?

4. What days of the week anchor you? Which days feel soothing and less stressful?

5. What objects, images, or rituals anchor us in the moment? What helps us the most if we have only a few minutes or seconds to take care of our nervous system? Some examples might be chewing gum, a mint, running our hands under cold water, a hand massage, grabbing a chocolate or cough drop, eating popcorn or something crunchy, texting a friend, looking at a picture or an image, three deep breaths, journaling a sentence or two, a one-minute walk, chewing on ice, holding a hand warmer, or moving ourselves to another location in the room. We could yawn, hum, or splash our faces with cold water.

6. What practices or things anchor us in the morning or evening? These might include a project we would like to take on, a 20-minute walk, 20 minutes of yoga, singing, playing a musical instrument, walking outdoors, sitting on our porch with a cup of tea and listening to nature, calling a friend, a five-minute focused attention practice, taking a drive, listening to music, a hot or cold shower, reading a favorite poem or book, lifting weights, or anything calming and soothing that we could do in 10 to 30 minutes that we might carve out of our day to help us prepare or release.

As I reflect on this chapter addressing the adult nervous system, I must emphasize that our students may need to borrow our calm throughout the school day; yet when we are running low or on empty, our brains move into survival and we become defensive, personalize behaviors, and lose sight of what is ours and what isn't. In other words, holding a compassionate presence begins with me! As we reflect on our ability to become a safe sanctuary for any student who needs one, we will also need to protect our boundaries and compassionately detach from what is out of our control.

Our schools will need to check in often with staff nervous system states. Collectively, we want to become aware of how we are collaborating, listening deeply to one another, and intentionally creating cultures of awareness; we must be courageous enough to speak to our own triggers, biases, to reflect on our self-talk, and to ask for help when we need it.

We will need to be intentional about what lies beneath the behaviors of our students and colleagues, as restorative practices mean very little if we are not connecting to the lived, embodied experiences and the stories that both adults and students carry in their nervous systems in all moments!

In the Resource Section of this book, you can find a list of regulatory (social and emotional) nervous system practices that I have created for adults. This is an evolving list, so feel free to look through these ideas and resources, and to share them with colleagues and family. Many of the practices in this section are also beneficial for children and youth. Below is an example of the social and emotional competencies through the lens of Applied Educational Neuroscience. The more we activate the pathways of ease, safety, and connection, the more accessible they become.

SEL Competencies for Adults

Social-Emotional Learning Practices for Educators

1. Sensorimotor Integration: the ability to have body awareness and recognize sensations in the body.

Gaining Sensorimotor Integration (also called Sensory-Body Integration) is an important skill for managing transitions, changing routines, increasing alertness for teaching, leading, learning, and improving emotional well-being. Sensorimotor Integration aligns with how we initially experience events and occurrences in our lives. It is the language of the body and lower regions of the brain. When we tune into our bodies and experience the sensations that accompany emotions and thoughts, we create an awareness of how to buffer our stressors and build the capacity for resilience! I will be sharing more of these practices in the Resource Section of the book. Below is a peek into adult awareness and regulation practices.

Corresponding CASEL Domain: Indiana-state Specific

Sensorimotor Integration is critically important for educators as they begin to interact with students who will be carrying in pain-based behaviors that often look and feel disruptive, oppositional, and defiant. Our brains and bodies hold implicit fragmented sensory memories which are embodied trauma and adversity experiences from our past. These fragmented and scattered memories are held below conscious awareness. The adversities in our lives often sub-consciously bubble to the surface without our conscious awareness, affecting how we perceive the pain and hurt through negative behaviors that are showing up in a child's or an adolescent's disposition, and therefore brain and body. Meeting ourselves with a gentle under-standing of our activated negative brain states (embodied memories of our adversities and trauma) will be foundational for educator emotional, social, and physiological well-being!

Educator Learning Outcome: Educators acknowledge and understand the significance and implication of the science of sensory language and cues through brain and body awareness.

Requirements and Materials: Willingness to take deep repetitive breaths, use journals, pens, computer or phone access for instructional videos and lectures.

Adult Nervous System Educator	
Indicator/Purpose	**Strategies & Practices**
1. Educators identify and actively participate in sensory practices and strategies for body and brain stress regulation to lessen and mitigate life stressors.	1a. Educators identify troubling sensations in the body by physically placing a hand and holding areas that feel tense, tight, painful, or tired, taking 5-10 slow deep breaths with an extended outbreath. Repeat a few times as needed. Following a repetition of deep breaths, identify two repairing sensory experiences that feel doable, actionable, and helpful in stress-filled moments. Ex.: movement, breath, being outdoors, warmth, pressure, coolness. 1b. Educators identify a bodily sensation and draw or journal what it looks like, using lines, shapes, colors, words, or images to explore how it communicates body and brain awareness. 1c. Educators identify 2-3 experiences where they need to pause, breathe deeply, and contemplate. (What sights, pieces of clothing, postures, sounds, tones of voice, scenarios, tangible felt experiences, etc., consistently push your buttons?) Following a repetition of deep breaths, identify two repairing sensory experiences that feel doable, actionable, and helpful in stress-filled moments. (3 deep breaths, a mint, cup of water, text a friend, write out thoughts, hand massage, short walk or move to another area with some deep breaths.) 1d. Focused Attention Practices: Focusing on a stimulus and extending our breath in a deep exhale engages the parasympathetic nervous system to slow our heart rate and lower our respiration and blood pressure. Our focus can be on a sound, taste, visualization, or movement while we are intentional about our breath and breathing. Some resources: • "30 Meditation Exercises & Activities to Practice Today," Leslie Riopel, https://positivepsychology.com/meditation-exercises-activities/ • "Break the Addiction to Negative Thoughts & Negative Emotions," Joe Dispenza, D.C., https://www.youtube.com/watch?v=AXrdVagSjjg • "Change Your Breath, Change Your Life," Lucas Rockwood, TEDxBarcelona, https://www.youtube.com/watch?v=_QTJOAI0UoU • Tension and Trauma Releasing Exercises: TRE® is an innovative series of exercises that assist the body in releasing deep muscular patterns of stress, tension, and trauma. The exercises safely activate a natural reflex mechanism of shaking or vibrating that releases muscular tension, calming the nervous system. Activating this mechanism in a safe, controlled environment, encourages the body back into a state of balance. Tension and Trauma Releasing Exercises are based on research showing that stress, tension, and trauma are both psychological and physical. TRE®'s reflexive muscle vibrations generally feel pleasant and soothing. After TRE®, many people report feelings of peace and well-being. TRE® has helped many thousands of people globally. https://traumaprevention.com/

Indicator/Purpose	Strategies & Practices
	• Emotional Freedom Technique/ Tapping: The practice consists of tapping with your fingertips on specific meridian points while talking through traumatic memories and a wide range of emotions.
2. Educators identify and befriend the pathways of the nervous system through the Polyvagal Theory with continual attention and awareness of how you experience sensations in your body. • The dorsal vagal system, the oldest pathway of the nervous system, assists us in immobilizing or collapsing when our bodies and brains meet significant threats. This is a reflexive survival response. • The sympathetic system, the second oldest pathway, mobilizes us to fight or run (fight-flight) when we perceive danger. This higher-level survival response on the autonomic hierarchy prompts us to action beyond simply shutting down. • The ventral vagal system, the newest pathway, creates a cohesive, rhythmic partnership between our brains and bodies when activated. It's the neural platform to support social connection and prosocial behaviors creating felt safety in our internal and external environments. The goal is not always regulation, but to recognize when you feel dysregulated. When we experience a regulated nervous system, we are able to move back and forth between pathways throughout our experiences. We begin to notice when we start moving away from the ventral vagal pathway.	2a. Resources supporting Polyvagal Theory and practices: • "Befriending Your Nervous System" is a presentation by trauma therapist Deb Dana on becoming aware of how our nervous system responds to our experiences, and how that can empower and relieve us. https://www.youtube.com/watch?v=TxpxyzZx_rw&t=3409s 2b. Regulatory practices that assist us in regulation and activating the brake on the vagus nerve, or parasympathetic pathways to a sense of calm: • Deep breaths with an extended outbreath • Sighing to regulate the nervous system • Movement to calm the nervous system (taking a walk, yoga, exercise, etc.) • Locating cues of safety for the nervous system in personal and professional environments (images, people, places in our homes or classrooms, a special e-mail or letter written to you, an object you can hold or see that brings some calm to your nervous system)

Guest Reflection From Sarah Guest, Elementary Educator and Neuro-Educational Consultant, Quesnel School District, British Columbia

In this final section of Chapter 2, graduate student and colleague Sarah Guest graciously shares the plasticity of her life with an account of her personal journey.

In 2017, I was teaching a grade 5/6/7 combination class of 24 students. It was my second year with many of the students, and the previous year we had accomplished an incredible goal. A Language Arts/Social Studies project begun in November 2016 snowballed (in the best ways possible) to culminate in the students realizing their passion for social justice work and advocating to their local stakeholders for recognition of contemporary veterans. Ultimately, the project completed with three new plaques honoring peacekeeping missions in Afghanistan and the Persian Gulf on our community cenotaph.

From my angle as their teacher, the planning was extensive, highly organized, and intentional; to be sure, we were covering many areas of the curriculum at all three grade levels. This wasn't the plan from the outset. Initially it was meant to be a letter-writing campaign to veterans over the holidays, to remember them after Remembrance Day. But one thing led to another, and when some of the veterans reached back to the students to say thank you for thinking of them during what was sometimes a very difficult, lonely time of year, the project became one of passion.

Some of the vets who reached back offered to share their experiences of combat and what it was like living with PTSD back on home turf. It was an eye-opening learning experience for all involved, learning that none of us could have ever been gifted by a book, and I had no idea what it was about to open up within my own being.

One day we were listening intently to a veteran share her vulnerable story and how she navigated the "normal" world with a head injury and PTSD as a result of her service, and as she recalled a memory of seeing a child crying next to the body of her deceased mother on the side of the war-torn road, I felt a catch in my throat as I tried to suppress my grief. The story made me feel small and helpless; it made me ache inside for my own son who was in his grade 1 classroom at another school in the district. Then as I was overcome by a wave crashing down on top of me, I was able to quietly excuse myself before I could release into the end of a quiet hallway the muffled sobs no longer willing to be stifled in my throat. Away from this vulnerable story, away from students and other adults who might see my weakness.

As educators do, I dug deep to steady myself, and within a few moments returned to the room with some dissociation to preserve my dignity. With that well-rehearsed emotional removal, I was able to see that most other adults and students had also been moved to tears. We carried on from that point with a spark to create some kind of lasting change for our community, as the students felt compelled to make sure that others knew of the sacrifices these men and women had made quietly and voluntarily, to be honored with dignity.

After writing to stakeholders, presentations to City Hall and Rotary, and doing their own fundraising, we were able to have three new plaques installed on the cenotaph less than a year after setting our goal.

That was in the fall of 2017, my eleventh year as an elementary classroom teacher. As our goal was realized, I also began getting migraine headaches. It was the classic, "work so hard, get to the finish line, and then collapse in a heap," and now I get the "sick" thing that many perfectionists and overachievers experience on a cyclical basis. I'd had a small stint of migraines a couple years prior, but they went away with a few life adjustments (better sleep, less stress). When they began again, I remember the fear they brought with them, and also my way of dealing with them, like most things that were wrong ... just fix it!

So I did, for a time. My fix happened to be a cocktail of over-the-counter acetaminophen and ibuprofen gulped down with a hasty swig of water right when the aura of visual fireworks came to obscure my vision. I found that if I caught it at the right time, the head-splitting pain could be interrupted just enough so that I could continue teaching. I operated this way for a few weeks, and the students were kind and supportive, knowing it was independent reading time if I was struck suddenly with vision loss. I carried on, again, until I couldn't.

It got to the point where I would marvel at how good I was at interrupting the onset of a migraine. And so, when the intensity and frequency increased to six migraines a week, and sometimes two in one day, I began to wonder if I possibly had a brain tumor. I went to my doctor to make sure. If it was a brain tumor, we were going to need to have that dealt with so that I could get back to my purpose: teaching.

My doctor normalized my migraines and their tenacious pattern as well as the medication he recommended I take to control them, but was reluctant to send me to a neurologist so that the actual *brain doctor* could find and remove my *brain tumor*. In my mind, I was there to get my referral and not a quick Band-Aid fix. I left with my referral to the neurologist and an angry GP in my wake, frustrated that I wouldn't just comply and take the meds! That was the last time I would see that doctor.

The problem with multiple migraines a week is eventually my brain became so exhausted, it wasn't functioning all that well even when I wasn't having symptoms. I couldn't tell where one ended and the next began. Defeated, I acquiesced, taking a couple weeks away from teaching to see what else was *maybe* going on.

The neurologist appointment came and went; I even had a migraine during his assessment. The best options I had were an abortive type of med to interrupt the migraine more effectively than the garden variety pain meds that I was using up to 18 per day. I would later learn that I was inducing rebound headaches as my body became dependent on the medication to keep the symptoms at bay. Eventually the symptoms just got louder and more obnoxious. Maybe because they weren't meant to be ignored?

Only after I began to surrender to the idea that I wasn't going to outsmart these symptoms—and this only came to pass as I was spending more time lying in my dark bedroom, not only missing out on my calling as an educator but barely able to interact with my son and husband in their day-to-day lives—did I begin to get curious. In that place of wondering, I was bombarded with harsh internal judgments but also a longing to be well. Without my work to distract me, as it had been such a safe, robust, and welcome distraction to myself for over a decade (not to mention a socially acceptable, even honorable distraction), I accepted my situation the best I could and got around to "just fix it"—finding that solution to the problem.

As you can imagine, it wasn't an easy fix. It was messy and complex, formed of many intricate layers, some fused together. Literally fused together, like the scar tissue fascia that blanketed the right side of my neck and shoulder and ran down my back, the result of a childhood trauma incident when I had been attacked by my caregiver at nine years old. An incident I had revisited and deconstructed with a therapist to resolve that trauma, yet somewhere in there, deep in my body, that physical trauma was only the tip of the iceberg. So much still unresolved, unexperienced, and unexpressed because I had never felt safe enough to stop and let the emotional deluge really catch up to me.

I had hit my wall and it had caught up with a fury.

Fast forward to 2022 for a moment. I am about to complete the final course in the Applied Educational Neuroscience Certification under the mentorship of Dr. Lori. I found her work in 2020 through a podcast about education and neuroscience, and I devoured it. So much of what she was infusing into the field of education was what I had been intuitively bringing into my life since I had left the education system in 2017. I had finally discovered the significance of adult brain and body state (the central pillar of AEN) and how, when left unchecked, it threatened to poison me and those who coexisted in my environment.

Those "few weeks off" actually transformed my life through three years away from the classroom to become my own teacher. I learned to interpret my body's cues as information rather than a nagging nuisance. I learned how to feel in my heart center; how joy or sadness took up space in my body, rather than existing under the constriction of anxiety that often bled into eventual numbness due to the sheer exhaustion of hyper vigilance. As I began to feel my way through the world as a whole person, I read and researched about trauma and adversity. I found practitioners, therapists, and doctors who met me with compassionate presence rather than judgment.

In the gift of those three years, I had lots of time to become better acquainted with my true self and my son, who had been missing my presence deeply and communicated it with outbursts of anger and disconnect. My insight allowed me to make connections to why and how my body was doing what it was doing; just like my son, it was only trying to communicate unmet needs.

In my perfect hindsight vision, I had come to realize how the day a vulnerable veteran bravely sharing their heartbreaking story about a child losing their mother had awakened my own fear of being severed from my son. I was alive, I was physically there in his life, but her story made me see how emotionally cut-off I had become from myself and, therefore, from him. I also began to consider how I had normalized my childhood trauma even though I had grown up in my own war-torn environment, harmed by the very people who were meant to care for me. There was no escaping this, and my body was protecting me by getting my attention the only way it could. By interrupting my intellectual mind, it forced me to stop living in distractions and instead recruit the space and resources needed to finally process what had been abandoned 27 years prior, my whole self. Living as a fraction was no longer sustainable. The greatest gift I could give my son was my health.

The migraines slowed gradually. The last one had its say in February of 2019. I returned to teaching in a behavior support role in 2020. It's a privilege to be part of this life-changing work of helping students and the adults who support them to understand the wisdom of our body and the symbiotic nature of how our nervous system works from within for our own safety, but also from without, for the shared safety and connection of others. Dr. Lori's work is a healing validation of how our suffering can transcend and serve a purpose much greater than a problem to be fixed, but instead a life to be reclaimed; seedlings of resilience, connection, and joy sprout from the once parched, now overturned rich soil. This is just one golden strand of my post-traumatic growth story, but in its weaving through the fabric of my lifetime, I find vitality and health as I am tucked safely inside—all of me, top to toe.

"Knowing yourself is the beginning of all wisdom"
ARISTOTLE

Chapter 3

When we understand that connection is the biggest driver for regulation, we are then able to share our calming presence to help others through their storms...

In co-regulatory practices, we are sharing a sanctuary of safety through our offered presence.

How Connections Can Heal Trauma—and Frighten Us, Too!

"Trauma happens in relationships, so it can only be healed in relationships."
ALANIS MORRISETTE

As I write this chapter addressing the power of connections, our world is hurting. From the words of Maria Shriver, "As Ukraine is being brutally attacked by Russia's brazen dictator Vladimir Putin, it made me think back to the times when my children were little and sick. I would hold them and ask them where they felt pain, but they were unable to pinpoint the location or the cause. They just knew it was everywhere, and so that's what they would say: 'Mommy, it hurts everywhere.' I feel like this quote aptly describes where we are as a world and as human beings right now. If the world could speak at this very moment, I think that it would say exactly what my children used to say: It hurts everywhere."[117]

We are all hurting from the pain of disconnection. We feel it in our bodies, minds, and hearts, and as neuroscientist and author Dr. Stephen Porges writes, "We carry our trauma stories in the pathways of our nervous systems."[118] We feel it in the collective nervous systems of our families and communities, and in the deeply woven fabric of this hurting yet resilient world. The conditions in Ukraine are unimaginable as we observe and deeply sense the fear, yet we also observe and sense the bravery and valorous leadership of Ukraine's president Volodymyr Zelenskyy, who is holding courageous space and honor for both his nation's anguish and its vital resilience. Human beings are social creatures, and we cannot survive without one another, but in this time of massive divides in our world, when our collective nervous systems hold the agony of war, racism, a global pandemic, and bitterly divided politics, coupled with the mental and emotional fragility of our children and youth experiencing toxic levels of stress, we have an opportunity to hold each other in our discomfort as we build the strong connections that nourish the human spirit and experience. We are only able to sit beside another fully when we begin to recognize the pain or peace living inside our own hearts and minds. Our inner awareness has the potential to serve a world. It is time.

Our early experiences become the prototypes and create the attachment dynamics for all our later connections. Psychiatrist Dr. Bessel Van Der Kolk states, "Children become attached to whoever functions as their primary caregiver. But the nature of that attach-ment—whether it is secure or insecure—makes a huge difference over the course of a child's life."[119]

Because human beings are profoundly social as we feel our way through experiences, conditions, relationships, and life, we cannot survive without one another. We also can activate one another's stress response systems, throwing us into survival autonomic states, where our threat and protection needs override our sense of felt safety that can be found with one another.

As I have shared, this 2021-22 school year has been such a chal-lenging year for our students, staff, and families. In the young brain and body, the nervous system is developing at unprecedented rates while survival responses and emotional reactivity are elevated as mid-brain regions holding those survival responses have emerged. Along with brain states of survival, the evolving nervous system embraces heightened emotional reactions that prioritize threat and safety over cognitive learning. The pandemic is and has been a continual threat to the collective nervous systems of our country and world, systems that biologically shut down accessibility to the frontal cortex for felt safety and ease of connection with another. I have also been wondering about the palpable state of the communal nervous systems in schools, districts, and communities. Which schools are functioning in survival fight-flight states? Within our schools, what is the collective nervous system of departments, grade levels, and administration or leadership when there is ramped-up emotional reactivity, which our students experience from the adults? Which schools feel a significant loss of energy and purpose? Which schools are hanging by a thread of hope, fighting the pull of this moment's educational demands? We need each other, but when our nervous systems are impacted by chronic unpredictability, isolation, and deep unrest, our tolerance for others lessens, and we may find ourselves unintentionally pushing people away. As author and therapist Resmaa Menakem writes, "Settled adult bodies produce settled bodies of children and youth."[120] Put another way, human beings are irrevocably contagious!

A few weeks ago, I was asked by a large school district's leadership to meet with all the schools' community liaisons that attend to the social, emotional, and physiological needs of students, staff, parents, and the community within each building. As I walked into the administration building's large, dimly lit, and chilly lecture hall, I was met with 40 adults who nonverbally mirrored this dimly lit, oppressive environment. They were not chilly or unfriendly, but they appeared untethered and lost, as their postures and facial expressions felt powerless to meet the challenges of all those needing connection and hungry for viable solutions for the people they served in their schools. I immediately snatched and tucked my hard drive containing a detailed slide deck back into my backpack, inconspicuously zipping it up as I held my breath for a second or two. My mouth felt as dry as sandpaper, and for a minute it was hard to swallow as I tried to find a deep breath. I had no idea how I could meet their presented challenges or even what words would feel comforting for the next 50 minutes. Pulling up a chair, I glanced over at the district's administrator and found that deep breath this time. Forty-plus pairs of eyes were watching me, then checking their phones, while slumping down in their chairs. I observed and allowed a few seconds to pass, possibly buying time! Suddenly I found a few words that validated what I was intuiting from this group. The words came slowly. "There is nothing in my presentation this afternoon that feels relevant and authentic for what you all must be experiencing right now. I want to hear and learn from you this afternoon, and better understand what you are facing inside your schools and communities." There was silence for what seemed like forever, but then a young woman spoke her heart. In a low voice, she began. "There is so much divisiveness in our school, and teachers are afraid to say what is truly on their hearts and minds, because what they say may not be supported or heard." This honest conversation opened a heartfelt discussion, because each adult validated and listened deeply to one another's stories. As the conversation continued, there was a growing sense of shared trust and safety. There were no solutions or strategies presented, no problems solved, yet there was a re-storying, or a retelling and reframing of the felt challenges that everyone was sharing. Through validation, newly formed connections became the protective factors as we cultivated a sense of belonging with one another on that Tuesday afternoon.

As I left the room, I felt lighter, as if I could effortlessly fly to my car. It was as though a soft, warm glow was radiating from the lecture hall that, just an hour ago, I'd entered feeling chilled, alone, and anxious. Now the room was filled with a burst of welcoming, pleasurable energy that I was reluctant to leave behind.

As I reflect on this day, it was nothing short of miraculous, because the emotional temperature collectively shifted. Through that hour of storytelling, we discovered relational wealth, the glue that we all needed and benefitted from as we left the administration building feeling more hopeful, flexible, and curious about next steps. When we validate one another, we are able to offer a compassionate presence which signals and is interpreted as reliable, and we then can begin to regulate our own physiology. Trauma therapist and author Deb Dana writes, "A regulated, flexible, and resilient system is built when the ruptures are recognized and repairs are made, and the ability to self-regulate is built from ongoing experiences of co-regulation."[121]

Pondering

There is so much talk about connection in our schools today. Relationships are mentioned and discussed in almost all professional development trainings, and we can become cognitively numb and ironically detached as we listen, integrate, and reflect on the healing properties of relational presence. I am thinking about our individual lives and collective presence, personally and professionally, as we address these questions:

1. When something celebratory happens in our lives, what do we do?

2. When we receive difficult news or encounter challenging experiences, what do we do or desire?

3. When we are lonely, how does that affect our thought processes and feelings?

4. When we are isolated from others, how do we often experience this in our nervous system?

5. When we say goodbye to a family member or friend, how do we experience this?

6. When we anticipate a gathering with others that we care for, how does that feel?

7. Why is rejection so difficult?

8. What is underneath bullying, social rejection, or humiliation?

9. When we mistake a voice or person for someone we know or admire, how does it feel first to anticipate meeting that person, then to be disappointed at not meeting them?

10. What creates that lump in our throat when we feel anxious, worried, or angry? Is it usually caused or correlated with other people?

11. How do biases impact human beings?

12. What creates the countless power struggles, divides, and conflicts among people, communities, and nations?

13. How has social media impacted the developing brains and bodies of our children and youth?

14. When I am alone and reflecting on an experience, condition, or happening, what or who is in my thoughts?

Social psychologist Dr. Matthew Lieberman explains, "Our biology is built to thirst for connection, because it is linked to our most basic survival needs."[122] Maybe our survival needs should include socialization on humanistic psychologist Abraham Maslow's Hierarchy of Needs? Mammalian infants cannot survive without the attachment of a caregiver to provide those food, water, and shelter needs.[123] Love and belonging may appear to be conveniences that we can live without, but we do not survive without another. World-renowned neuroscientist Paul MacLearn wrote, "A sense of separation is a condition that makes being a mammal so painful."[124]

So why do we hurt one another, aggressively fight, and compete fiercely with violence if we are biologically wired to connect with one another? I feel that partial answers to this question may be centered around our nervous system states. In survival states, our nervous system is in protection, and we will defend our survival or a perceived threat or danger at all costs, as we will explore throughout this chapter.

Empathy and Compassion

There are significant nervous system state differences between empathy and compassion. Klimecki et al. (2014) suggests that "the excessive sharing of other's negative emotion (i.e. empathy) may be maladaptive, and that compassion training dampens down emotional and empathic distress and strengthens resilience."[125] It has been suggested that empathy is mirroring another's distress inside our own elevated and aligned sympathetic or fight-flight pathway.[126] Foundational to compassion is respecting the individual's capacity to experience their own pain, allowing the fear to be expressed without judgment or negative evaluation.[127] Compassionate presence validates but also allows the lived experiences of others to be expressed in a safe, nurturing space as the compassionate presence is held in the social engagement system (prefrontal cortex) where we are attempting not to fix, but to respect those painful experiences in a warm, detached state. Dr. Stephen Porges writes, "Compassion functionally allows one who has lost or is suffering not to be defensive about the loss and not to experience shame for the loss."[128]

On that Tuesday afternoon that I spent with the school liaisons, there was a felt compassion, rather than empathy, that became transformative in the healing and reparative discussions. This is communal neuroplasticity, and it begins with a relational, compassionate presence.

Social Nervous Systems

Our physiological states are inherently social. This is true for all of us, but the brain and nervous system development of children and youth is constantly being shaped by experiences with others and the perceptions of those experiences and environments in the early years. The chronic behavioral challenges from many of our students are often communicating nervous system pathways functioning in sensitized threat-and-protect survival states. Our educators have also felt and experienced tremendous anxiety, and possibly an immobilized or collapsed nervous system state, when our brains and bodies feel overwhelmed by the chronic unpredictability of these past few years. How do we begin to move through the adversities and trauma experienced from the global unrest occurring during and in the aftermath of a pandemic? Scientist and author Dr. Stephen Porges says, "Cues of felt safety are an efficient and profound antidote for trauma."[129]

As schools address emotional and social health in the upcoming years, our children, youth, and staff will benefit greatly when we integrate **Nervous System-Aligned Trauma-Responsive Teaching** with a heavy focus on connection: being intentional about creating an emotional resonance with one another in our buildings, classrooms, and districts. When we prioritize sensory regulation over cognition, we create pathways to the prefrontal cortex, generating access to the executive functions and cognitive skills (reasoning, problem solving, attention, working memory, and emotional regulation) that we require for emotional, social, and cognitive well-being. As I listen to educators across the country and world, we are recognizing that social and emotional development does not occur through purchased programs or 30 minutes of a social-emotional lesson pushed into the day. When we cultivate trauma-accommodating and responsive teaching practices to create environments that embrace social and racial equity, cue safety and connection, and are aligned with the application of nervous system science and health, we see learning gaps lessen and well-being deepen for staff and students. It is a start, but it is not enough to only ask, "What happened to you?" We need to follow this question with others:

- "What do you need?"

- "How can we work through this together?"

- "Can we meet each other where we are?"

- "What are we missing?"

Secure connections with others allow us to hold one another's experiences as we speak to another's capacity for listening. This is **co-regulation**, our biological imperative to share our emotional availability in a safe, trusted, and nested space. When we meet each other where we are, we are working within a relational window of tolerance.

Our nervous systems need each other, and we must prioritize frequent check-ins with our staff, our students, and ourselves. We refer to these as **touch points** within the framework of applied educational neuroscience, as these micro-moments, minutes, or extended times of connection can strengthen one another's sense of autonomy while validating and noticing what is going right and well!

Attachment to another is the carrier of all development. Our nature is to seek relationship coupled with warm nurturance. Dr. Louis Cozolino, a professor of psychology at Pepperdine University who lectures worldwide on psychotherapy, trauma, and attachment, states, "At the most basic level, we shape one another's embodied brains from pre-birth to death."[130] If our developing nervous systems experience chronic unpredictability and isolation—with levels of stress that are prolonged, extreme, and unpredictable—our stress response systems become sensitized and dysfunctional, resulting in behaviors that are misinterpreted and misunderstood. Our children and youth will need co-regulatory practices (moments of feeling seen, heard, and understood) as their brain and body development is moving through a heightened pruning and proliferation of synaptic connections (brain growth), preparing for efficiency and specialization during the adolescent years and through young adulthood.[131]

Nonverbal Communication and Connection

It is becoming increasingly evident that facial expressions, postures, gestures, and even the way we tilt our heads through nonverbal communication connect us in constant communication exchanges with those around us. It is within this interpersonal matrix that our nervous systems and brains have evolved to be sculpted and co-regulated by one another. Dr. Stephen Porges writes, "The face-heart connection concurrently enables an individual to signal safety through patterns of facial expressions and vocal intonations which dampen stress-related physiological states, support growth and restoration to the nervous system. Social communication and the ability to co-regulate another lead to a sense of connectedness which is a defining feature of the human experience."[132] From a neurobiological perspective, an educator's safe, available presence resembles that of a parent's or caregiver's presence in cultivating ways to share experiences that model unconditional acceptance, trust, and guidance in building a child's brain. Both can strengthen emotional regulation by providing a haven that supports the learning process. This "secure environment" optimizes neuroplasticity, allowing for new learning.[133] Psychologist and author Dr. Louis Cozolino writes, "Among the many possible implications of this finding for the classroom is the fact that teacher-student attunement isn't a 'nice addition' to the learning experience, but a core requirement. This is especially true in cases where children come to class with social, emotional, or intellectual challenges. The social brain takes into account both what we are learning and from whom we are learning it."[134] Stress in the learning environment, traumatic unconscious memories from past experiences, or high levels of tension in a student's life outside of the classroom can all impair learning by inhibiting the neuroplastic functions of the brain. As stated previously, when we hold another's experience, we cultivate an environment where a relational window of tolerance activates neurochemicals that can enhance a sense of belonging and trust with another.

Because of our shared ancestry with other mammals, we too have a biological inclination for connection addressing our social-emotional health and survival. Our need for social interaction is evidenced by the fact that loneliness can be as painful as physical ailments, and so much so, that loneliness can be correlated with earlier death.[135] Psychologist and author Dr. Matthew Lieberman writes, "Why have our brains been constructed to make us feel so much pain at the loss of a loved one? Our brains evolved to experience threats to our social connections in much the same way as they experience physical pain. By activating the same neural circuitry that causes us to feel physical pain, our experience of social pain helps to ensure the survival of our children by helping to keep them close to their parents. The neural link between social and physical pain also ensures that staying socially connected will be a lifelong need, like food and warmth."[136] Knowing the relationship between social and physical pain, as a society, community, and school, should we not begin to prioritize and treat social pain as we have traditionally addressed physical pain and injuries? Conventionally, our schools have not focused on the social connections that drive well-being, but the pandemic has recently shone a spotlight on the social challenges we feel and experience through the lost and distorted sense of belonging that our students are carrying into classrooms. Although our nervous systems are built for attachment and connection, our classrooms are focused on everything but connection. We now know that social interaction and shared presence are healing to our nervous systems, promoting growth and sustainability so we can learn and thrive.[137] We will explore shared connection practices at the end of this chapter as we address nervous system states for sustainable co-regulation and growing emotional well-being.

Connection, Protection, and Disconnection Through the Polyvagal Theory

"It is difficult to give children a sense of security unless you have it yourself. If you have it, they catch it from you."
WILLIAM MENNINGER

The evolutionary biology lesson about mammals and their upbringing gives us a lens in understanding how and why the nervous systems around us work the way they do. When we understand that we are not automatically hardwired or programmed to self-regulate on our own, we can give each other a bit more grace as we witness emotional disruptions. When we understand that connection is the biggest driver for regulation, we are then able to share our calming presence to help others through their storms. Having the perspective that "students should know better" or "they need to be able to handle their emotions" goes against what we know about how our nervous systems develop and thrive. Practicing co-regulation over time with a trusted adult can assist children and youth to generate and then feel the needed pause, or a safe and soothing emotional sensation before we act on impulses. Emotional regulation takes practice, guidance, and safe spaces and is likened to an endurance event. We need each other over and over and over again! Just as we need to provide extra chances or opportunities for academic learning, we also need to acquire a growth mindset when it comes to the plasticity of our emotional regulation skills.

Let's take some time to identify those in our social circles who "anchor" us. Anchors keep us grounded, as we discussed in Chapter 2. When we are in rough waters, these individuals stabilize and reinforce us when we need them the most. Who are your anchors when you need moments of co-regulation? What settings anchor you in moments of needed grounding or calm? Our touch points or anchors are not always people, but can be places and spaces that soothe our dysregulated nervous systems.

We are constantly sending out signals to others with invitations to connect, or unintentionally sending signals of threat or danger which can cue survival responses in others. As I have written, this occurs through our body language, facial expressions, tone of voice, posture, gestures, and eye contact. As we think about co-regulating, are we sharing with those around us that we are a safe individual to trust and confide in, or are we telling them that we ourselves are uncomfortable and not in a place to regulate beside them? If our goal is to co-regulate with an individual, building secure connections, we need to understand that our brains and bodies send and seek cues of safety and danger, as we are in conversation at all moments with our autonomic nervous systems. This search is often unconscious as we sense safety and danger from one another, so we will need to be aware of our nonverbal communication.

Co-regulation can occur through our eyes, ears, voices, face, and head movements. Our eyes signal safety and trust, and our ears listen for sounds of welcome or danger. There is so much co-regulatory energy within our tones of voice that it is not surprising we are emotionally contagious when we experience the uneasy or settling tones of another. We unconsciously listen for frequency, patterns, rhythmic sounds, intensity, and tones. Studies out of UC Berkeley refer to these emotional expressions as "vocal bursts."[138] Vocal bursts are the nonverbal sounds we make when we feel understood, activated, triggered, annoyed, or settled. Examples include "ahh," "ohhh," "ugh," "humph," and so forth—sounds recognized throughout the U.S. and among other English-speaking populations. The most recent study explored 24 emotions expressed nonverbally. Dr. Alan Cowen, lead author on this study, said that the voice is a powerful, emotional tool when it comes to expressing how we feel in a variety of experiences and environments.[139]

Neuroplasticity and Discipline

In our schools, homes, and communities, when adults (whether caregivers, parents, or educators) do not understand the biological significance of co-regulation, co-regulation can be likened to rewarding unwanted behaviors; therefore, the practices of co-regulation feel uncomfortable compared to our traditional views of discipline around unwanted behaviors. For example, if a student just cursed at us or yelled across the room, our gut reaction is to implement our power and control by giving immediate consequences. But co-regulation is always required for a sustainable and meaningful behavioral change, which actually flows from a shift in adult perceptual understanding, modeling, and leadership. Behavioral management is about adults, not about children and youth! We need to deeply understand that it takes a calm nervous system to calm a nervous system. An example of a co-regulatory moment with a student might be a gentle, compassionate question or validation when we ourselves have found some calm. "I can tell you are experiencing something bigger than this. What do you need right now?" The student may be surprised with our question or noticed observations because their primary objective may have been to unconsciously expect our traditional response: being sent out of the classroom and left alone. In co-regulatory practices, we are sharing a sanctuary of safety through our offered presence. When we give a student the opportunity to be seen and heard, we can begin to turn a crisis into an opportunity to connect. We are building rapport and helping to build nervous system pathways that say, "I am safe and I see you." When a student is moving to a mobilized fight-flight state, they cannot process or productively think, "Why did I do that? What caused me to act this way? Was that a good idea?" because they don't have access to their prefrontal cortex in this moment. In survival nervous system states, all those critical thinking skills aren't activated in the cortex because the student's sympathetic fight-flight nervous system pathway is in charge. For students who carry into the classroom chronic and toxic levels of stress, traditional discipline procedures of yelling, threatening, or isolating can unintentionally reactivate their stress responses and possibly be retraumatizing.

We must first co-regulate to create felt safety so that the student's sympathetic nervous system can calm down and their parasympathetic ventral vagal pathway (activating the prefrontal cortex) can come onboard again. Only then can we set the scene for those authentic disciplinary and learning conversations that guide us to sustainable behavioral changes where consequences become learning opportunities and supportive experiences. While it may look like rewarding or coddling a student who is "misbehaving" by responding with a calm voice and offering movement, space, time, attention, a second chance, and then a conversation, we are co-regulating that student's nervous system, creating nervous system plasticity changes so they can access the cortex to share in those necessary learning moments. Our students may not have the capacity or capability to self-regulate. Either because of where they are developmentally or because of the chronic pain they carry each day, they are not in a nervous system state where they are able to self-regulate. Perhaps the child or adolescent has not had the modeling from caregivers to know what a co-regulatory experience feels and looks like. When we understand that chronic behavioral challenges are nervous system challenges, we realize that by attending to the autonomic nervous system needs of students, we are ensuring relational nervous system-aligned states that are capable of holding connection and safety. Building and strengthening connections in early development is a continual neural exercise in cultivating human resiliency, encouraging deeper, more impactful, and creative learning in the long run. This doesn't mean giving students a pass for misbehavior. There are consequences (intentional and meaningful experiences) for poor choices, but co-regulating the feelings and sensations that a student is experiencing is the initial step, and one that is critical for a sustainable change in behavior and overall well-being.

Trying to co-regulate a dysregulated child can be difficult. It's not as easy as saying "I'm going to stop how I'm feeling right now and attend to your needs." Emotions are contagious, students push our buttons, and we can unintentionally enter the conflict or power struggle as our own nervous systems escalate and we suddenly mobilize our energy in a threat-and-protect response. We need to be aware of our own autonomic state and ask ourselves if we are able to share an authentic and warm presence with this child or adolescent. If we try to respond to an upset child when we are showing signs of frustration, our bodies will give us away even if we are using a script of words that we hope will comfort that child. Our neuroception (autonomic intuition) picks up on the body language, voice tones, and facial expressions before it attends to the content of what is being said. Our nervous systems will give away our internal feelings of safety or felt disconnection.

When we are in our social engagement system, our ventral vagal pathway has the ability to control and interact with a number of parts on our face and neck.[140] The ventral vagal system not only provides a "brake" to decrease the heart rate, but it also allows us to be more fluid with our head tilt and orientation of our neck and skull.[141] This head tilt isn't something we comfortably do when we feel confronted or in danger. A head tilt is often used to signal, "I am comfortable with you and showing vulnerability through this movement because I trust you will not hurt me." Our ventral vagal system also interacts with our larynx and pharynx, involving vocalizing, swallowing, and breathing.[142] So, when we are comfortable, we can utilize a variety of vocal tonality. We can be expressive and speak in silly or "motherese" ways (think how your mom might have spoken to you as a baby to encourage play or attention). We are able to swallow and breathe in a slower pattern that keeps our heart rate lower.[143] Furthermore, our middle ear muscle is tightened to attune our hearing to the higher ranges associated with the human voice.[144] Human voices are typically at a higher pitch than the lower roaring and rumbling that our ancestral predators may have had. And lastly, and maybe most obvious, is how the ventral vagal system impacts our facial expressions. The ventral vagal pathway innervates many facial muscles around our eyes, eyebrows, and mouth that indicate emotional expression.[145] When we feel safe and connected, we can emote with our face those safe, inviting cues. The amount of tension in our brow, the social gaze we can provide with our eyelids, the pursing of our lips are all signs that can indicate we are regulated. The neuroception of others around us are picking up on those signals or cues. When others can see the expressions we have, hear our vocal tonality, and sense our breathing patterns and body language, they can be comforted by our states of regulation. Our nervous system is literally communicating to other nervous systems that "we feel safe, and I hope my safety will invite your safety!" On the other hand, we can also share that we are not safe, and to another nervous system, we might feel like a threat.

Polyvagal Safety: You Know It When You See It!

Think of the flipside to all of these vagal innervations. If we are feeling safe, we tilt our head and show deference or an invitation to connect. Do you think we do that when in fight-flight? No! We stiffen up and don't offer any body language that shows vulnerability. When we are in our social engagement state, we can talk to someone with expression and interest, but when we are emotionally activated and mobilizing to defend and protect, we don't have the biological resources or ability to use much variety other than loudness and possibly a faster talking pace.

This is why when some people present to an audience, they have that deer-in-headlights expression and a shaky monotone voice: because they are so nervous, they can't access the ability to diversify the sound of their voice. When someone is in trouble or feels in danger, their vagal tone drops in the middle ear to expand the muscles, and therefore they might focus on the lower tones of sound. When in danger, our focus needs to be picking up on the sounds that could be threats to us: the lower voices of predators. If we see a student covering their ears when stressed, it is probably not that they are actively trying to avoid listening to us. The auditory information coming into their ears is too overwhelming and creates sensations and feelings of danger or threat, making them feel unsafe. Let's think of our own breathing patterns. Someone who no longer has the ventral vagal brake on, slowing the heart down, will have a faster breathing rate and faster heartbeat when they are in their sympathetic nervous system. They will feel like they can't swallow. Think of the facial expressions of someone who is in their fight-flight state or even in their collapsed brain-body state. It can be pretty easy to tell when someone is upset by looking at their face, but what we will notice is that they don't have much variety or control over expression. As Dr. Stephen Porges states, "We wear our hearts on our faces."[146] Maybe we can see and hear the brokenness of a heart? Individuals in an immobilized or collapsed state can carry a flat affect with very little expression or muscle tone. All these cues indicate that a person is *not* in their social engagement system and that their prefrontal cortex is offline. When we are interacting with someone and they can sense these signals from us, their neuroception is sensing that "I may not be safe," and these sensations and emotions are contagious!

As I have continually noted, before we co-regulate with our students, we must be aware of our own autonomic states. Are we feeling regulated at this moment to deal with a student who needs us? And we must be honest, because our facial expressions and body language won't lie. If we are authentically calm, then we can sit beside our students and spend some time validating their emotions, giving some encouragement, and finding what they need to feel better before we begin to discuss what went wrong and how to repair. But what if we aren't ready to share our nervous system with a student? Do not force it! It may be tempting to address the situation or conflict right away, but engaging without being regulated will only lead to an escalation of emotions for both student and adult. Be transparent with the student, modeling those regulatory practices that you would love for students to adopt. "I need a moment to calm myself down before we figure this out. I'm going to grab a drink of water. What would feel calming to you for the next couple of minutes?" By allowing ourselves to take some deep breaths and tap into a sensory practice or one of our anchors that can begin to soothe us, we will be better able to communicate with words and body language that are aligned and authentic in building relational trust. If we are honest enough with ourselves, realizing that we may not have the capacity to help this student now, or that our relationship isn't as solid as it needs to be for this interaction, we might want to ask the student if there is another adult in the building that he or she could sit with for a while. It's OK if we are not always "that person" for all our students; we do not have to be! By modeling with transparency, we show students that we need to be aware of our brain and body states and that we, too, are learning ways to ground and settle our nervous systems. This modeling is so powerful for our children and youth to observe.

Relationships are the key to co-regulation. Touch points can be moments of mini-co-regulatory encounters that build the foundation for growing positive relationships. Co-regulation is always mutual and is a reciprocal interaction that leans into facial expressions, gestures, and vocalizations. When we make the time to connect prior to emotional, heated, or controversial moments, we are ensuring that our students will trust us even during conflicts. Touch points can be in the form of intentional conversations or through shared experiences, greetings, goodbyes, or transitional moments that we embody with our students. We have this relational window of opportunity to sit beside our children and youth, attuning to their biological instinct to attach, as there is so much development during a nine-month academic school year! Our connections through these touch points of check-ins, validation, and feedback practices occur all year long as our students' nervous system needs will continually change. And while some students may be easier to get to know, there is evidence that it only takes two minutes a day for ten consecutive school days sitting beside a student, strengthening, and improving our relationship with them. These two-minute conversations can occur in the hallway, transitioning between specials, before the bell rings, during dismissal, or even during independent work time.[147] Asking students about themselves and getting to know them is an accessible way to increase connection in your classroom. When we embrace relational plasticity, we are focusing upon the healing, nurturing, and supportive partnerships that build resiliency while widening the windows of relational tolerance.

Principal and colleague Michael Cox has written a list of questions that may help to lessen the awkwardness of these initial two-minute conversations with our students. We hope you will find these conversation starters helpful. It is very important to listen to a student's responses without judging their answers. We are not trying to solve their problems or give them advice on how they should live their lives at this time, but rather building a rapport so that our words will feel impactful to them down the road.

Validate their opinions with statements like:
- That must be fun for you.
- That must frustrate you.
- I'm glad you find enjoyment in that.
- I'm sorry to hear that makes you sad.
- That sounds interesting. Tell me more about that.
- Really? How does that work?

Here a few conversation starters on subjects about which almost everyone has an opinion!
- What is your favorite food?
    - Where do you get to eat that?
    - Does someone make it at home?
    - What place has the best _____?
- So what's for dinner tonight?
    - Is that a regular meal for you?
    - Have you always liked that?
    - Would you rather have had something different?
- What is your favorite kind of music?
    - Who is your favorite artist?
    - What speaks to you about their music?
- What do you like to do in your free time?
    - Are there other people that do this with you?
    - Where do you usually do this?
    - Are there any cool clothes or accessories you need to do this?
    - Who taught you how to _____?
    - Where were you the first time you _____?
- What annoys you the most about school?
- What do you enjoy about school?

- Do you like movies?
  - What kind of movies are your favorite?
  - Do you think it would be cool to be an actor?
  - Have you ever acted or been part of a stage crew?
- Hey I've noticed _____
- Shoes, hair, electronic device, stickers shirts that show a certain interest, etc.
- Follow Up:
  - Cool, tell me what is it you like about that?
  - Is there a club you are involved in for this?
  - Who else around here does that kind of stuff?
  - Where do you get _____ like that?
  - If you could travel anywhere, where would you go? - OR -
  - What would be your dream vacation?
    - What do you like about _____?
    - Who would you go with?
  - What is your dream job?
  - Would you rather live on the beach, in the mountains, in a city, or on a farm?

As therapist and author Arielle Schwartz says, "In reality, we all have relational vulnerabilities and imperfect attachments to varying degrees."[148] Acknowledging our disconnection from others allows us to share authentically as we work through feelings of loss, rejection, loneliness, and anger. Co-regulation is taught. Co-regulation can occur through how we begin a day or class period, or how we end our time together with our students. Deepened connections occur through these organic, fluid moments that are built into our class periods and days.

Bodies, Brains, and Negative Peer Behavior

With an increase in behavioral challenges from many of our students in this current school year, these escalations and meltdowns can feel scary or dysregulating to the nervous systems of students who observe negative peer behavior ("bad" behavior, like aggression, defiance, eloping, or shut-down responses).[149] We often try to protect children and youth from these uncomfortable situations by simply not addressing them. But this can unintentionally create added anxiety because the unknown is met with a student's personal interpretation of a peer's outburst or a meltdown. Our brains predict experiences based on past experiences, and we encounter a visceral sensory/brainstem response, which is usually a sensation experienced in our bodies when we see another person struggling.

If a child or youth hears someone yelling, a door slamming, a classmate sobbing, or harsh-sounding tones of voice, their hearts begin beating fast, breathing becomes shallow, and they can feel tension and tightness in their bodies. These sensory signals occur immediately before we recognize how we are feeling or thinking. Emotions are contagious, so other students in the room begin mirroring or picking up on the dysregulation of classmates, and possibly the teacher or staff member.

As I have said, many students are currently carrying toxic levels of stress into schools, which creates an altered stress response state that can trigger a survival response like defiance, avoidance, or aggression. The nervous system is designed to protect us, and our students need to know this.

When our nervous systems are operating on high volume, we can feel edgy and irritated, and our anger can be explosive toward a perceived threat, or anything that feels unsafe, as we begin to defend ourselves. Adults and students alike can misinterpret this reaction as intentional or deliberate.

But when we take care of each other before a crisis, we are building cultures of awareness and communal practices that feel predictable and rhythmic to our students.

Many people need glasses so they can see well. Some need hearing aids for improved hearing. Crutches help us to walk when we are injured. If we have a headache or body pain, we treat it with medicine, a trip to the doctor, or a cold compress. If we are exhausted, we sleep. If we have a cut or wound, we treat it with ointment, an antibiotic, and a covering. Our emotions often need accommodations as well. When we feel lonely, many of us need connection. When we feel afraid or worried, we may need to feel a hug or the closeness of someone we trust, but we can often ask for connection in the most unloving ways.

When we are chronically anxious, sad, or angry, we can look normal on the outside, but our wounds or injuries are invisible. This is what we need to share with our students during morning or afternoon gatherings before we have eruptions. Our students need to understand that most negative peer behavior is communicating pain that feels unmanageable inside the nervous system of a friend or classmate. Our students need to understand the neuroscience of how they feel and, therefore, how their bodies sometimes react when they are upset or see negative peer behavior. These discussions need to happen all year long as we learn about our nervous systems and the superpower of plasticity that we carry in our own brains and bodies.

Children and youth are resilient in their personal responses when adults are authentic and honest, explaining what lies beneath behaviors. We never have to share the personal conditions or experiences that a student is working through. But we do benefit when we have these open conversations with our classes in an environment that is calm and collaborative.

At the end of this chapter is a simple survey that your school could send out on a regular basis to better understand students' feelings of safety and connection.

Neuroplasticity Is Our Human Superpower

Neuroplasticity is our brain's and nervous system's ability to structurally and functionally change with every experience we encounter. The more we practice these rituals of morning or afternoon discussions as a part of our routines, the more we begin to understand that behaviors are only the signals of an anxious or dysregulated nervous system, and therefore, we can respond to one another with more ease as we care for our own nervous systems, no matter what is happening around us.

I have been studying the neurophysiology and the definition of "play" through the lens of Polyvagal Theory, and the social and affective neurosciences. Dr. Stephen Porges suggests that "play" is a neural exercise in which our nervous systems toggle between sympathetic (fight-flight) pathways as we mobilize energy and work from the cortex, with activation in our social engagement system.[150] Play requires mutual and collaborative interactions between mammals while integrating our social engagement center as a regulator of our fight-flight responses.[151] During the past few years, our schools have lost the face-to-face interaction between students and teachers, between classmates. Whether we were virtually learning, wearing masks, or inside school environments that often felt unsafe, we could not read each other emotionally. Nonverbal communication is how humans and other social mammals cue safety and threat, and we were cut off from that means of communication! Playing in isolation or with a toy or video game cannot carry the face-to-face interaction that provides a shift from calm to defensive and back to calm, cultivating a resilient and flexible nervous system. We might begin to open class meetings in circles, seeing one another as we explain the physiology of how we connect with others nonverbally, through the cues of facial expression, posture, gestures, and vocal tones. As we learn about the neural pathways in our nervous systems that produce relational connection, we can interact with these reflective questions. (We will need to set up guidelines for these questions, so we do not use specific names.)

1. Can you describe a time when someone's face signaled discomfort or fear to you? What does a face look like to you that feels safe and friendly?

2. Was there a time when all you heard was the tone and sound of another person's voice and knew how they were feeling, no matter what their words said?

3. Can you share a time when your facial expression or posture conveyed how you were feeling, and someone noticed this?

4. What gestures cue safety or threat for you? (Leaning forward, closed arms, pointing fingers, open arms, hands on lap, hands up in the air, etc.)

5. Can you think of a time when your words and nonverbal communication did not match?

6. Can you think of a time when someone you were talking to made you feel confused because their words did not match their non-verbal communication?

7. When you feel dysregulated, where are you? Who are you with? Where does this happen most often?

Ask yourself these questions:

8. What do I notice about sensations in my body when I feel unsafe, dysregulated, threatened, or in danger?

9. What cues safety for me? What people? Places? Settings or environments? What experiences feel calming to my nervous system?

10. Have I noticed patterns to my autonomic nervous system states? What are those? Months? Days of the week? Following specific events or experiences? Night? Morning? Before school? Weekends? Holidays? Specific people?

When we establish new routines, procedures, or ways of responding to an experience, the conditions begin to feel more controllable or adaptable with repetitive practice.

Here are some suggestions for beginning to cultivate intentional neuroplasticity with our students when negative peer behavior leaves them feeling fearful or confused.

- When holding class meetings or convocations, take an opportunity to share how invisible pain is just as important to address as physical and visible injuries or wounds.

- This is a time when we teach our children and youth about the brain and the nervous system. We talk about how impossible it is to think clearly or learn when we are feeling anxious, angry, or sad.

- We discuss that behaviors are just clues or signals covering up the deeper injury or wound. We share stories of times when we felt lonely, hurt, disconnected, or super angry.

· We discuss how our brain is always trying to protect us when we begin to feel rough or dysregulated. This is called a survival response, and in this state, we feel as if a bear is chasing us.

Below are a few resources that can help students of all ages better understand how their nervous system functions under stress.

1. Create classroom community meetings or gatherings at the beginning or end of the class period or day so everyone can choose to share how they are feeling in their nervous systems. We need to provide ways for students to check in with their nervous systems and the templates below are great ways everyone can share how they are feeling.

2. Help students express their sensations, feelings, thoughts, strengths, and preferences. Journaling, drawing, and creating art are powerful ways to accomplish this. We can provide this opportunity as part of our routines and procedures, because this feels predictable and safe and is always a choice.

3. Provide opportunities for students to step into leadership roles if the class encounters negative peer behavior. As we create these collaborative environments, we plan procedures that can help students respond to disruptions caused by negative peer behavior. For example, Jane will oversee turning down the lights. Tyesha will pass out books or journals for students to read or write out their thoughts. Sy will turn on some soft rhythmic music, and Tamara will relay to the office that our classroom may need some assistance. What other roles and responsibilities could we provide for our students when we have mounting chaos and confusion?

4. During morning or afternoon gatherings, have students create a menu of three or four "in the moment" practices they can begin to implement if they are feeling anxious or worried. Integrating these practices every day gives students access to a sensory and regulatory toolbox that helps them remain calm when they are in emotionally rough waters.

Collaborative Regulatory and Connection Practices

Below are nervous system-aligned connection practices that focus on collaboration and cooperation to create a culture of relational and harmonious attunement. A huge thank you to my graduate students in Cohort Six for sharing practices that begin to build connection.

Developed by Kiah Pienfield, Middle School Educator, Darrington School District, Washington

1. Who Are You? We Want to Know!

Getting to know one another through questions is a great check-in at the beginning of a school year, midway through, and end of the year. Student responses can be graphed, shared, and discussed. We also invite our students to create some of their own questions that they would like to share with our class. How would our responses change the culture in our classrooms? How could these responses help us to meet students where they are if we know their preferences, interests, and self-reflective responses?

1. Do you prefer going with the flow or having a plan? (Flow or plan)

2. Where would you rather spend the day relaxing? (The beach/lake or the mountains?)

3. Do you prefer to keep up with the news? (Yes or no)

4. How would you rather experience a story? (Books or movies/TV?)

5. This one's controversial... which do you prefer? Dogs (woof) or cats (meow)?

6. Can money buy happiness? (Yes or no)

7. Which is more important? (Helping others or taking care of ourselves?)

8. Sometimes I think nobody understands how I feel. (Agree or disagree)

9. OK, if you were a bird, which would you be? (Hummingbird or eagle)

10. Now you are going to write a word or phrase. If I were in charge, everyone would have...

11. The most important thing school doesn't teach you is...

12. One day I hope that I will be able to...

13. I hope other people think that I am...

14. My favorite thing to do to relax is...

15. My motto/mantra/word of the year is...

Developed by Kimberly Richards, District Behavior Resource Teacher, TM Roberts Elementary School, Cranbrook, British Columbia

2. Collaborative Art

To begin sessions, I often engage in shared drawings with students. This is where one person takes a turn creating a mark on the page, and then indicates that they are ready for their partner to take a turn. It continues until the students determine that the image is complete, or until we provide a time limit. It is an amazing way to connect, see into their world, and share some laughs when their mark-making becomes interactive. The students have choice in their medium (for example, watercolors, markers, oil pastels, or crayons), and if they chat or not during this time. It is a good low-risk activity that creates a great back-and-forth rhythm and co-regulation. It can be practiced by partnering with an adult or between students, building community and safety if done (often and over time) as a class image or smartboard creation, eventually leading to multiple shared drawings with partners or classmates.

Developed by Trish Giese, First-Grade Teacher, Homan Elementary School, Schererville, Indiana

3. Back-to-Back Drawings

As we have learned from the Applied Educational Neuroscience certification courses, a focused-attention practice is a brain exercise for quieting the thousands of thoughts that distract and frustrate us each day. When the mind is quiet and focused, we're able to be present with a specific sound, sight, or taste. Research repeatedly shows that quieting our minds ignites our parasympathetic nervous system, reducing heart rate and blood pressure while enhancing our coping strategies to effectively handle the day-to-day challenges that keep coming. Our thinking improves, and our emotions begin to regulate so that we can approach an experience with variable options. Art therapy does just that and more!

To help contextualize this creation for my first-grade class, I would do this after our lunch/recess break. Generally after recess, our students come in dysregulated and need some time to calm down and get their brains ready for an afternoon of learning. I try to incorporate this practice once a week. Students always work with a different partner to build relationships between students.

Items needed: Clipboard/paper/pencil/object/shape/piece of simple abstract art

Time frame: 10-15 minutes (this might take a little longer in the beginning)

• Students will be grouped into pairs.

• They will sit with their backs turned from each other.

• One person will be partner A and the other will be partner B.

• Give one person an image, such as a shape or a collection of shapes. You can also gather examples of simple abstract art from your art teacher for students to use.

• Partner A will be instructed not to show their partner the image or shape they received. Partner B will be instructed not to peek at their partner's image.

• Partner A will have the drawing/shape and describe it to their partner who cannot see the image. Partner B will try to recreate the image to the best of their ability.

• Set a timer of three minutes or whatever you feel is an appropriate time. The timer limits students from going off task.

• Then the partners will switch places and repeat with a new image.

- When the pairs are finished, they will compare images.
- If students are describing a shape, they cannot say the name of the shape to the other partner.

Debriefing questions:

- What did you learn when you described the image?
- What was hard about that activity?
- What did you learn while drawing?
- What are some lessons that you learned from this activity that might be used in the future?
- How did that make you feel?
- Was this something you would like to do again?

My class starts math right after this practice, so it ties in nicely if we are using shapes. I hope you give this a try! (It also results in some healthy laughter when the creations are shared and compared.)

One More Practice by Lori Desautels

To complement these practices supplied by my graduate students, I would like to add one more activity that I shared with my graduate students to model as they designed their bell work, or transitional meetings.

4. Give Me Yours and I'll Give You Mine

The focused attention practice we call "Give Me Yours and I'll Give You Mine" has become a staple in our classroom meetings. Students visually document something that is stuck in their mind or that they feel is impacting them mentally. They fold up their pieces of paper, exchange with a classmate, and that pair does a moment of deep breathing together. Sometimes students ask to share what they wrote or drew with the class or with me, but often they just appreciate the ability to express it in a nonverbal way. I always ask students to reflect on how the experience has impacted them. A common theme in their responses is that being able to put something on a piece of paper instead of just internalizing the worry puts them in a better mental space to learn. We used to do this once a week, but now they request to do it daily, and I love that it is such a meaningful outlet for them.

Guest Reflections From Pennie Gregory, Assistant Director of Secondary Special Services, Wayne Township MSD (Indianapolis)

In this final section of Chapter 3, Pennie Gregory shares how a positive academic environment helped her overcome adverse childhood experiences—and thrive as a result!

Years ago, as a special education inclusion teacher, I took the Adverse Childhood Experiences (ACEs) quiz. The quiz was ten yes or no questions about traumatic experiences that may occur before the age of 18. Every *yes* represented a point. The higher your ACEs score, the more likely you were at risk for certain challenges like substance abuse problems, lack of education, lack of job opportunities, or health problems later in life. My ACEs score was a seven out of ten. Seven! This score was high, and it meant that I had experienced trauma like fear of being physically hurt, not feeling loved by my family, divorced parents, a household member with mental illness, verbal abuse, etc. I will be honest—I did not want people to know. As I listened to my colleagues, I realized no one else in the room had a score over three, let alone one as high as seven. I was ashamed of my score and chose not to share. But life has a funny way of demanding your truth.

Ironically, over the years, I have talked a lot about ACEs and trauma. As a matter of fact, in many ways, this subject matter has become central to my work as a special educator. Many students who have special needs and require individualized education plans have also endured adverse childhood experiences. I found myself listening to stories of neglect, abuse, gaps in education, mental health struggles, etc.: stories very similar to mine in many ways. I became aware that I was very lucky. How in the world did I navigate school? Not only did I navigate school, but I essentially found great success in school. I have been able to graduate high school, earn an undergrad degree, get my master's degree, and in a few weeks, I will be starting coursework for my doctorate degree at Harvard University. Remember that ACEs score of seven? Crazy, right?! But why? What was different about my story?

I think the real question is *who* is different in my story? No matter what I was experiencing at home, I was able to leave that behind me when I went to school. I grew up in Gary, IN, and despite the very negative connotation associated with Gary, I was pretty lucky that I grew up there. Most of my teachers looked like me, lived in my community, and expected me to be excellent. My teachers did not focus on what was happening in my home. They focused on the genius they believed I held inside of me, and because of this, I remember feeling safe at school and having an overwhelming sense of belonging. One winter, there was a terrible snowstorm. My mother told me no one would be at school, but I was determined to go. She relented, and I walked to school. She was right. I was the only student there with my teacher. I couldn't have been happier! I can also remember watching the clock in my classroom, dreading when it would be 3 p.m. I did not want to go home. School was predictable and safe—home was not. This was because of my teachers! I did not know it at the time, and I am not sure they did either (this was in the 1980s), but these supportive relationships were actually helping my brain grow, a concept known today as neuroplasticity.

Robin S. Sharma wrote, "Everything is created twice: first in the mind, and then in reality." This is important because trauma impacts your body and mind. Because trauma is often not just one single event, but ongoing exposure to negative experiences, the brain creates pathways that signal the body to be in constant flight, fight, freeze, or fawn response mode. Neuroplasticity is literally changing your mind by building new and better neuro pathways! This was a massively empowering concept to me. As a child, I could not always control what happened, but as an adult, I can choose to heal not only my body, but my brain, too! I can rewire negative, harmful thinking to positive, productive thinking that can help create the life I want and deserve.

But this isn't just about me. Now, when I meet students who have had adverse childhood experiences, I know that my care and my love can literally create new connections in their brains and change their predicted negative outcomes. The story does not have to end where the trauma begins; we can begin anew again and again and again!

The roots of resilience ... are to be found in the sense of being understood by and existing in the mind and heart of a loving, attuned, and self-possessed other.

DIANA FOSHA

STAFF & STUDENT SURVEYS
OF REGULATORY RESOURCES & ANCHORS

In these surveys, we want to address sensory practices that can create a sense of calm and safety within your nervous system.

What would happen if I checked in with my nervous system to decipher what I need or what feels calming? What if I began the school year with integrated, periodic check-ins with staff and students using these surveys of regulatory resources that anchor felt safety?

Resources
You can find the full surveys in the Resource Section of the book, or scan the QR code for a downloadable version.

Chapter 4

The nests we build can nurture our young.
The nests we build can make room for mistakes.
The nests we build can be relational.
The nests we build can hold collaboration.
The nests we build can hold and sustain a new lens for discipline.
The nests we build can hold unconditional love and acceptance for ourselves and our children and youth.

Building the Nest

"Radical simply means pulling things up by the root."
ANGELA DAVIS

"Radical education" is something that I have been pondering for the past several years, and living through a global pandemic has heightened and fastened my curiosity, questions, and desire to look deeply into the bio-social and emotional needs and shifts that our schools will need to summon. As I travel through schools and districts across the country and world, the questions below are on my mind and in my heart, as well as the minds and hearts of many of the educators, parents, and communities that I sit beside.

1. How would you define a radical shift in education?

2. What cultivates revolutionary shifts in how we address social, emotional, and equitable conditions and experiences within our schools and universities at this time?

3. Moving forward, where do we begin to specifically focus as we speak to the adversities and trauma that impact our children, youth, schools, and communities?

4. How can we create parent communities and collaborations that feel safe and connected when interacting and supporting schools?

5. How do schools support our families and communities in ways that invite deep connection?

6. How can we address the trauma of racial discrimination that is so pervasive across this nation and the world?

Questions are critical in this time. They engineer change, but we are often impatient; although we feel the strain and drain that have only intensified during these past few years, we sometimes find ourselves doing, talking, meeting, and recycling the same conversations. We still hold onto our traditional conventions, protocols, and practices because they feel familiar and reliable.

This global pandemic may become less severe, but its effects on schools will linger: children coping with the death of their caregivers; staff shortages in education; academic fatigue; the balancing act of keeping kids healthy and safe; our students struggling with the social skills they missed and forgetting how to be with each other; educators' mental and emotional weariness; and K-12 students with the highest rates of anxiety and depression we have ever tracked and recorded.[152]

Schools are now prioritizing mental health programs, tutoring, and other academic recovery efforts—work that is likely to stretch past the three years they have to use their federal relief funds.[153] "Our hardest and most important work lies ahead," the U.S. education secretary, Miguel Cardona, said recently.[154]

From our book *Unwritten, The Story of a Living System,* published in 2016, Michael McKnight and I wrote these words in the introduction:

Schools are not machines. Schools are a network of human beings who feel, think, behave, and function within a human system that is alive and never static. Schools are living systems! This living system of sentient beings is neurobiologically wired to feel and sense, connect, think, and to experience deep joy as well as deep disappointment and pain. This system is wired to thrive, even through difficult times. Have we lost our way through the primordial landscape of our innate purpose and genius? We can begin to think and to feel differently. Deep learning is profoundly relational, and connection to one another is a prerequisite for our collective emotional, social, spiritual, and cognitive growth and development.[155]

Our current educational story continues to be rooted in scarcity and deficiency as the pandemic has highlighted our challenges, but seeking awareness and applying our discoveries can generate hope and the plasticity of possibility. Many of our children and youth are unable to learn in these current educational environments. Students leave by either formally dropping out, or checking out socially and emotionally, unable to access the **cortex** (the learning part of the brain) as they sit beside us in classrooms and schools.

We are facing teaching shortages and are awakening to the many unsustainable conditions and mindsets within our schools. As we question those conditions and mindsets, we are learning that these paradigm shifts begin within each adult, moving inward and listening to the stories of our own nervous systems. A trauma-responsive school deeply understands that the ability to be present in ourselves is the greatest intervention that we can share with our students. How can we create an emotionally safe space, presence, and environment for these stories to be shared so that students and staff begin to feel validated and feel their purposes ignited? Are our schools at times inflicting new wounds upon students through the unconscious (or even conscious) ways in which teachers are taught to uphold the white supremacist thinking that produces racism in our schools? Our challenge is to explore the ways in which neutral behaviors can be read through a hostile lens.

We need to be aware of how our schools can be places of adversity for many of our students of color when current inequitable conditions, alongside racial and generational trauma, support experiences of rejection and dehumanization. These students must contend daily with persons, environments, and systems that have not embraced their humanity or deeply understood the contextual issues of racism, loss, conflict, and community violence.[156] When our sense of belonging and purpose are diminished, we struggle to reach, try, and engage! When our purpose is acknowledged, validated, and shared by and with another, this co-regulatory experience can foster self-reflection, mental rest, a sense of belonging, and an exploration of possibility through the lens of resiliency.

I ask myself: "Does my language validate or invalidate my students' stories, perceptions, and beliefs? Am I unintentionally pathologizing a feeling or belief, unable to recognize and hold an experience that I do not understand through the lens of my white, Eurocentric values? Am I checking in with my nervous system? Am I able to find a sense of grounded curiosity and openness for my own learning and evolution as I sit beside the children and youth in my care?"

Why Build a Nest?
We Begin With Breathing
Psychiatrist and trauma expert Dr. Bessel Van Der Kolk tells us:

Learning how to breathe calmly and remaining in a state of relative physical relaxation, even while moving through painful experiences, is an essential tool for recovery and resiliency. When you deliberately take a few slow deep breaths, you will notice the effects of the parasympathetic brake on your arousal state. The more you stay focused on your breathing, the more you will benefit, particularly if you pay attention until the very end of the outbreath and then wait a moment before you inhale again. As you continue to breathe and notice the air moving in and out of your lungs, you may think about the role that oxygen plays in nourishing your body and bathing your tissues with energy you need to feel alive and engaged.[157]

One of the most foundational lessons we have received from contemporary neuroscience is that a sense of ourselves is intimately connected to our bodies.[158] If we are not listening to what our bodies need, we are unable to take care of them. This is why sensory awareness can foster emotional regulation. Our body awareness through sensory recognition also changes our sense of time, shifting us to the present moment. So often our children and youth walk into schools carrying the heavy baggage of past experiences that feel hurtful, untethered, and out of their control. When we teach our children how to manage their breath and become aware of these bodily sensations, they begin to experience a sense control that feels empowering in this instant, preparing the nervous system to receive experiences in the present moment.

So why construct a nest? I have been researching the unique nests built by a variety of species of birds throughout the world. These nests are built from many diverse materials, such as interwoven sticks, twigs, plant fibers, feathers, spider silk, and clay, to name just a few. Many of these nests are built by communities of birds collectively stitching leaves together, digging trenches into sand banks and riverbanks as they prepare a safe and comfortable environment for their young.[159] There is much detail, patience, and preparation in the specificity of nest construction as they attend to the bio-social threats, dangers, and needs their offspring may encounter. Birds and mammals form complex social groups, often involving intricate vocal communication, and both groups care for their offspring for an extended period of time as well, as opposed to most ectothermic animals, which don't offer a high level of parental care.[160]

The construction of these nests translates into our schools' capacity to tap into our students' diverse cultures in ways that let us begin identifying young people's strengths, gifts, and unique identities, as the adults hold the vision of what the child or adolescent may not be able to see just yet. And when we sit beside our students inside this culture of awareness, we are meeting them in their personal brain and nervous system development and state. The nests, or the emotional and physical environments that we create, begin paying attention to the anxiety, pain, internalized oppression, and emotional injuries that our students carry into classrooms. This creates a finely tuned awareness that we need as we begin cultivating points of connection to lessen the felt tension and uneasiness through touch points of validation and advocacy, to launch safe, connected, and equitable environments. Nests embrace and deliver the anchors for our students to hold experiences that feel strength-filled and purposeful.

Thinking about the materials and the construction of these school and classroom nests, we educators also need safe, sturdy, and reliable nests: environments and experiences that strengthen our collaboration, enhance our commitment, and validate our personal and professional personhood.

In the natural world, animals build nests to hold the entire family, an idea that is significant as we think about the nests that feel secure and comforting to adults. What spaces have we constructed for our-selves? How strong are they? Are they constructed from the diversity of experiences that have grown us, even when we resisted? Are those spaces within the nests created from trust, hope, respect, imagination, validation, and empathy? Are they more than just spaces of survival? We are no different than our students. We, too, need to trust those around us so that we can begin to develop the emotional and mental fitness that births a deeper meaning and purpose inside our own lives. Emotions are contagious, and our children and youth are observing how we move through our experiences, navigating the nests we have created. As educator Nel Noddings has stated, "At a time when the traditional structures of caring have deteriorated, schools must become places where teachers and students live together, talk with each other, take delight in each other's company...it is obvious that children will work harder and do things for people they like and trust."[161]

As we explore intentional neuroplasticity, we are learning that it is with purpose, with focus, and with one another that we can begin to thrive, and this is hopeful! In *Unwritten, The Story of a Living System*, I created the acronym THRIVE for a concept that becomes tangible and definitive when we put the conditions from the acronym into action.[162] To thrive is to unfold in one's unique way in school environments that focus on the cognitive, emotional, social, physical, and spiritual needs of all staff and students. Using the acronym THRIVE, we began by defining this as:

T—Trust: Trust is built through our ability to empathize with our students and care for them. Building trust is a slow process, and with our most troubled children, an endurance event. Trust is built within environments of a caring and shared presence from adults as well as students.

H—(Active) Hope: All children and youth need to have a possible vision of their hoped-for future. In *Other People's Children*, Lisa Delpit describes her experience with hope and "turnaround teachers" this way: "They [teachers] held visions of us that we could not imagine for ourselves. All children need to see new possibilities, and all children need a reason to come to school the next day."[163]

R—Respect: Respect must be demonstrated by adults and modeled for children. Children raised in disrespectful ways cannot possibly show respect. Adults, regardless of the child's behaviors, need to always model respect and dignity for the child. One of our great challenges is to recognize that our most troubled and struggling children and youth will only begin to respond to us when we can demonstrate that we can see them "at their worst" and still provide care, structure, and support in a respectful manner. We must take the initial steps to model respectfulness and dignity to our most difficult children and youth.

I—Imagination and Innovation: In some professions, there are certainties that act as rules to follow and hold true for the majority of problems or circumstances that may come up. Teaching is not one of those professions! There are very few certainties in our work. Many times, we have found ourselves surprised to actually see what has worked in the classroom and what has turned out to be a disaster. Many times, what we try as teachers does not work according to our plans. We must consciously recognize that our ability to imagine different ways of teaching a concept, or interacting with a dysregulated student, is a skill that we can develop over time. Our ability to innovate, to problem solve, and come up with a new idea or plan allows us to face many of the failed efforts that are unavoidable for teachers. We learn, we change, and we go on. Our ability to reflect, to own and speak to our mistakes, and then to try again, may be one of the most important lessons we model to our children and youth.

V—Validation: What is validation and why is it important? When we validate a student, we are essentially saying, "I see and understand how you are feeling. Your feelings are important to me, and it's OK that you feel that way." Validation provides "psychological air," or the emotional relief and safety that allows another the experience of feeling felt and understood. We do not need to agree with what the person is feeling, but we do need to acknowledge it. It is about valuing another person's experience and feelings. Validation is the gateway for allowing someone their experience and self-reflection. Sometimes, simply being heard is enough to begin the healing process. How attentive are we when our colleagues are in need of validation?

E—Empathize: Empathy is our ability to see an event from another person's point of view, whether our student or our colleague, feeling their emotion as if it were our own. Empathy is the key to seeing beneath a student's surface behavior as we walk inside their private realities, exploring a nervous system that may be functioning in survival. Survival states occur when the nervous system is flooded with sensory information that is coming too fast, too soon, and feels too much. It can also include nervous system states where the adversity or trauma lasts too long. Author Steven Covey explains: "Seek first to understand, and then be understood."[164] Empathy and validation open the door to the conversations we need to have with our children and youth. These conversations can set the trajectory for emotional connections, which begin to create the nervous system's plasticity for developing a foundation that children and adolescents can trust.

Re-imagining and Constructing the Nest Through Breath and Self-Reflection

We begin constructing the nest with the healing and resilient power of awareness, breath, and self-reflection. As I mentioned in earlier chapters, the human body regenerates body tissues every day, working at a cellular level, and when we change our patterns of breathing, we are able to restore a balance to the nervous system.[165] According to physicians and authors Dr. Richard Brown and Dr. Patricia Gerbarg, "The stresses of our modern day life induce negative emotions such as anxiety, anger, frustration, and stress accelerates the decline in physical health due to inflammation and immune dysfunction."[166] The authors continue by explaining that the daily use of breath practices coupled with self-reflection can unlock the metal casing around the heart, enabling a re-remembering and reconnection in our relationships and with ourselves.[167]

From the early writings of D.T. Suzuki, the renowned Zen master: "As soon as we deconstruct, deliberate, and conceptualize, the original unconsciousness is lost, and a thought interferes... The arrow is off the string, but does not fly straight to the target, nor does the target stand where it is. Calculation, which is miscalculation, sets in... Man is a thinking reed, but his great works are done when he is not calculating and thinking. 'Childlikeness' has to be restored with practice, intention, and training in self-forgetfulness."[168] Perhaps this is why it is said that great poetry, art, and music are born in silence and arise from the quiet depths of our unconscious.[169] Author Timothy Gallwey writes, "True expressions of love are said to come from a source that lies beneath words and thoughts, and sometimes we need one another to tap into that source as we uncover our inner knowing and strengths."[170]

For many people in the world, quieting the mind or shutting off our thinking brain feels unfamiliar and even unsafe, as our daily realities are often noisy, busy, filled with doing and talking. For these reasons, quiet environments and experiences often elude us and can feel strange, as if these moments are abnormal. We may feel the disapproval of those around us when we focus on quiet mindfulness. Depending on how acutely we respond to others' disapproval, this perceived disapproval may throw us into survival states, unsettling our own nervous systems. What is interesting and so often misunderstood is that human beings are sensing and feeling creatures who think. Cognition, the thinking and learning aspects of brain development, are the final brain regions to evolve preceded by sensing our internal and external environments and feeling our way through life experiences.[171] We require felt safety so that we can become aware of our experiences, to feel how we feel without the fear of rejection or abandonment, and to therefore learn purposefully and deeply.

In the western part of the world, meditation practices are often misinterpreted and undervalued within the context of education. Meditation can be a spiritual practice, but it is more accurately defined as an executive function practice. Why? When we focus on a stimulus such as a taste, sound, visualization, or touch integrating our focused breath, we provide experiences to the brain and body that can exercise and therefore strengthen our ability to focus and pay attention. Focused Attention Practices address the frontal lobes of our brains, increasing an oxygenated blood flow that strengthens working memory, attuning and sharpening our attention to provide clarity inside our thought processes while increasing our capacity to reason and problem solve. Deep breathing practices not only dampen down our stress response systems, but they also cultivate stress resilience by activating the parasympathetic pathway of the nervous system. This is the healing, restorative, and calming route of the nervous system.[172]

I usually speak about the origin of how Focused Attention Practices came to be when I am invited to share the application of educational neuroscience and trauma-responsive practices at conferences, presentations, and seminars. However, until now, I have never written specifically about how these sensory and breathing practices came to be identified as Focused Attention Practices and how their use is unfolding in our schools.

About 12 years ago, when I was teaching in the College of Education at Marian University in Indianapolis, Indiana, I was given a course release that allowed me to return to the K-12 public school classrooms and co-teach with the grade-level teachers and staff. I was exhilarated and skeptical because I would be back in the classroom (where I began as a self-contained special education teacher with students carrying a label of emotionally disturbed), and I would be modeling, sharing, and teaching these practices myself! I needed to sit with my mistakes, reflect on the challenges these practices would evoke, and know firsthand how students and staff would receive, reject, and hopefully begin to integrate these exercises into a school day or class period.

What I researched and discovered through the lens of developmental and contemplative neurosciences is that these breathing and movement practices could activate the frontal lobes of the brain, which is where our executive functions reside. This area of the brain was the last to evolve, so we were actually providing a few minutes each day to "work out" these areas, and the students likened this concept with…going to the gym. I realized that when we slowed down or sped up our breathing, our physiological states shifted, and we began to truly enhance our concentration, and even enjoy this time together. What should we call these practices? How could we replace the word meditation and yet not lose the meaning of focusing on a stimulus? We were focusing our attention and increasing the amount of time each day that we practiced. That was it! Focused Attention Practices were born, and we then added movement, taste, sound, and texture with our focused breathing.

In the first school where I was placed, two half days a week in the fifth-grade classrooms, I began co-teaching Brain- and Nervous System-Aligned Bell Work and Focused Attention Practices to build engagement while quieting the stress response systems as part of our morning meetings, end-of-the-day gatherings, transitions, or any time our classes needed to refocus and begin again. My two co-teachers and principal were so invested, and their leadership was a game changer for how the students received these new practices. When the adults in schools join in, learn, appreciate, and share the value of new strategies or practices, our students will feel this positive contagion in their nervous systems. They will observe, try it out, and feel safe enough to share what they liked and what was not pleasant or helpful as they discover their voices and the latitude to make the adjustments they might need to personalize their own practices. Deanna and Sarah, my initial co-teachers, always gave the students a choice to participate, and in return asked for them to respect their classmates who were participating by finding a quiet activity that they could enjoy. Those who chose not to participate were given a couple of options that felt calming as they prepared for the day, during transitions, or before returning home. What was so encouraging to witness were the moments students asked for a Focused Attention Practice! This happened when schedules changed, or there were interruptions during the morning meeting gatherings. Gradually more students began participating, and over the semester, we extended the time we took for these practices from ten seconds to five minutes. We continually reflected upon the process and discussed it with our students. The students began signing up to lead the Focused Attention Practices. Nine years later, during the second year of the pandemic, our third-

and fourth-grade students began to share these practices with their parents and recorded videos of their families practicing together.

Even today, more than ten years after we introduced these practices, many adults are still uncomfortable with teaching children and youth breathing practices in traditional school settings. Knowing this resistance would be a reality, I began delving deeper into the contemplative and developmental research and literature to discover the significant positive impact that deep rhythmic breath can have on the developing brain and nervous system. I realized that we could not acquire buy-in without exploring and sharing the neuroscience of breath practices, but there was something else. Our students needed and desired to know the science of *why* these Focused Attention Practices matter so much to our nervous systems. We began teaching students about their neuroanatomy and the parts of the brain and body that responded to a long slow breath or faster movement, rhythm, pressure, vocalization, heat, or a cold sensation. I wrote about many of these practices in my last book, *Connections Over Compliance: Rewiring Our Perceptions of Discipline,* but just like the many facets and disciplines of neuroscience, the applications of this growing body of research continue to shift and change. At the end of this chapter, and in the Resource Section of this book, I will share new Focused Attention Practices that prepare the nervous system for accessing the cortex, so that we begin to feel safe, connected, and calmer. There are Focused Attention Practices that can energize our nervous system when we feel sluggish and tired. These practices can ramp up our heart rate, alerting our brain and body with movement, faster breathing, and novelty. Depending upon the nervous system state of the student, we can determine which practice best meets the needs of our students' nervous systems.

A Variety of Different Breathing and Movement Practices

Breathing is one of the only biologically known ways to calm the autonomic nervous system. There are no known drugs that have the sole ability to engage the parasympathetic system to turn on and "calm you down." When we breathe deeply with an extended outbreath, we can lead our body into sensing safety. Think about the differences we sense in our bodies between a deep inhale and long slow exhale. When do we breathe quickly and take a preparatory inhale? We might be gasping in surprise, or because we're nervous, or we're about to do something that makes us anxious. When we take a longer inhale than exhale, we are engaging our sympathetic system and telling our body that we need to prepare by getting a lot of oxygen into our system. On the other hand, if we are slowly breathing and allowing ourselves to exhale as we rid our bodies of the carbon dioxide in our breath, that signals that we are in a safe space to breathe. We don't have to ramp ourselves up any more, and we can rest. By breathing with a focus on the inhale through the nose and an exhale through the mouth, and by consciously deciding how we want to feel (either calmed down or energized), we can adjust our breathing patterns to suit our needs. Therefore, we utilize Focused Attention Practices; they biologically support our desire to center ourselves with the simplicity of our breath. Remember that breathing is only one of many options, and taking deep breaths may not feel comfortable to your nervous system. The most important thing is being aware of what does feel soothing to us as we explore a variety of practices! Below is a practice that we can integrate in the early mornings or evenings and even when it is cold, because the chill of the air can activate the parasympathetic pathway of our nervous system, calming and soothing our bodies and brains. We can share practices for our staff and students to integrate at home, and not just at school.

The Resonance of Sound and Breath

Take some belly breaths: A few long, deep belly breaths coupled with calming sounds can provide rhythmic healing to a worn-out nervous system. Before you go to sleep or first thing when you awaken, step outside, and just listen to the night or morning sounds. Sit comfortably, and for two or three minutes take a few deep breaths, exhaling a few seconds longer than you inhale. Listen to the rhythm of the crickets, katydids, morning birds, or any sounds that may arise.

Following a Focused Attention Practice, we create a space and some time for reflection. It can be easy to skip this and just move on, assuming that the experience was useful. But it is important to give everyone a chance to let the moment sink in. What we are hoping to achieve, as well as a moment of regulation, is an opportunity to build on our embodied or disembodied sensory experiences. When we reflect on the moment that we just experienced, it allows growing awareness with adjustments in our practices that might feel safer or calming. Some reflection questions we can ask are:

- How did that make you feel? How did your body respond? What sensations did you recognize?

- Did you like this one? Would you do it again? How would you change this to meet your needs?

- Was that enough time to get what you needed? Or was it too long?

- What sensations did you notice in your body before, during, and after?

- Is there a different way you would have introduced or implemented this Focused Attention Practice?

We don't need to have our students or staff respond, but it is important that we at least pose the questions and model our own preferences, giving the space and time for them to think about how they might answer internally. Gathering feedback on what our students and we enjoy practicing allows us to provide practices that will ensure further engagement in the future. These practices are always an option and can be modified in hundreds of ways.

Focused Attention Practices take time and repetition before they feel more comfortable or enjoyable. We need to give our students and ourselves the time and space to feel more relaxed with them, building endurance in how long we can focus our attention. We begin with just a few seconds and build our attention and focus each day! Students and staff tend to comment that at first, they weren't sure about the practices, because they hadn't had the opportunity to focus on a specific sensation in the past; but once they trust the process, they begin to enjoy the practices and start requesting them. If you hear people comment that they feel a little sleepy when you get started, that is normal. With Focused Attention Practices, we don't want to judge how they make us feel. Maybe we can decrease how much time we allot for one practice or another. Maybe we can involve more sensory options in our routine: include movement, grab some lotion, make the breathing quicker or with more intentional inhales then exhales, or create doodling and drawing options within the breathing practice. Focused Attention Practices can take a variety of forms.

What are some ways that we can be creative with our Focused Attention Practices?

- Look online for videos of mindfulness or Focused Attention Practices.
  - Some Focused Attention Practices are just about breathing, while others involve a script to follow as you think about a visual image or check in with a body scan.
- Include doodling or drawing images.
- Play music and ask students to notice the different instruments or sounds.
- Play clips of sounds and ask if students can identify them.
- Involve other objects, like lotion, essential oils, ice cubes, weights, stones, or any items that provide a texture.
- Think about what senses you'd like to engage.
  - Taste/mouthfeel: mints, hot candies, sour candies, gum, crushed ice, small chocolates
  - Visual: breathing GIFs, natural landscapes, screensavers, and WindowSwap (a website showing views from other people's windows @ https://www.window-swap.com/)
  - Touch: sensory tools like fidgets, tennis balls, Velcro, bubble wrap, kinetic sand, pipe cleaners

We may find that sitting still and doing a Focused Attention Practice is uncomfortable. For some people, being told to sit still and be mindful activates their survival/immobilized state, which can feel very threatening. That would mean that we are in such immediate danger that we can't escape it and can only freeze like a deer in the headlights. Some of us need to move in order to feel safe.

Focused Attention Practices are great ways to start the day or bridge the energy after transitions. They don't have to be confined to classrooms. When adults are learning about Focused Attention Practices with students, learning together as a staff and student body creates a co-embodied experience for everyone. Imagine how much more focused our staff could be during an after-school meeting if we gave them the space to attune to their brains and bodies before we work together as a team! Or what if we integrated these practices as a routine before school started, or as an opportunity for staff to breathe together before the day starts? Imagine how connected and prepared we could feel if we supported our colleagues' nervous systems this way, and how this positive energy could ripple down into the regulation of our classrooms!

We need to give ourselves time to explore a variety of practices and ask ourselves why we enjoyed one over another. Was there something in our environment that made it difficult for us to immerse ourselves in the experience? These aren't practices that work well when we are trying to multitask or when there is much distraction and chaos, as it takes time and practice to work through those disruptions and share these nuggets of insight with our students. Consider these questions as you review your experience:

- Was it too loud or were there too many visual distractions that kept you from being engaged in your internal monologue?

- What do you need to help you focus? Maybe noise-cancelling headphones and closing your eyes?

- Was it too quiet? Would you benefit from white noise or an audio recording of natural sounds to ease you into comfort?

When we are curious about what makes us comfortable, it allows us to explore and find more of what cultivates ease and safety. And when we feel safe and comforted, we are more regulated, aware, and flexible in our thinking processes.

Co-Regulatory Focused Attention Practices

Our nervous systems are designed to ask the question, "Am I safe?" "Safe" can mean physical safety in the environment or relational safety with those around us. In the previous chapters, I discussed the challenges for our students as they returned to school in year three of a pandemic. There was a significant social loss, and the verbal and physical aggression was palpable. The reason is that prolonged isolation is a condition in which our nervous systems adapt to aloneness, so being with others needs to be re-experienced. Building collaboration, cooperation, and negotiation often requires time and practice. When we feel felt by another person, our physiological states can sense safety and trust. Co-regulation is sharing embodied experiences with another so that we can both find protection and well-being. Co-regulation can change the power dynamic between two people so that a shared experience brings safety. The ability to self-regulate is constructed from ongoing experiences of co-regulation. We can find a rhythm of safety and collaboration through this dyadic process of predictable, emotionally available, and consistent connections with other autonomic systems. Below are some examples of how we can integrate a combination of Focused Attention Practices through co-regulation to build relationships and a sense of safety and connection in the classroom:

1. Dedicate This One

In this Focused Attention Practice, we create an image or write down a few words that we want to share with someone we appreciate. As we think of this person, we breathe deeply for one minute sharing our love, hope, and any words of comfort that we want to send them. We then share our dedication with a partner. We can draw, write out, or visualize our appreciation.

2. Regulating With Your Partner

Choose a partner. Without talking, find a rhythm in your own breathing, and see if your partner can match the breathing rhythm. What about a drumming or movement rhythm? Change it up as each person takes the lead. Did you find a pattern, rhythm, or even a beat to your dual breathing or movement? Maybe one student could begin a rhythm, and the other could add to it and repeat a few times until they have created a patterned collaborative rhythm.

3. Mirror Me

In this co-regulatory practice, one partner creates a variety of body movements that the other person must mirror. We then switch partners, and the other leads the movements.

4. Dual Drawing and Dual Journaling

Create dual storytelling through journaling, storytelling, or drawing. (This may be something that you and your students have already done.) In this co-regulatory practice, partners share a sheet of paper for one minute. When the time starts, one partner draws a line or shape and then passes it back to the other person for their line or shape. We continue doing this for one minute without speaking. When the time is up, we can share our dual masterpiece, giving it a title, and any description that feels appropriate to both of us. We can create the same format with dual journaling or storytelling. For one minute, students pass back and forth a sheet of paper, contributing a sentence or two at a time to create a collective story. We can provide prompts of places, objects, or other themes, connecting the story to what we are learning and to each other. Maybe we write about our similarities, differences, interests, passions, etc.

5. Faces, Eyes, Gestures, and Postures

It is important to notice another person's eyes, listen to their voice, and watch their gestures and posture. These facial expressions and body languages tell us how someone is feeling, and they are signals for us as we interact with them. To be aware of their body language is to understand how we need to respond. People "listen" more to body language than the words that people say. It is also very important for us to understand our own body language!

A. What do you share through your eyes, face, and body when you are angry? Worried? Anxious?

B. Can you think of a time when you read the body language of a friend or an adult and you felt comfortable and safe?

C. Can you think of a time when you read the body language of someone that, for you, felt uncomfortable or unsafe?
- Their eyes are signaling_____.
- Their tone of voice sounds_____.
- Their face is expressing_____.
- Their posture and the way they move their hands and arms tell me _____.

D. What about you when you're angry?
- When I am angry my eyes are signaling_____.
- When I am angry, my tone of voice _____.
- When I am angry, my face is expressing_____.
- When I am angry, my arms, hands, and posture_____.

E. What about when you're worried?
- When I am worried my eyes are signaling_____.
- When I am worried, my tone of voice is_____.
- When I am worried, my face is expressing_____.
- When I am worried, my arms, hands, and posture_____.

F. What about when you feel safe?
- When I am safe, my eyes are signaling_____.
- When I am safe, my tone of voice is_____.
- When I am safe, my face is expressing_____.
- When I am safe, my arms, hands, and posture _____.

G. What about when you feel scared?
- When I am scared, my eyes are signaling_____.
- When I am scared, my tone of voice is_____.
- When I am scared, my face is expressing_____.
- When I am scared, my arms, hands, and posture_____.[173]

Building Bell Work Into the Nest

Procedures and Practices

Neurologist Dr. Judy Willis writes:

Every class, assignment, and experience shapes the human brain. Understanding how the brain processes information into learning, knowing more about what it takes for students' brains to be maximally responsive to information input, and finding explanations for how and why successful practices and strategies work are ways neuroscience research is providing keys to the interventions and strategies best suited for individuals and specific topics.[174]

We know that our brains seek patterns that feel pleasurable and meaningful, and sometimes we seek unhealthy or unsafe patterns because these also feel familiar and comforting based on past experiences. Dr. Willis has observed that mammalian brains use patterns based on memories of previous experiences to interpret the millions of bits of sensory information that flood our nervous system in all moments.[175] These memory patterns are initiated to predict the best response to novelty, whether it is experience, objects, people, or sensations and pleasure that can also be connected to motivation.[176] As everything that we learn enters the body from sensory nerves, we cannot possibly negotiate all this information and data on a conscious level, because the brain is wired for survival—and this volume of data would be overwhelming! The nervous system is very selective about what sensory information is worthy enough of our attention to reach the prefrontal cortex. The **reticular activating system (RAS)**, our attention and sensory filter, lives in the lower midbrain regions, and if our lessons or content are not selected by this primitive filter, the information may not reach the cortex, the higher brain where cognitive information is processed.[177] Dr. Willis states, "The RAS is key to arousing or tuning into the brain's level of receptivity for input. Preference is for sensory input regarding changes in the expected pattern of the mammal's environment. For an animal, the consideration might be: What has changed from the last time this animal was in this field or tree? For a student, it might be: What has changed in the classroom from the last day or the last week?"[178] When there is felt threat, danger, or feelings of being unsafe, it is unlikely that any potentially essential information will reach the cortex. We have discussed at length how stress and trauma change brain architecture, impacting the student's ability to retain information while producing significant cognitive deficits in overall intellectual, social, and emotional functioning and school performance.

Understanding the impact of trauma and adversity on the developing brain and nervous system allows us to be intentional when applying these understandings to the learning environment—or nest. When our nest is trusting, friendly, collaborative, and sensitive to the lived experiences our students carry in, it will reduce feelings of threat or danger, allowing the stress response systems to calm. With this calming, our children and youth gradually move away from protective survival states, as we hold and nourish them with a presence that generates poignant compassion. This is intentional neuroplasticity. We begin to create the conditions of felt safety while reflecting on our own nervous system states, allowing our nonverbal communication to invite connection. Our ever-changing nervous systems reflect our neuroception and therefore our perceptions of environments, relationships, and experiences. In schools, we have the potential to build stronger neural networks through relational presence while weakening neural networks and connections that produce fear and anxiety. Practice makes permanent, and we are teaching this brain science to our students. Students begin to feel proud, more motivated, and inspired to change, knowing that the brain and its synapses are plastic. That means they know there is always room to discover, relearn, and begin again!

Brain- and Nervous System-Aligned Bell Work is built into our routines and procedures. It embraces educator nervous system states, because when we are excited, enthused, passionate, and curious, our students experience this by contagion. This type of bell work is predictable because students learn that, during certain times each day, we will address our nervous systems, feelings, and thoughts in novel practices and discussion through morning gatherings, during transitions, and end-of-the-day rituals. We will check in with our nervous system states and discover how our bodies and brains respond to stress, adversity, positive emotion, behaviors, and the superpower of plasticity! We are not adding to educators' plates, as this application of Applied Educational Neuroscience *is* the plate. When we spend time preparing our nervous systems with novelty, movement, art, collaboration, questions, intentional feedback, and check-ins, we are meeting our students in their unique nervous system state functioning. These brain-aligned procedures and practices can activate the brain's level of receptivity for input while fostering a safe learning environment. Dr. Judy Willis says, "Although curiosity and novelty are powerful attention grabbers, the value of consistent routines should not be overlooked, especially in times of stress. These rituals and practices begin to build trust and give us feedback about the amount of trust that is developing through our efforts at community and relationship building."[179]

Discipline

Social/Cultural/Emotional Nests

Getting out in front of negative behaviors is the radical change in our discipline protocols we are needing to cultivate for the sustainable behavioral challenges that have been lost inside reactionary responses. Educators' nervous system states, Focused Attention Practices, and Brain- and Nervous System-Aligned Bell Work are conditions and practices that cultivate a new paradigm shift of discipline. After introducing this theory in my last book, *Connections Over Compliance: Rewiring Our Perceptions of Discipline*, I have further explored the co-regulatory experiences built into our procedures and routines that set the emotional temperature for staff, students, and parents. A regulated and flexible nervous system is developed when the ruptures between people are recognized, repairs are intentionally made, and the ability to self-regulate is constructed from ongoing experiences of co-regulation. This is true throughout our lifetimes.[180] Sometimes, however, rather than a co-regulating experience, we find ourselves unintentionally engaged in mutual dysregulation with one another or with a student. When we follow a child into anger or anxiety, when we follow a colleague into frustration or irritation, we find ourselves in opposition to others—and this is never where we intended to be! We rupture with our students, and there is little to no repair. Discipline challenges before, during, and following this global pandemic have been exhausting to navigate, describe, and understand. The pandemic created isolating, unpredictable, and devastating conditions. During this time, so many communities, families and individuals suffered from the adversities of sickness, death, poverty, racial disparities, and lack of access to foundational needs coupled with the racial violence and aggression that generations of people have embodied and will continue to embody. The collective nervous system dysregulation of our communities and schools is felt deeply by the developing brains and bodies of our children and youth, showing up in so-called behaviors that we persist in misunderstanding. For these reasons, it is accurate to say that we have been **crisis teaching** in this challenging time. So many of us have been living in survival states that our ability to reflect, pause, and ground ourselves in the present moment has been unattainable. In these survival states, our sense of felt safety diminishes as our **relational window of tolerance** lessens and often closes us off to the students who ask for love in the most unloving ways.

If we are unable to feel, we struggle with the restorative practices of somatic empathy. Somatic empathy is being aware and attuned to the sensations that are being expressed in the bodies of others through postures, gestures, facial expressions, and vocal tones. When we begin to intentionally resonate with our own inner worlds, we can tap into the internal worlds of our children and youth. This is discipline. This is plasticity. Discipline is a practice that shares an embodied experience of reclaiming a sense of belonging and resiliency with another person. Discipline holds a compassionate presence that sees and values another's lived experiences. This is intentional plasticity.

When the adults in our schools create this paradigm shift, deeply understanding that discipline is about us, and not about our children and youth, we will see a transformation in the behavioral challenges, engagement, and the revitalizing of purpose and possibility through the preventative relational and nervous system-aligned adult practices. Co-regulation is sitting beside our children and youth, helping them to revisit the parts of themselves encased in the defensive and protective habits that have helped them survive. This co-regulatory experience requires adults to revisit the parts of themselves that developed similar defensive and protective habits needed to help them survive. When we see the origins of our conflict cycles, adult and youth, those cycles begin to wear down as schools cultivate and hold a culture of awareness and are intentional about supporting and creating a space for self-leadership.

Below are some examples of Brain- and Nervous System-Aligned Bell Work and Focused Attention Practices. These are as meaningful and purposeful for adults as they are for our children and youth. They are built into our procedures, routines, and rituals, meeting each other where we are in our nervous system states and with what we might enjoy, or describe as safe, grounding, and thought-provoking. In the Resource Section of this book, I will share more of these regulatory and connection practices.

Energizing Focused Attention Practices

1. Breath of Fire or Dragon Breath
This is an energizing or sympathetic nervous system breath that helps create attention and energy in our nervous system before we begin an assignment, performance, or an activity requiring concentration and some added energy. For 20 seconds, stick out your tongue and pant like a dog. Try to do this quickly, limiting your breath movements to your belly. Stop and take two long deep breaths. Repeat the breath of fire with your mouth closed for ten seconds, and then sit quietly for a minute and notice any sensations in your body or brain. What do you notice? Can you feel the energy move faster in specific areas throughout your body?

2. Energize
In this breath exercise, think of a performer preparing for an event. We take a long deep breath in and then exhale quickly and fast. We see athletes using this breath to prime their brains and bodies

before a competitive event. It is important to start with five or ten breaths and then build up to 30, but this takes time. We can use this powerful breath to energize our brains and bodies when we are feeling tired, unfocused, and sluggish.

3. Fist Pumping

Stretch arms out to each side (shoulder height) with elbows straight, opening and closing our fists with an energizing breath of fire. We begin for 30 seconds. Then we take a long, slow, deep breaths and begin again for 30-60 seconds. This exercise brings an oxygen flow to the brain, as our fingers act like a remote control for the brain waking us up with this repetition. We begin to focus on the movement and breath. Flip our hands over, then open and close the fists again for another minute. This strengthens the nervous system.

4. Crossing Movements

Make a fist with the thumb inside and straighten arms out to a 60-degree angle. Inhale with straight arms, and on the exhale bend them to cross at the forearms in front of our forehead. Next, inhale with straight arms at a 60-degree angle and cross behind our head. When we repeat the cycle 20-30 times, this powerful breath exercise releases calcium deposits in the shoulders and increases an improved blood flow to the brain.

5. Twisting and Swirling

Sitting with legs stretched out in front, place each hand (your open palm) on your temple, just above your ear, and inhale as you twist your trunk to the left, then exhale as you twist to the right. Keep your spine vertical and straight with a firm pressure on each temple. Your elbows are out as you twist. This exercise balances the parasympathetic and sympathetic nervous systems with the breath and twisting motions as we energize for focus.

6. Punch and Grab

Standing with our feet about three feet apart, we make fists with our hands. One arm at a time, we reach in front of us, opening our fist on the inhale and closing it and drawing it back to our body on the exhale. We move back and forth with a powerful inhale and exhale, opening and closing our fists, alternating arms as we pretend to open our hand to what we need on the strong inhale, and then grabbing it as we close our fist and pull our arm back to our body on the strong exhale. This is much like a boxing movement with one arm at a time at any speed that feels comfortable to you. The faster you move, the more energy you create!

7. Push It Away
Clasp hands at chest level and inhale. Then, keeping hands clasped, we push them out in front of us, opening our palms but still clasping our fingers, as our arms straighten with palms facing out. When we push out, this is our exhale. On the inhale, we bring our hands back toward our chest keeping the hands clasped. Do this quickly with a powerful breath for one minute! (We can imagine a thought or color or something that we want to bring into our lives on the inhale, and on the exhale, we can imagine pushing out or away a feeling, thought, or experience that we want to release.)

8. Fly Away
Fly like the most beautiful bird, flapping your wings as you move your arms up and down, fanning the air with your beautiful wings and deep breath! Begin with your fingertips on the ground, and then with straight arms, inhale as you lift your arms above your head so that the backs of your hands touch each other. On the exhale, drop your fingertips to the ground. Repeat this movement with your powerful breath for one minute. This not only energizes our nervous system, but it also builds plasticity. Our arms get tired very quickly, so try starting with 10-20 arm movements. Build up to 100 in a minute as you continue the breath that aligns with the speed of your movements.

Calming Focused Attention Practices

1. Golden Cord
We imagine a golden cord with a glittering ball attached. The cord connects our chest to our belly. As we take a deep breath in, we see

the glittering ball move up along the golden cord into our chest, and as we exhale, we see the glittering ball move back down the cord into our belly. You can imagine this movement happening as fast or slow as you would like. Try this exercise for one minute as you focus on your breath and the vision of glittering movement.

2. Paint Breathing

Each student receives a drinking straw and a dab of acrylic or oil paint on a paper plate or sheet of paper. After we inhale through our nose, we exhale long and slow through the straw so that the air from our exhale moves the paint around the paper. When we are intentional about a long, low exhale, we activate the parasympathetic pathway, slowing down our heart rate and lowering our blood pressure. This Focused Attention Practice can also be done without paint or a straw; we breathe in through our nose, and then we purse our lips and breathe out long and slow, emptying our belly with all our breath.

3. Labyrinth Movement and Breathing

Students can use chalk, spray paint, or even yarn or string to create their personal labyrinth path. This can take place in a large indoor area or outside. Instead of a traditional labyrinth, students can also create a maze, an intricate path with different shapes and passages that begin at a certain point and end at another. The Focused Attention Practice is creating a unique labyrinth or maze design, and then moving through it with deep breaths as you wind around your creation. We can implement these in a variety of ways. Some of the variations might include listening to music while walking, walking backward, taking giant steps that align with our inhale or exhale, or any movement that might be engaging for a particular age group. Classes can also collectively design one large labyrinth or maze.

4. Butterfly Hug

This Focused Attention Practice resembles tapping, which I shared in my last book. We begin by holding our hands in front of us with our palms facing inward. Crossing our hands, we interlock our thumbs, and place our interlocked thumbs on our upper chest around the clavicle bone. With fingertips pointed upward, we begin tapping our chests as the butterfly wings begin to flutter. As we take deep breaths, our wings can rhythmically match our breaths, or we can just let our butterflies flutter around at their own rhythm and pace. We flutter the wings and breathe intentionally for about 30 seconds, building up to a minute or two. If our butterflies get tired, they can rest on our chest as we take in a few more deep breaths without the fluttering.

5. Sighing

With a huge deep breath, let out the largest sigh you can! This is not a scream or shout, but the swirling sound your voice creates when you let all the respiratory and vocal energy go. Sighing can lead to yawning, and giant yawns are calming to the nervous system. Maybe we try three sighs in a row.

6. Vision Quest

We begin by focusing on one specific object in our room or whatever our setting. After we focus on our object for approximately ten seconds, we begin to broaden our gaze and create a gentler, more open vision of our setting, which can directly impact our parasympathetic nervous system. As we focus ten more seconds on this broadened view with our softened vision, our heart rate, respiration, and blood pressure all lower! What did you notice around your first point of focus? What could you see at the corners of your eyes? We share with each other all that we observed and how this experience felt to our nervous systems.

7. Box and the Boat

We write or draw an image of a worry or something that is troubling us on a piece of paper. Maybe we simply imagine this worry or problem without drawing it. We then place our worries into a real or imaginary wooden box, and then place that box into an imaginary boat. In our minds, we watch that boat begin to sail away down a long, winding river. As we imagine this scene, we breathe in peacefulness and breathe out our worries. We can do this for a couple of minutes as we breathe deeply with the lifting away of a sadness, worry, or anxious time. We then conclude this Focused Attention Practice with questions: How did this feel? What helped you to work through this problem or challenge? Is there something missing from this practice that we could add? How would you change this practice so that it feels safe and comforting to you? (For inspiration, spend some time with this YouTube video of the view from a boat quietly traveling along the Nile River:

https://www.youtube.com/watch?v=cySBHyKZDsM)

8. Physiological Sigh

We discuss and share how we feel at that moment when, after we have been crying, our tears or sobs suddenly begin to lessen; or that moment when our breathing changes as we begin to relax and fall asleep at night. Our bodies naturally take in one or two quick inhales of breath, and then a long exhale follows. Mammals do this breath without being taught how, because it is the natural way that we release tension, tightness, and stress. (I always model this breath a few times before I ask students to try it out.)

9. Giraffe Breath

Following the Physiological Sigh, it feels good to do the Giraffe Breath. For this Focused Attention Practice, we took a blank piece of paper and turned it vertically. With our eyes closed, or just looking away from the paper, we took four long breaths while making a line from the bottom to the top with our inhale, and then from the top to the bottom with our exhale. Part of the challenge was trying to align these lines without looking as we drew them, increasing our spatial and motor skill awareness. The students loved it!

Brain- and Nervous System-Aligned Bell Work

1. Symbols, Rituals, and Predictability

In this Focused Attention Practice, we begin the morning with a discussion of symbols and rituals, and why the brain loves these! Our brains predict what will happen next based on our own experiences.

Our brains learn through repetition, prediction, and associations so that we can make meaning out of our experiences and will know what to do the next time there is a similar situation. The students shared their responses to the following questions, bringing in their personal experiences of what rituals are important in their own lives.

A. What are symbols?

B. How would symbols be connected or rituals or routines? Why do you think these feel soothing or comforting to us? (Remember that our brains and nervous systems struggle with unpredictability and anything that feels unfamiliar.)

C. Can you share any rituals, symbols, or routines in your own life that feel safe and comfortable to you?

D. Can you think of a routine or ritual that you would love to begin and practice that is currently not a part of your day-to-day life?

The students select their own symbol (I brought in hand-woven bracelets, but rocks, buttons, coins, or anything will do) that they personally connect with to help them remember their strengths, power, identity, and all that they value. This symbol is a reminder that YOU bring unique parts of who you are into everything you feel, think, create, and do! Students were given a large sheet of paper and markers, with the instructions to think of an image, sentence, power word, or design that they could connect to their object as they integrate this symbol into their life, creating new rituals or practices that feel soothing, calming, and comforting. They could create this for themselves or for a family member or friend.

2. "What Shall We Do With the Angry Monster?"

In this practice, I instructed the students to watch the first two minutes and 46 seconds carefully, and be ready to predict the end of this four-minute video: https://www.youtube.com/watch?v=bs_0m-CUEPQ&t=167s. As we watched together, I stopped the video at 2:46, and the students turned to partners or their small group and began discussing, predicting, and writing their thoughts about the ending. After a couple of minutes, we restarted the video and watched until the end. The reactions of the students (and adults) were palpable as we emotionally responded and checked our predictions. We then discussed how we often misunderstand and misinterpret the reasons that a person behaves or acts the way they do! Our perspectives are often mistaken when we assume that we know the lived experiences of another. Here are a few guiding questions that we can integrate as we share this bell work with students and staff.

A. Can you think of a time when someone hurt your feelings because they misunderstood you?

B. Do you have a memory of a time when you became angry with a friend or classmate, but then when you learned why they were acting a certain way, you felt confused, and then felt bad for them?

C. Our brains have a negative bias, and our emotions are contagious. When we see something or someone who looks hurtful, mean, or disruptive, we become protective and defensive. When has this happened to you, a family member, or a friend?

D. What is the moral or theme of this little video? Is there a lesson for us to take with us into our own lives?

3. Nervous System Tree

When we are aware of how we feel, which people or experiences trigger us, and how we can help ourselves to find the people, places, and experiences that calm our nervous system, we can run interference or mitigate the stressors that move in and out of our lives. This Brain- and Nervous System-Aligned Bell Work is for everyone! We create our nervous system trees all year long as our lives are continually changing with neuroplasticity. When we are intentional about identifying and naming our strengths, interests, passions, identity, and values, we can access those more easily because they are within our awareness. The image below is just one example of the hundreds of ways that staff, students, and even families can create their own nervous system trees.

We began working on this a few minutes each day for a couple of weeks. The trunk of the tree represents our values, identities, passions, and strengths. The branches represent our dreams, wishes, and possible future goals or plans, while the leaves help us to identify the people or relationships in our lives that are supportive. The storm clouds are our stressors, and the sunshine represents the things, places, and practices that help us to experience some safety and peace. These resources might include simple practices such as taking a walk, talking to a friend or someone we trust, chewing gum, sucking on a mint, taking a hot bath, or listening to music. Below the nervous system tree are a few examples of the many practices that students and staff can explore as we have the opportunity to create our own personalized list of regulatory practices. The entire list of regulatory practices can be found on my website:

www.revelationsineducation.com.

Download these charts:

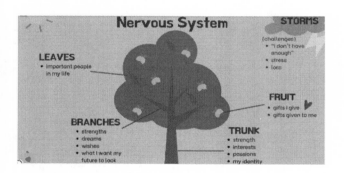

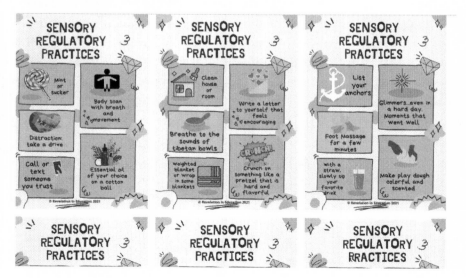

4. The Reveal

This Brain- and Nervous System-Aligned Bell Work is enjoyable and exciting for adults and students. It can be accomplished virtually or in person. We begin the day with an object hidden under a towel. It is that simple. This object could be related to subject matter or a theme that has been discussed in class. Sometimes, I will choose an object related to the nervous system or the brain. As I hold up the covered object, the students or staff listen carefully to the first clue. They begin writing their guesses on a sheet of paper, and they have the option of sharing with a partner or in a small group. I ask them to take two deep breaths, and then I slowly reveal a sliver or piece of the object with another clue. We continue with two deep breaths and another reveal that shows them more of the object. After two or three clues, each followed by deep breaths, they usually discover the hidden object. During the pandemic, I could engage them virtually with this practice as I held objects in front of the computer camera while they breathed with clues and wrote their guesses in the chat box. What happened next was wonderful! The students wanted to lead the bell work from their homes, so they took turns finding objects around the house, covering them with a towel, and leading us in the reveal. This was so special because when the students led, they shared personal items that they revered as parts of themselves. We learned about each other while having so much fun! This practice brought all of us to the present, preparing for learning and higher engagement. Students and staff can also bring their favorite items to school for an in-person reveal day. This bell work incorporated breathing, novelty, movement, and guessing. Our nervous system loves to predict and guess.

Guest Reflections From Dr. Dustin Springer, Principal, Gray Hawk Elementary School, Basehor, Kansas

---

As we ponder and become curious about the nests that we cultivate in our classrooms through co-regulation practices and connection that prepare our nervous systems for cognitive, emotional, and social well-being, in this final section of Chapter 3, Dustin Springer shares his story of how Gray Hawk Elementary, in its first year, has been intentional about practices that create touch points for staff and students—or nests for all students in his building!

Gray Hawk Nests

When I experienced my own paradigm shift around 2017, I began to embrace the idea of "keeping the word YES in my heart" and ensuring that I led with a servant's heart. I have embraced that mindset as a principal.

Opening a brand-new elementary school has not been without countless challenges. Establishing a culture that has a foundation built on love, compassion, kindness, and service is a challenge that our staff and students have embraced; but like anything new, we must seek to do this in a way that best meets the needs of all. While academics are at the core of what we do in schools, now more than ever I believe the social and emotional well-being of our communities is what is *most* important and should be the guiding factor in what we are doing to support one another in being able to be the best we can be in life.

Not necessarily knowing this new community, my deep desire to remain focused on social and emotional wellness assisted my mission to ensure that we were breathing life into our children at every opportunity. With this in mind, we implemented "nests" as a strategy to address a variety of challenges that we were all facing in opening a new school. We noticed that our students were getting along very well, but through discussions as a staff, we also came to the conclusion that, of our 242 students, we were concerned about 32 of them having a positive connection with another loving adult outside of their classroom walls. Even one student concern is too many, but after our staff identified 13% of our student population that concerned us, we knew that something had to be done.

As a young boy, I once watched a robin build a nest in the light on our front porch, and I was amazed at the strength, commitment, and love that little bird took in creating a home to lay her eggs. That nest represented safety, commitment, love, perseverance—so many things that we are trying to build in our Gray Hawks—so it was quite apropos that we would implement nests in our school. Nests are a school-wide strategy where every student in grades K-5 is randomly placed into a group led by a kind and caring adult other than their own classroom teacher. Each nest mixes together a variety of students from all grades. We come together every other Monday for 50 minutes to build relationships, learn about each other, and focus on opportunities to grow together as better humans. The beauty of nests is that children will remain in the same nest throughout the time they are at our school. We use that time every other week to focus on breathing life into our children—and if I am being honest, into ourselves as well.

We know that our brains have plasticity, which means that they can change and adapt as a result of experiences. Every two weeks, we provide a new experience by focusing on different areas where we can grow. One week, we focused on empathy and what it takes to walk in another person's shoes. Another week, we tackled childhood hunger and ways that we could give back and support others facing this challenge in our community. While another time, our students from our Structured Learning Classroom planned a school-wide nest introducing autism and showing that we all have things that make us unique, and that is really what being a Gray Hawk is all about! We need to celebrate our differences in order to really embrace and understand our similarities.

Nests have been an incredible growing opportunity for our entire Gray Hawk Community. Our brains crave novelty and change, and we have noticed a change in our students. Through these bi-weekly experiences, our students have become more empathic. Our students have sought ways to give back and take care of one another through acts of kindness and service. Our students have led with servant hearts and ensured that they have kept the word "YES" in their own hearts.

While we have not followed up as a staff to discuss if we have additional concerns about any of our students, let alone the 13% we identified back in early October, I am very proud to say that 241 of our 242 Gray Hawks (99.6%) recently were able to identify at least one other adult besides their classroom teacher that they know loves and cares about them. That is a pretty amazing thing! Now is the time that we will come together as a Gray Hawk staff and embrace that one child who did not feel a connection. We will not leave one behind. We are certainly better together. Like the nest that the robin built so many years ago on my front porch, our nests represent love, commitment, endurance, and more importantly, safety that every child deserves to feel and experience. Our commitment to continue to breathe life into children remains our top priority!

"We cannot live only for ourselves. A thousand fibers connect us."
HERMAN MELVILLE

Chapter 5

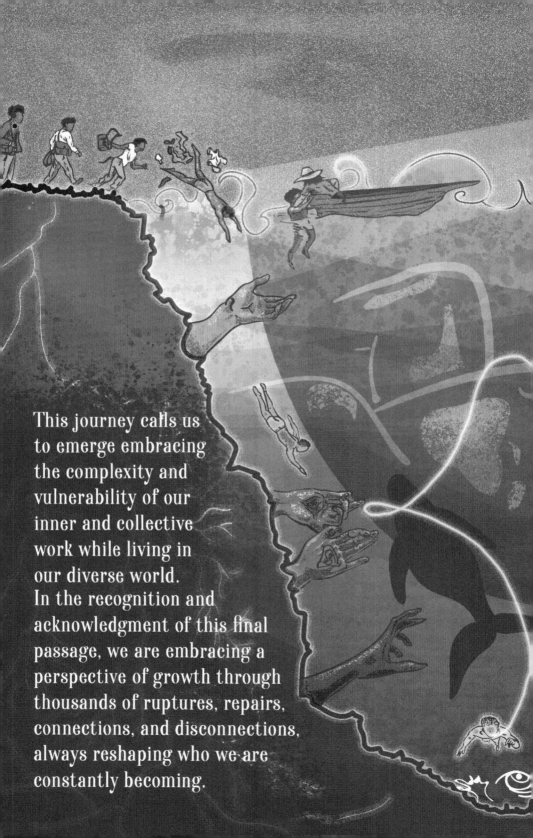

This journey calls us
to emerge embracing
the complexity and
vulnerability of our
inner and collective
work while living in
our diverse world.
In the recognition and
acknowledgment of this final
passage, we are embracing a
perspective of growth through
thousands of ruptures, repairs,
connections, and disconnections,
always reshaping who we are
constantly becoming.

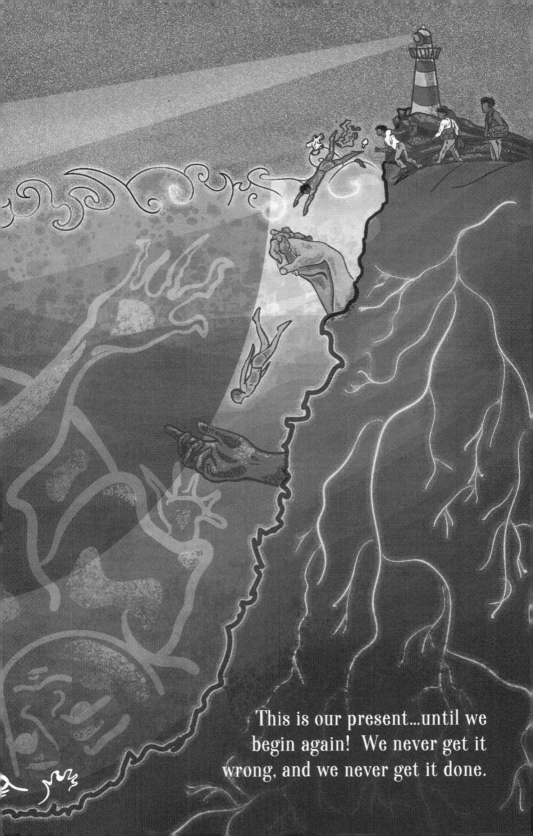

This is our present...until we
begin again! We never get it
wrong, and we never get it done.

Storytelling in Our Schools

"If we want to support each other's inner lives, we must remember a simple truth: the human soul does not want to be fixed, it wants simply to be seen and heard. If we want to see and hear a person's soul, there is another truth we must remember: the soul is like a wild animal—tough, resilient, and yet shy. When we go crashing through the woods shouting for it to come out so we can help it, the soul will stay in hiding. But if we are willing to sit quietly and wait for a while, the soul may show itself."

PARKER PALMER

Our Journeys Toward Growth and the Re-Storying of Discipline

Trauma is a wordless story that is held in our bodies. What we sometimes do not fully embrace is that our bodies also hold the stories of resiliency. The body is where we live life. The body is where we cling to fear, anger, anxiety, and a host of other emotions, but it is also where we carry hope and possibilities. We know and recognize that:

1. In times of chronic adversity and trauma, our bodies care only about survival, and they have evolved to be highly effective managers in their protective responses when we feel threatened or unsafe.

2. Trauma is personal to each individual and can live on in our nervous systems long after the traumatic events have passed.

3. Trauma therapist and author Resmaa Menakem says, "Trauma is a soul wound and occurs in multiple ways:

- Through families in which one family member abuses or mistreats another.

- Through unsafe or abusive racialized systems, structures, institutions, and cultural norms.

• Through our genes. Recent work in human genetics suggests that trauma is passed on in our DNA expression, through the biochemistry of the human egg, sperm, and womb."[181]

4. Trauma is fast, reactive, and can leave out the thinking regions of the brain; and therefore, during the healing process, we need to ground ourselves, leaning into the pain or discomfort as we become curious about what we are experiencing in our bodies.[182]

The body not only holds our trauma, but it also embraces our healing. Our bodies are instruments for one another's healing, as we have the capacity to listen deeply to another person's pain through the resonance of the emergent third within the "in-between" space that Dr. Albert Wong describes as "magic resonance."[183] When we listen with our bodies and not just our ears, our bodies become the intervention that shares a gentle presence with another. We can listen to our own bodies as well, learning to slow down as we lean into the complex, intricate communication between every organ and system inside our bodies. If trauma can be passed down through generations, then so can healing and growth.

This chapter is about healing and storytelling. We are social creatures holding collective experiences. Neuroscientist and author, Dr. Louis Cozolino writes, "Our social brains evolved within oral traditions that relied upon storytelling to store learning and wisdom, transmitting tribal culture from generation to generation. Stories play a significant role in emotional regulation and group connectedness, as well as serving as templates of behavior."[184]

During the first year and a half of life, the brain's right hemisphere holds our emotional, visual, and sensory experiences. Our emotional development occurs without words as we depend on our caregivers to meet our sensory experiences through touch, gentle eye gaze, soothing tones, predictability, and the emotional availability that helps us integrate and organize our emotional experiences.[185] The left hemisphere enters its sensitive growth period during the middle of the second year, when spoken language begins to develop and "hot" emotional experiences can be integrated and translated into words, gradually impacting our ability to regulate our sensory and emotional experiences.[186]

The integration of our developing emotional and sensory systems happens with our caregivers, those who can receive and hold our experiences with warmth, touch, rhythm, and predictability. We need others to assist us in attempting to make sense of the often-fragmented sensations and overwhelming emotions that originate from a tattered, shredded implicit traumatic memory. Creating and sharing our stories helps us to remember where we have been, where we are, and where we are going. For many of us, the memories we retain from past experiences are not conscious and can hit us hard during ordinary moments through smells, tones of voice, sounds, and other sensory experiences, because at the time of the traumatic event, these memories did not become encoded or time-stamped as explicit, cohesive, and clear memories. Why? The **hippocampus** (a limbic system structure that processes memories with the amygdala, our brain's emotional center) can begin to atrophy, unable to consolidate memory when there is heightened chronic emotional distress. This is why it can feel as if a previous traumatic experience is happening right now in the present moment.[187]

For many children and youth, a teacher may be the first adult in their lives who can hold space, reflect, and feel the depth of a young person's experience, which can reduce the anxiety, stress, and uncertainty from feeling so alone, scattered, and story-less. Dr. Louis Cozolino writes, "A strong gauge from the power of stories is reflected in the faces of listeners."[188] In other words, we can literally see the power of a story as we tell it. Have you ever noticed how a trusted other receives our stories? They tend to lean in, tilt their heads, hold eye contact, and focus as if these shared words are the most important words they could hear.

As we become aware of the plasticity of our nervous systems, resiliency correlates with the flexibility of our system. The research shows that, as we begin to metabolize the traumatic sensations and feelings that keep us stuck in survival states (in moments when there is no present danger), our bodies may be detecting sensations of threat; in survival, our bodies are trying to protect us. We cannot talk anyone out of those felt sensations of danger. Trauma is about past energy that is lodged in the body, and when we recognize what those sensations are communicating—tears, tightness, constriction, shortened breath, flashes of heat, tingling—we can begin to normalize those sensations, knowing that our bodies are trying to digest and slowly release some of the trapped energy from sensory fragments of past experiences.

If we know that the discomfort of these bodily sensations is allowing us to understand how we are metabolizing an experience, we can feel relieved and even empowered by them. My daughter Sarah shared: "Momma, when my anxiety feels to be diminishing, following frightening sensations, like when I can't get my breath or I feel frozen and heavy, it feels like it did when I was little, and my fever broke. I feel relieved."

The stories we begin to tell ourselves are co-constructed from our experiences with parents, caregivers, and peers. These self-evolving stories begin nonverbally, which is how we sense and feel our experiences in our first few years of life. They can become powerful tools in the cultivation and maintenance of an evolving sense of self that serves to perpetuate both healthy and unhealthy aspects of identity, autonomy, and a growing sense of purpose.[189] When our personal narratives are negative, they impact our perceptions of the world, relationships, and ability to emotionally regulate, settle into ourselves, and deeply learn.

Our Historical Trauma and Living Stories: The Science of Epigenetics

As we begin to process the plasticity of change, growth, and hope, it is often helpful to realize that the hardships, adversities, and traumas we lug around are not always ours. When we, and when those in our families, have experienced the suffering of inherited trauma, our unspoken distress can cultivate malignant fears, perpetuating the felt brokenness and generational chains of pain that leave us locked up with shame and guilt. Trauma therapist Mark Wolynn says, "The traumas we inherit or experience firsthand cannot only create a legacy of distress, but also forge a legacy of strength and resilience that can be felt for generations."[190] Writing, sharing, and reflecting on our living stories helps us to question and explore the truer sources of their origins. Without language, our experiences often go undeclared, and are more likely to be stored as fragments of memory, images, bodily sensations, and emotions with little context.[191]

"Tragedies varying in type and intensity—such as abandonment, suicide, war, or the early death of a child, parent, or sibling—can send shock waves of distress cascading from one generation to the next. Recent developments in the fields of cellular biology, neuroscience, epigenetics, and developmental psychology underscore the importance of exploring at least three generations of family history in order to understand the mechanism behind patterns of trauma and suffering."[192] Epigenetics is the emergent field that studies the heritable changes in gene function without a change in the gene sequence.[193] In other words, our environment, relationships, lived experiences, and a host of other factors impact how our DNA is expressed. Traditionally, science believed that our genetic inheritance was transmitted through the chromosomal DNA, which determines eye color, hair, and other physical traits, but now we are learning that these physical traits make up approximately two percent of our total DNA.[194]

The other 98% consists of **noncoding DNA** (ncDNA), which holds the emotional and behavioral traits, and is impacted by stressors such as toxins in the environment, insufficient nutrition, and the trauma and adversities that produce chronic levels of stress in our bodies and lives.[195] The noncoding DNA helps us prepare for life as it transmits information that ensures we will have the specific traits needed to adapt to our environment through development.[196] According to neuroscientist Dr. Rachel Yehuda, epigenetic changes biologically set us up to adapt with the trauma that past generations experienced.[197] This is resiliency that is built into our nervous systems. We're born with an innate set of skills or toolkit that allows us to adapt to stress-filled conditions.[198] But these adaptations can be harmful as well, because if the mother is experiencing heightened chronic adversity and trauma during pregnancy and is producing excessive cortisol and adrenaline, these stress hormones can cross the placenta and enter the fetus's bloodstream, as well as produce chemical signals in the cells to either activate or silence a specific gene.[199] "There's something in the environment that affects the internal environment, and before you know it a gene is functioning in a different way," states Dr. Yehuda.[200]

We do not have to be who our ancestors were. We can make choices that we previously did not know would affect the emotional, social, and physiological outcomes of our lives. We can begin to reclaim and re-story our personal agency, helping our children and youth to embrace their positive identity development. This research suggests that when we metabolize our pain and heal our trauma, we make room in our nervous systems for growth.[201]

Trauma is unique to each body, and we have an opportunity in our homes, schools, and communities to attune to the inimitable emotional and social nervous system pathways that hold the stories of our children and youth as they communicate these states of functioning through behaviors, emotions, and relationships. Below are the words from a room message that high school educator Monte Syrie wrote to his students as part of a daily practice in his English classes. I liken his messages to love notes and touch points that students breathe in the moment they step into his classroom. These notes of compassion are making a difference in how students relate, feel, learn, and experience their worlds.

"You are the primary source of your learning story. That's why I go to you (the source). I don't want anything to get lost in my translation, because long after your story is forgotten here, you will still carry it with you. So, let's get the story straight. For you. It's yours." – Sy[202]

Metabolizing our own pain and suffering from ongoing or past adversity can occur with communal stories. Sharing our stories initiates trust, which is the oxygen for cultivating spaces where we begin to feel seen and heard without judgment or fear of rejection. There is a powerful connection between social acceptance and learning.[203]

Co-regulation is holding a compassionate presence with another person. Co-regulation does not interrupt, judge, offer advice, or rush in with its own stories. Trauma therapist Resmaa Menakem states, "Although they don't realize it, people visit my office to be with my settled, regulated nervous system. Over time, their repeated contact with my nervous system helps their nervous systems settle. This does not happen through a process of mirroring, or cognitive training, or verbal communication. What takes place is energetic, chemical, biological—a synching of vibrations and energies."[204]

As educators, we spend hours upon hours with students who are sometimes scanning the environment to find a settled, receiving space and a person who feels safe and trusted to them. A student's neuroception (autonomic intuition) is always seeking that energetic, chemical, biological synching of vibrations and energy that Resmaa Menakem mentions above. Human beings are hungry for feeling settled. We are no different than our children and youth. We, too, walk into our buildings, offices, and districts desiring to settle into connected safety. Humans are predominantly nonverbal communicators sending energetic messages into the world in all moments and for these reasons, we need to become aware of how our nervous system state is receiving other nervous systems, while exploring if we are indeed providing a safe landing place for another person. We cannot always be regulated, or provide that safe space to land, but we can learn to be aware when we are dysregulated, unsettled, and unknowingly cueing resistance. Learning to settle our bodies and practicing wise, compassionate self-care offers a positive contagion for those around us.

> *"I can't believe what you say, because I see what you do."*
> JAMES BALDWIN

Resmaa Menakem writes:

Genuine healing is a temporarily disruptive process. And this is true for the collective American body. Just as the human body creates inflammation to physically heal, wise social activism creates the social and cultural disruptions needed to help a culture heal and grow up, holding the diverse cultures, histories of systemic racism, and the embodied lived experiences of all who work and live beside us. These disruptions might be called compassionate agitation.[205]

When the brain and nervous system try on new ideas and ascribe to unaccustomed behaviors, these experiences feel threatening to the nervous system because they are unfamiliar, not practiced, and can throw us into survival states if we are not prepared to meet ourselves and others with a compassionate presence inside these new experiences.

Our nervous systems are filled with our cultures that embrace how our brains and bodies hold, reenact, or reject histories of racism, war, and generational trauma through the stories we tell and the conditions we ignore or refuse to acknowledge or question. Our cultures live in our bodies, and they have a much stronger hold over us than cognitive ideas, principles, and laws.[206] How do we connect with our embodied culture? Question, listen deeply, and begin attuning to our own stories that our nervous systems are communicating in all moments. We have rarely been taught how to listen within. Trauma therapist Deb Dana writes:

> The nervous system speaks its own language, and in order to listen, we need to understand that language. Becoming fluent in a new language takes time and practice. When we enter the conversation with curiosity, we begin to connect with the energy that is just beneath the surface of awareness and hear the autonomic stories that are shaping our days.[207]

ACTIVITY: The Story and Map of Our Nervous Systems

Following are practices and questions for adults and students that guide us in the exploration of our nervous systems' stories. In other words, our bodies and brains are always in a bi-directional conversation communicating our experience of the present moment and the patterns and repetitions of those experiences. One example of these nervous system conversations is the tension that I feel in my body when I approach a person, place, event, or situation. With awareness of this tightness or tension, I may be able to access the calming breath, a certain physical movement, or words said to myself that can validate and begin to cultivate a sense of grounding and relief. After reviewing the descriptions, the questions propel us into deeper reflection as we explore our stories through the nervous system.

Story of Connection (Ventral Vagal Regulation):

Concepts and keywords: connect, collaborate, cooperate, self-compassion, compassion for others, curiosity, wonder, reflective, empathy

Story of Protection (Sympathetic Mobilization):

Concepts and keywords: driven to compete, moved to judgment, critical of others, downward comparison, argumentative, "I have to be better than others!"

Story of Disconnection (Dorsal Vagal Immobilization):

Concepts and keywords: loss of hope, numb, self-critical shame, dissociation, collapse, "I'm never going to measure up."

Stories of Blended States (Healing Awareness of Autonomic System):

- Ventral/Sympathetic: playfulness, enthusiasm, creative, in the flow with excitement
- Ventral/Dorsal: reflective, **interoceptive**, sometimes hard to access
- Dorsal/Sympathetic: immobilized and stuck yet fired up (deer in headlights)[208]

Questions for Reflection

1. Can we find short-term and longer-term cues of safety for ourselves? Can we plan for them ahead of a crisis?

2. What states do I find often? Are those states pleasing or dysregulating?

3. When I feel dysregulated, where am I? Who am I with? Where does this happen most often?

4. What do I notice about sensations in my body when I feel unsafe, dysregulated, threatened, or in danger?

5. What cues safety for me? What people? Places? Settings or environments? What experiences feel calming to my nervous system?

6. Have I noticed patterns to my autonomic nervous system states? What are those? When do they occur (months, days of the week, night, morning, following specific events or experiences, before school, weekends, holidays)? Do they occur around specific people?

7. What does my self-talk feel and sound like? Does it include words or phrases that feel negative?

8. Do I find myself calling up and rethinking old memories?

Develop Maps of Our Individual and Collective Nervous Systems

Following are prompts that can be helpful in identifying how we feel, how we relate to others, and how we experience our internal and external worlds when functioning from a specific hierarchal nervous system state or experiencing a blended autonomic state. If I am in a blended state, I may feel like being alone so that I can reflect, take a quiet walk, or write in my journal. This is an example of the social engagement and dorsal states combined. If a group of students are running out to recess excited to play, this condition is a blended state of social engagement and sympathetic states; the students are mobilizing energy and excitement while feeling safe and connected as they anticipate play. It may be helpful to fill in the following prompts based on your perceptions and experiences when moving through these different states.

Ventral Vagal—Safe/Connected (Cortex Activated):

- I am....

- Others are...

- The world is...

- The word or phrase that I feel, live, or use when I am feeling a sense of safety and connection: ____ [209]

Sympathetic—Fight-Flight (Limbic System Activated):

- I am...

- Others are...

- The world is ...

- The word or phrase that I feel, live, or use when I am feeling a sense of threat or danger and need protection: ____ [210]

Dorsal Vagal—Immobilized/ Collapsed (Brain Stem Activated):

- I am...

- Others are...

- The world is...

- The word or phrase that I feel, live, or use when I am feeling a sense of threat, danger, or feel immobilized: ____

- What type of thoughts, feelings, sensations, or experiences keep me stuck in fight-flight or immobilized/collapsed? [211]

- What helps me to stay calm, regulated, and connected to the environment around me?

- How do I ask for assistance? Is it hard for me to reach out to others?

Our Autonomic States in Our Schools

The Story of Discipline

The following questions are intended to be surveyed individually, followed by a collective, authentic discussion with our colleagues that may assist us in exploring our biases, perceptions, and the stories we unconsciously bring with us each day affecting how we engage, discipline, and interact with our students.

Guiding Questions (Student Interaction)

1. Do certain students trigger or activate me more than others?

2. Are my responses to each student's behavior the same?

3. Which students do I redirect most often?

4. What behaviors do they show?

5. What behaviors do I expect to see?

6. What emotion do I feel when certain students do not follow my directions?

7. Which behaviors push my buttons the most?

8. What time in the day do I feel the most calm and happy with my students?

9. How do I interpret a silent classroom or a classroom filled with student chatter?

9. In my class, to which students do I feel the closest? Why do I feel that connection to them?

10. In my class, which students are my "favorites"? Why?

11. Do I understand the cultural identity of my students? If not, what can I do to learn more?

12. Do I attempt to make connections to my students' culture and backgrounds in an authentic way?

13. Do my students feel safe to be their authentic selves?

14. Am I creating a community of inclusion and equitable access? (Note: Everyone getting what they need doesn't look like the same thing for everyone.)

15. Do we have to make people feel bad to change their behavior?

After answering these questions, create a ten-word story sharing your personal views and perceptions of school discipline. Sharing these stories is a wonderful opportunity to collect the perceptual data from colleagues that will help us begin to see patterns and themes addressing where we are and how we can move forward.

Discipline Practices

To deeply understand our discipline practices and the values that we have attached to these practices, while exploring how we view behaviors, consequences, and infractions, it is essential that we delve into our discipline stories and histories. The questions below may activate survival sensations in your own nervous system, so please breathe into these questions with loving compassion for yourself. As Carl Jung wrote, "The answers to our most important questions are to be found in the shadow. The shadow is the repository of our pain, shame, and the demons of our inner lives."[212] Maybe we can learn to acknowledge and befriend our shadows, knowing that they are a part of our emotional realities in our classrooms, homes, and schools.

Once we have reflected on these questions individually, we can come together with our colleagues to share our stories that generate many of the thoughts, beliefs, and perceptions that we carry into our present educational practices.

1. How were you disciplined as a child?

2. Typically, for what kinds of behaviors and infractions were you disciplined?

3. Who disciplined you most often?

4. When you remember your own childhood discipline, what three words, sensations, or feelings come to mind?

5. How did you feel after you were punished or disciplined?

6. What did you usually do or say to yourself after you were disciplined?

7. After you were disciplined, how did you repair with the adult? Or did you repair?

8. Did you feel safe when you were disciplined?

9. Through moments of discipline, did you feel connected to the adults?

10. What thoughts, feelings, beliefs, or stories from these past experiences are activated today?

"Children who come to be designated as unteachable are usually fighting a heroic battle for survival."
LOUIS COZOLINO

Schools, Organizations, and District Conversations That Share Our Stories

In this section, schools have the opportunity to explore and discuss the questions below as we rethink procedures and discipline guidelines, discussing how these may or may not reflect and align with our understanding of behaviors, consequences, and the adversities that many of our students carry into our schools. Wisdom is the sharing of knowledge and experience, offered with compassion, and presented in a way that assists others in their healing and growth.[213]

Adult Nervous Systems

Have we provided time and space for school staff to check in with each other as we address the adult brain and body states, providing opportunities before, during, and after school for self-care? What would this look like? *A trauma-responsive school shifts its discipline lens with a heavy focus on the adult brain and body state.* As every adult in the building touches the school experiences of our children and youth, our schools have the opportunity to orchestrate and integrate touch points during the school day for adults and students. Many of the following questions address the inclusion of our support staff in our school policies and discipline protocols.

Steps Along the Path

Joseph Campbell, an American mythologist who studied myths from all over the world, created the famous Hero's Journey, a monomyth that explains how each individual goes through continuous cycles of change and transformation. Nothing could be more accurate as we apply this monomyth to educators, students, and schools, because the teaching and learning process and emotional connection are real-life cycles of continual challenges, births of new ideas, successes, and transformations.

As I reflect upon these past few years and the impact of a global pandemic, along with the individual heroic journeys that I observed within my own life and the lives of those teachers I've worked beside, I return to a stronger reflection practice that also recognizes the hero's thousand faces: getting up in the morning with chronic unpredictability and facing the social and emotional losses of my students and colleagues, all while paying attention to the nervous system states of my students and myself. I'm learning that modeling our own Hero's Journey for our students provides a powerful teaching and life tool. It offers opportunities for reflection, problem solving, hindsight, foresight, and cognitive flexibility for sitting beside students whose struggles, celebrations, and identities change and develop unceasingly. By cultivating present moment awareness and feeling all of the experiences, no matter how difficult, on our educational journey, we can begin to model empathy and understanding for one another. We can embrace all that we do, experiencing it as a heroic adventure with no predictable outcomes. Each moment, hour, day, week, and month, we enter a cycle and travel toward change, challenges, and new beginnings. The questions below can help us untangle the feelings, thoughts, and behaviors that often seem so overwhelming in our classrooms, schools, and homes.

Questions Driving Our School or District's Heroic Journeys Toward Post-Traumatic Growth and Resiliency

1. Are we preparing our transportation personnel with the under-standing and practices of applied educational neuroscience, which includes a trauma-accommodating lens and focus? (Our bus drivers are first responders, able to observe students outside of classrooms, and they can often see students' lived experiences and patterns of interaction each day. They also have the capacity to build relationships while tapping into the strengths, interests, and passions of our children and youth that teachers and administrators cannot see or explore.)

2. How many of our students have referrals from bus behaviors before they walk inside our schools?

3. Do we see patterns and gaps from these bus referrals showing that the adult's nervous system might be reacting from a fight-flight state, personalizing the behaviors that feel disrespectful, oppositional, insubordinate, and disruptive?

4. How can our food service providers integrate positive touch points during lunch and down time in our lunchrooms and commons areas? (There is an opportunity to connect with a smile, greeting, ges-ture, or check-in as our students move through the lunch lines.)

5. Have we empowered and informed our instructional assistants, custodians, office staff, and coaches to be trauma-accommodating? Have they learned that most chronic negative behaviors are signals from a nervous system that may be feeling unsafe and disconnected?

6. How are we preparing our office staff to be the informed, as gentle mediators for parents and students who come to the school office, dean's office, or a traditional school environment where con-flict, power struggles, and punitive communication leave everyone feeling defeated and depleted?

7. What do the first 10-20 minutes look and feel like in this class-room and in this building? As we walk through the halls and in and out of classrooms, how do these spaces impact how adults and stu-dents are experiencing school?

8. Is there a coherent rhythm to the collective student body and staff, or is there collective dysregulation? A coherent rhythm in a school shares a healthy rupture-and-repair culture and climate that includes a welcoming tone to student and educator voices, relational presence, and an authentic feeling that mistakes are celebrated as growth factors.

9. What is the autonomic state that our school is functioning within today, this week, during the past month, or throughout the semester? Can we notice patterns or gaps where we are collectively functioning in fight-flight or immobilized-shut down?

10. How can we begin to create routines and procedures that meet the adults where they are in their nervous system? How can we create routines and procedures to meet students where they are at the beginning of class periods, during advisory, or at the end of the school day? How are we visibly caring for one another in our buildings and districts?

11. How can we share our own day-to-day heroic journeys with each other, so that there is felt support in strengthening relationships in our buildings and districts? Stories help to reframe challenging experiences. "What we can reframe, we can tame."

12. How can we transform our current discipline practices and protocols by integrating the practices inspired by Joseph Campbell's Hero's Journey?

13. How would Restorative Circles change if they were story-focused? (Our brains respond to patterns, analogies, and predictable experiences. We make sense of our experiences, perceptions, and worlds through stories.)

14. How can we model the Hero's Journey for our students through adult Restorative Circles sharing our own passages of struggle, challenge, hope and growth? (It would be to our shared advantage if students could observe staff modeling these discussions and resolutions. To learn more about how we might do this, see "Social and Emotional Competencies for Educators" in the Resource Section.)

15. Can we begin to share the science beneath our behaviors, so that we are intentionally discussing our neuroanatomy instead of pathologizing anxiety, depression, emotional disturbances, or behavior disorders?

16. Do students have a voice, choices, and autonomy that celebrates identities, values, and the rich cultures that we all carry into our schools every day?

17. Are students given opportunities and experiences for shared reflection?

18. Are Focused Attention Practices a core procedure in our buildings and districts?

Review and Reflection of Current School Discipline Policies and Practices

Knowing our educational history with regard to our school policies, codes of conduct, and current discipline data is vital in understanding how we move forward. Addressing the plasticity of current practices requires reflection, discussion, and an invitation to be authentically heard and seen. These changes take practice and time. As with any new perception or mindset, patience and time are our allies in accepting that we will encounter resistance and setbacks. Many of our schools have functioned in status quo (survival states) for so long that this flawed state of functioning has become so familiar that any systemic change will feel threatening and overwhelming. There is certainty in misery.

Racial, historical, and generational trauma have traditionally contributed to our punitive discipline practices. Our unchallenged or unacknowledged beliefs around pain-based behaviors have intensified and often unintentionally deepened the soul wounds of our children and youth. We can actively disrupt the corrosive effects of discrimination through the individual and collective work of addressing our biases and the myth of neutrality, which simply allows silence to support racism and oppression.[214] The global pandemic has opened the reticent and proverbial doors for us to look at—if we're willing to see—the racial and cultural disparities built into our systems of education protocols and worn-out policies. Are we willing to accept the understanding that education requires autonomic state regulation? We have an opportunity to begin cultivating a paradigm shift as we begin to rewrite our personal and collective narratives into an awareness that can gently guide our behaviors, provide emotional security, and deepen our understanding of how our own nervous systems and the shared nervous system of our schools can initiate the felt relational safety to ignite and inspire radical emotional, social, and cognitive well-being. Dr. Louis Cozolino states, "Although it is difficult to predict the exact knowledge and skills our students will need to succeed later in life, they all need to become the hero of their own story. A central part of this journey are the adults who sit beside them as guides, modeling their hero journeys."[215]

Consider these questions:

- How many of our schools' practices and codes of conduct are reactive?

- How many of our schools' practices and codes of conduct require student obedience?

- When looking at our consequences, can we create a list of current practices that are aligned to those consequences?

- Is there a current assessment or process to verify that these current practices are working?

- What current strategies or practices do our districts implement to reward or incentivize student behaviors?

- How many of our current practices and strategies are preventative? In other words, are there any current discipline practices we would define as Tier One practices?

- Do our current practices address the physiological states of pain-based behaviors?

- What are our current school rules and classroom rules?

- In reviewing student handbooks and discipline codes, what are two or three sentences that would describe your current discipline protocols?

• In two or three sentences, what changes or steps could build the resiliency and plasticity of relational discipline and engagement, guided by the social and emotional well-being of staff and students?

The Hero's Journey Through the Cultures of Our Home, Schools, and Communities

Following is an adapted Hero's Journey outline with questions addressing our personal voyages and those of our schools. It is my hope that these journeys will be shared with our students as well, because young people need to recognize the stories that they carry into their relationships, behaviors, and maps of the world: the things that drive their everyday feelings, thoughts, and belief systems.

Our schools and districts hold collective nervous system states, states that impact our relationships with one another and the connections that we have with our students. Each school, department, or grade level has an opportunity to come together at specific times, whether in professional learning communities (PLCs), at grade level assemblies, or department and staff meetings, to reflect on our individual and collective journeys that can lead us to recognize and embrace the resiliency that is built into our cells—but is also learned.

The students can begin exploring the Hero's Journey as a part of their classroom procedures, during brain-aligned check-ins, integrated into the subject matter, and during end-of-the-day rituals and procedures. In the Resource Section of the book, we have created guiding questions and activities for our students of all ages to explore their stories and journeys with one another.

When we recognize our challenges, when we identify and celebrate our authenticity, when we rely on one another as emotional buffers, we begin to build the social connections that our children and youth need as they move into young adulthood. The Hero's Journey offers a way to reframe our experiences as we share our stories of challenges, hope, and the renewal that is possible in all moments of our lives. When we reflect on our nervous system's journey, we begin to create a greater capacity for growth.

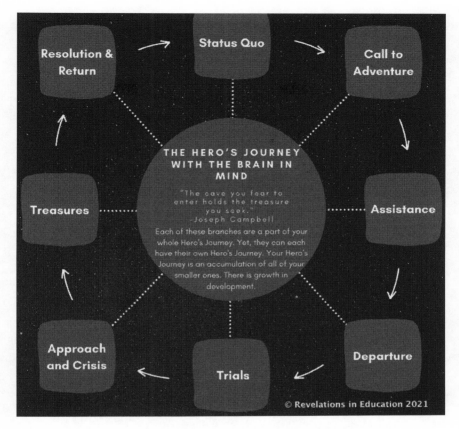

The cave you fear to enter holds the treasure you seek.

JOSEPH CAMPBELL

    The Hero's Journey is a cycle of passages or life movements through thousands of thresholds or doorways in all moments of our lives. These passages can often provide contrast through reflection of our lived experiences during our social, emotional, and physiological development. Our brain and body are always communicating and collaborating to mitigate the felt stressors while prioritizing our survival and working to protect us so that we can return to our home of felt safety. When we journey inside our fears, anxieties, and restlessness, this can naturally feel overwhelming and scary. Our brain is a complex organ and our body is a complex system, working together to integrate and organize our lived experiences as they occur. We may have days-long, weeks-long, months-long, and years-long hero journeys through the adversities of our lives; this is a part of our human evolution, providing the needed narratives that, when acknowledged and shared, can be transformative as we move through our future experiences.

Through this global pandemic, each of us has navigated our way through loss and overwhelming sensations, as our stress response systems have become highly sensitized because of the chronic unpredictability through which we have traveled. As we begin this collective and personal journey, we may feel uncomfortable and edgy, exploring the unresolved tension that is so difficult to keep contained. But with intention, practice, time, and one another's support, the plasticity of our nervous systems provides a bit of renewed meaning inside our lives, mixed with a little relief and peace seeded in the smallest moments.

As our children and youth are traveling through their day-to-day heroic journeys, traversing these moments and times of chronic unpredictability and possible isolation, relationships matter more than ever. Without a trusted other, adversities can become lodged in the developing nervous systems, where they create anxiety, depression, and a desperate longing for felt safety. Brene Brown writes, "When someone shares their hopes and dreams with us, we are witnessing deep courage and vulnerability. Celebrating their successes is easy, but when disappointment and deep loss happens, it's an incredible opportunity for meaningful connection."[216]

Hope grows.

"No, no! The adventures first, explanations take such a dreadful time."
LEWIS CARROLL

Ordinary Worlds

We begin the Hero's Journey in our ordinary worlds. In every experience, our brains and bodies adjust, change, and adapt to our environments, to people, perceptions, feelings, and thoughts. These changes cultivate neuroplasticity. We can begin this cultivation intentionally when we become aware of our embodied experiences, embrace confusion, and wonder about change as we befriend our ability to self-reflect. Author Adam Grant states, "I need time to wonder about my confusion. Confusion can be a cue that there's new territory to be explored or a fresh puzzle to be solved."[217]

I hope the final pages of this chapter provide an opportunity for reflection that you will explore individually and with your schools. Each passage is followed by guiding questions to ponder. The Hero's Journey is shared through a nervous system-aligned lens, addressing the four pillars of the Applied Educational Neuroscience and the Polyvagal framework.

Status Quo

We begin with the acknowledgement of our ordinary existence. Life feels somewhat neutral, and we may be functioning from blended brain and body states of felt safety, with added emotional excitement or restlessness originating from our sympathetic or fight-flight pathway. We are typically moving through our everyday experiences within our usual routines. In this state, our restlessness and growing discontent may be slightly felt, but we continue to move through life with automaticity. We are not questioning much about the experiences that we encounter during this initial part of the journey. Your Hero's Journey could be taking place as you read these words or reflect on a past transformative time.

APPLICATION TO YOUR PERSONAL HERO'S JOURNEY
(Status Quo)

Think about how the status quo stage felt prior to the moment that you realized you are on a journey (and that moment of realization could be right now). Recall what your state was before a change in your thought processes, feelings, relationships, or experiences started you on your Hero's Journey.

1. What felt safe and comfortable in those moments?

2. Was there anything that felt inspiring or exciting in this time?

3. How would you describe your life at this point? If you could

have drawn or journaled what those moments felt like, what colors would you have used? What lines and shapes describe that moment? What places, people, animals, or things remain part of that shift when you think about it now?

4. How do you feel in your body when you are expecting that something is about to change?

5. What would you have identified your brain and body state to be at that moment when something was about to change? Please refer to the table below.

BRAIN AND BODY STATE

Ventral Vagal (Social Engagement):
Feeling calm, grounded, balanced, peaceful, curious, mindful

Sympathetic (Fight-Flight):
Feelings of irritation, anxiety, worry, frustration, growing anger

Dorsal Vagal (Collapse):
Feeling numb, untethered, abandoned, lost, heavy, disconnected, stuck

Blended Ventral Vagal and Sympathetic (Play):
Feeling anticipation, excitement, nervousness, jittery, playful, silly, scattered

Blended Ventral Vagal and Dorsal Vagal (Quiet Reflection):
Feelings of quiet, stillness, serenity, lull, hush

Blended Sympathetic and Dorsal Vagal (Alert But Stuck):
Feelings of a racing heart, being frozen, unsteady, fast and heavy, trapped and anxious[218]

APPLICATION TO THE SCHOOL'S OR DISTRICT'S
HERO'S JOURNEY (Status Quo)

1. As a staff, what was the communal autonomic nervous system state in our building or district prior to the moment that we realized we were on a journey?

2. In two or three sentences, words, or images, how would the school staff describe their felt states of nervous system functioning in this time or the recent past? We might want to think about student and staff morale, behaviors, engagement, and restorative work. What else?

3. What feels comfortable or unsafe and threatening in this time?

4. How would you describe the life energy inside of your school or district at this point? If you could draw or journal what moments felt like in that status quo state of your journey, what colors would you use? What lines and shapes describe that time? What places, people, animals, or things represent the felt existence of where the school was during status quo?

5. Which of the autonomic nervous states shown below most accurately describe what staff members are experiencing in this time? Please refer to the previous **Brain and Body State** table.

Call to Adventure

As we recall or begin our Hero's Journey, it is in this initial stage that we feel yearning, growing challenges, and the call of unfamiliar emotions, places, sensations, and unpredictable outcomes. As we feel doors opening for us, we might feel unprepared to venture into the unknown, yet we might also feel called to explore, wonder, and be curious amidst the chaos this change is generating in our lives. As a shift in body and brain states activates our emotional and sensory brains, we become increasingly nervous, anxious, unsure, closed down, or hyperactive. We might begin to feel stuck or frozen in time like a block of ice, as our nervous systems are **downregulating** and switching pathways, which produces feelings of a loss of control over our current situations and experiences as we become increasingly dysregulated. We might sense that changes are happening too fast and too soon! It feels like too much stimulation. There is an overwhelming felt sense in our bellies, chests, and other body and brain areas that we experience as tightness, tension, itchiness, teariness, shakiness, or other edgy sensations. Intense questioning and doubts begin to arise.

- What is different?
- What should I do?
- What can I do?
- Is this dangerous?
- Is this safe?
- What is wrong with me?
- How can I get through this?
- Where is this fear coming from?
- Why am I shaking?
- Where is all my energy? I feel cold, numb, and unable to move.
- I am confused and worn out.
- What is going to happen?
- How can I be sure of anything?
- Who can I call? Who is there for me?
- Can I trust them?
- When will this be over?

APPLICATION TO YOUR PERSONAL HERO'S JOURNEY
(Call to Adventure)

1. When was a time that you felt a call to adventure?

2. How did you feel at that moment? What do you remember feeling in your body? What was going on in your head?

3. What led to that point?

4. At the time, did you notice that this was a call to adventure? Did you realize then how monumental that moment would end up being for you?

5. What were your doubts during this stage? What were your hopes?

6. What would you have identified your brain and body state to be at this moment?

7. What resources or supports did you need in this state?

APPLICATION TO THE SCHOOL'S OR DISTRICT'S HERO'S JOURNEY (Call to Adventure)

1. When was a time that your school or district was being called to make a change? Are you currently experiencing this call?

2. How has the staff responded to the growing tension, discomfort, and feelings of unfamiliarity connected to these calls for change?

3. What experiences, people, places, or conditions contribute to this call for change?

4. What are our doubts at this time? What are our hopes?

5. What resources and supports might our school or district need to anticipate as we move into unfamiliar and resistant territory?

6. What would you identify your own brain and body state to be at this moment?

7. What resources or supports do you personally need in this state?

8. Which of the autonomic nervous states shown below most accurately describe what staff members are experiencing in this time? Please refer to the **Brain and Body State** table.

Assistance

During this passage or transition, we realize that we'll need the help of someone who is possibly more experienced, or who has shared similar challenges to what we're experiencing. In this part of the journey, we begin to seek the resources and supports that feel calming, soothing, and protective as we meet the challenges before us. Sometimes the assistance appears without asking. Other times, what initially feels to be an obstacle is a gift of assistance. Who or what are the emotional buffers in our lives that can co-regulate and help us drain off the accumulating negative emotion as we meet the challenges? We need each other! Repair and growth are often unable to occur unless there is another to sit beside us in our pain, hurt, and conflict. Co-regulation equalizes the relationship of power between two people. It is of mutual benefit when there are ruptures and opportunities to repair circumstances and relationships. In this time of assistance, we may need a friend or someone we trust to help us feel safe and connected to everything that seems to be shifting so quickly. Assistance often occurs when we have connections with others. Our nervous systems need other nervous systems.

APPLICATION TO YOUR PERSONAL HERO'S JOURNEY (Assistance)

1. What people did I need at this moment?

2. What places felt calming to me?

3. What things did I need around me to feel safe?

APPLICATION TO THE SCHOOL'S OR DISTRICT'S HERO'S JOURNEY (Assistance)

1. What people, organizations, relationships, and growth approaches could support us as we move through these school and district shifts?

2. Do we have the support of our staff?

3. Where is the resistance? How are we handling the resistance?

4. How do we cultivate a safe and trusting space for the adults in our buildings?

5. Are our voices, concerns, and identities being recognized and acknowledged?

6. What would we identify our brain and body state to be at this time? Please refer to the **Brain and Body State** table.

Departure

It's time to step outside our comfort zone and try new ways of being with the situations or relationships that have fueled change and challenge. We cross the thresholds of sameness by paying attention to our neuroception, which is our nervous system's response to felt internal, external, and relational stimuli. It is always activated, sensing safety or threat.

We have left the ordinary world. Our brains and bodies may be moving to fight-flight pathways, where our heart rate is faster and we feel irritated, excited, scared, anxious or all of those feelings at once! We also may feel numb, heavy, and alone. This is an immobilized shutdown fear response as our nervous systems are preparing to endlessly protect us.

APPLICATION TO YOUR PERSONAL HERO'S JOURNEY (Departure)

1. What did you depart from and what were you moving toward?

2. During this time, many people relay that they felt intense heaviness and confusion. What concerns did you think about or feel in your body during this time?

3. Could you sense any hope about the felt risks you were experiencing during this challenging time?

APPLICATION TO THE SCHOOL'S OR DISTRICT'S HERO'S JOURNEY (Departure)

1. What is changing in your school or district? What are you weeding out and leaving behind as these practices, mindsets, and policies no longer serve your staff collectively?

2. What is the school experiencing internally as these changes occur?

3. When we think of departure from old ways, where is the resistance? How can we work through this resistance together?

4. Is there a sense of hope through the chaos of change? If not,

what resources could assist in providing additional leadership that will begin to plant seeds of hope? What could this look like for your school or district?

5. What would we identify our brain and body state to be at this time? Please refer to the **Brain and Body State** table.

Trials

We now begin to feel and sense the intensity of the growing conflict and challenges before us, as the old ways of being and doing begin to crumble away. Our survival can feel threatened in this time, as our attention may be focused on everything that feels unfamiliar, unsafe, or dangerous. During this part of the journey, we often resist change, becoming angry and confused about the challenges unfolding as our negative emotions arise. We may begin to ask the difficult questions that could lead to additional deep dives into discomfort, fear, and a loss of control. We may also notice how our own activators (triggers) can unintentionally escalate the impending challenge or perceived crisis.

APPLICATION TO YOUR
PERSONAL HERO'S JOURNEY (Trials)

1. What felt the hardest or most painful when things changed at this time in your life?

2. What feels comforting to you when you feel sad, lost, hopeless, or alone? What did you need during this time? What do you need now?

3. What smells, tastes, sounds, visual images, or thoughts bubble up when you think of the changes you were experiencing during this part of your journey?

APPLICATION TO THE SCHOOL'S OR DISTRICT'S
HERO'S JOURNEY (Trials)

1. What are the most difficult challenges facing this school or district in this time?

2. How will this school or distract cope with the felt stress during these systemic shifts?

3. How is this school or district checking in with the staff during this transition?

4. How are families being informed and included during these changes?

5. How are students experiencing these trials of transformation? How are we meeting our families and students with these changes?

6. What does it feel like in your body as you move through this stage? Where do you identify your brain and body state to be at this moment? Please refer to the **Brain and Body State** table.

Approach and Crisis: Our Darkest Hour

This is the hour where we approach our worst fear. We feel that a change in relationship, environment, conversation, or circumstance is inevitable and necessary. We begin to understand that the status quo can no longer be sustained. We enter a type of crisis and intense difficulty. We understand that crises induce movement and change. On the other side of the crisis is opportunity, which allows us to learn and grow from our darkest hours, yet we are still unable to sense this opportunity here and now. We face our vulnerabilities, activators, worn-out belief systems, and long-held practiced thoughts and private logic. During times of high stress, our need for connection intensifies, providing emotional first aid that can buffer growing distress. Our brains and bodies are emotionally over-reactive in this hour, and our nervous systems might be engaging the sympathetic nervous system pathway, preparing us to fight or flee. We may have shifted to the immobilized pathway of feeling stuck, shut down, numb, and hope-less. It is here that we unknowingly begin to die to our old self. In other words, we may be leaving old relationships, habits, behaviors, and settings (small or large shifts) as we journey into courageous new territory.

APPLICATION TO YOUR PERSONAL HERO'S JOURNEY
(Approach and Crisis)

1. What vulnerabilities, activators, or old beliefs were you challenging head-on during this time?

2. What were you scared to lose during this time?

3. What did it feel like in your body as you transitioned through this stage?

4. How would you have described your nervous system state at this time?

APPLICATION TO THE SCHOOL'S OR DISTRICT'S
HERO'S JOURNEY (Approach and Crisis)

1. As a staff, how are we handling these trials collectively? Are we checking in with our own nervous systems? Do we feel safe in this time to share our emotional and mental states?

2. In a collective survival state, what are the most reasonable and realistic coping strategies or practices for our staff or community?

3. Are there pockets of strength? How can we access those strengths during this time?

4. How are we addressing those who are resisting? How can we support or validate this resistance as well?

5. What is our school's or district's greatest fear?

6. How would we identify our school's or district's collective brain and body state at this time? Please refer to the **Brain and Body State** table.

Treasures

On our Hero's Journey, we claim our treasures by learning new aspects about ourselves through difficult times. We discover new sensations, feelings, or thoughts within ourselves. Maybe our opinions and views have changed. We begin to see an alternative or opportunity that we could not have recognized or identified before this journey.

We assess those opportunities with a blend of hesitancy and hope. Maybe we have learned how to care for ourselves in different ways. We begin learning and understanding that feeling depressed, angry, anxious, irritated, or numb is not a human flaw; we are simply receiving a range of normal communications form our nervous system as it brilliantly protects us while we address past or ongoing chronic adversity and trauma. We begin learning to acknowledge how we feel, and we sense our experiences knowing that our nervous systems can find their way home, or find their balance. Finally, the survival patterns of our behaviors in the past may no longer serve us in the present. Acknowledging this can fill us with hope.

APPLICATION TO YOUR PERSONAL HERO'S JOURNEY
(Treasures)

1. What new things did you learn about yourself through this passage?

2. What thought processes or mindsets have shifted? Did any of your opinions and views change?

3. In what ways did you give yourself grace during this period as you became curious about past habits of survival and ways of thinking and experiencing your internal and external worlds?

4. What did it feel like in your body as you moved through this stage? How would you have described your nervous system's state at this time?

5. What thoughts, sensations, and feelings do you want to grow and nurture?

6. What thoughts and feelings do you want to weed out?

7. Imagining your nervous system as a garden of flowers or vegetables, how did you care for it?

8. Who waters your garden? Who is your sunlight?

9. How do you care for your own garden, providing water and sunlight, protecting it from the winds and storms that produce unsettling or dysregulating emotions, feelings, or behaviors?

10. Have you given time for your garden to seed and begin growing?

For a deeper dive into the garden of our nervous systems, I share in more detail through questions and activities in my previous book, **Connections Over Compliance: Rewiring Our Perceptions of Discipline.**[219]

APPLICATION TO THE SCHOOL'S OR DISTRICT'S HERO'S JOURNEY (Treasures)

1. How is this school or district moving forward with these transformative changes?

2. A discovered and often misunderstood treasure is when we are able to validate the fear, anxiety, resistance, and restlessness mutually shared by staff. Has your school or district discovered this treasure?

3. What has this school or district learned collectively?

4. How are thought processes and approaches to growth being shared and communicated?

5. Did any of your opinions and views change during this collective shift?

6. As a building or district, can we identify and recognize the treasures from this journey together?

7. In what ways did you give yourself grace as you became curious about past practices and mindsets of survival? How or where have you landed inside this collective shift?

8. What did it feel like in your body as you moved through this stage? What did the collective body of the school or district experience from your viewpoint? Please refer to the **Brain and Body State** table.

Resolution and Return

As we leave the special world of transformation and return to our ordinary worlds, we begin to see how we can convert obstacles into doorways, which is good for those of us who have experienced many obstacles, because we can now see and access many doors! Those doorways can lead us home to ourselves. We begin to find our strengths, passions, renewed sense of purpose and autonomy, and the ability to reflect upon or review the conditions and experiences that no longer serve us. We may commence to steady our balance, leaning into the presence of our nervous system's communication, which is always sharing (or sometimes shouting!) its guidance to help us feel and sense our physiological states. We know that hardships, loss, and moments of sadness and despair will always be a part of our lives, but we can now approach our contentious experiences with a bit more awareness and compassion for ourselves. We might gradually begin to recognize and celebrate the powerful, beneficial flexibility and resiliency of our nervous system. Trauma therapist and author Resmaa Menakem affirms, "Like trauma, resilience can ripple outward, changing the lives of people, families, neighborhoods, and communities in positive ways. Resilience is much more than the ability to bounce back from adversity. Resilience is learned and intrinsic, manifesting both individually and collectively. It is nurtured from the words and actions of people who care for you and from your relationships with them."[220]

APPLICATION TO YOUR PERSONAL HERO'S JOURNEY
(Resolution and Return)

1. What did you discover that interests you now? What new strengths did you acquire? What feels troubling or out of control?

2. What have you confidently left behind? What have you hesitantly left behind? What have you confidently kept?

3. What did it feel like in your body as you transitioned to this stage?

4. How would you have identified your brain and body state at this time?

5. What thoughts, feelings, or behaviors do you continue to reluctantly practice, still pondering and questioning?

6. As you move through this passage of the Hero's Journey, is there a thought, feeling, or behavior that you would like to intentionally begin practicing?

APPLICATION TO THE SCHOOL'S OR DISTRICT'S HERO'S JOURNEY (Resolution and Return)

1. What has changed within our school or district?

2. Do we share a deeper understanding of how connection through conflicts has contributed to the coherent narrative of relational wealth cuing safety in difficult moments?

3. How have these changes impacted the student body?

4. How have our parents been impacted, and what does this look like moving forward for our parent community? For our school community?

5. Is there a lingering feeling of unease, restlessness, hope, or confusion? How would the staff describe the state of school's or district's collective nervous system?

6. How do we move forward, and what might this look like as we return to status quo?

7. How would we have identified our brain and body state at this time? Please refer to the **Brain and Body State** table.

As we arrive at this stage in our transformational journeys, we may be sensing that there is an accessible portal leading to the other side of our pain and suffering. Maybe we are setting new boundaries, asking for what we want, standing firm beside our values, pulling into our sense of self-worth. Maybe we have released relationships and experiences that have felt toxic even in their familiarity. Maybe we are feeling some isolation and rejection because we have traversed the changes of the Hero's Journey feeling somewhat alone or isolated. From the words of author and therapist Arielle Schwartz, "Your worth is not dependent upon your external situations, relationships, or actions. In truth, self-worth is your birthright. It is the birthright of every human being. Your worth was always there, just waiting for you to claim it."[221]

A Return to Status Quo

Author and educator Parker Palmer states:

Encounters with mentors and subjects can awaken a sense of self and yield clues to who we are, but when we listen primarily for what we 'ought' to be doing with our lives, we may find ourselves hounded by external expectations that can distort our identity, self-worth, and integrity. When I follow my oughts, I find myself doing work that is ethically laudable but not mine to do. A vocation that is not mine, no matter how externally valued, does violence to the self—in the precise sense that it violates my identity and integrity on behalf of some abstract norm.[222]

We have upgraded to a new level for now. This journey calls us to emerge embracing the complexity and vulnerability of our inner and collective work while living in our diverse world. In the recognition and acknowledgment of this final passage, we are embracing a perspective of growth through thousands of ruptures, repairs, connections, and disconnections, always reshaping who we are constantly becoming. This is our present...until we begin again! We never get it wrong, and we never get it done.

APPLICATION TO YOUR PERSONAL HERO'S JOURNEY
(Status Quo)

1. How do you sense the world and feel right now? How would you describe your current mindset or story of self? What colors, shapes or images describe or define the subtle or larger shifts and changes?

2. What advice would you have given to your earlier "status quo" self?

3. What experiences or lessons have you learned about relationships, past lived experiences, and your relationship with yourself?

APPLICATION TO THE SCHOOL'S OR DISTRICT'S
HERO'S JOURNEY (Status Quo)

1. How is your school or district adjusting to and experiencing these changes?

2. What advice would you share with other schools or districts as you have collectively traveled through this crisis?

3. What feels different? What feels familiar?

4. How does the school or district envision next steps?

5. How would we have identified our brain and body state at this time? Please refer to the **Brain and Body State** table

The Story of Our Nervous System Is an Open Book

When we approach our journeys in the light of our stories, the coherence of exploring these stories helps us to live with the dichotomies, conflicts, ambiguities, and polarities in our lives. We might discover a soft grace that wraps us in the warmth of lost trust, forgotten self-worth, and the threads of a fabric that are ready to be sewn. We get to write our own stories. We get to revise our stories in all moments. We get to take responsibility for our stories, as we reflect on our willingness to persevere and stay engaged during times of deep pain and struggle.

Resiliency is not the finish line. Resiliency is not something we attain and shelve. Resiliency is not something that one has, and that another does not. Resiliency is about the recognition, flexibility, courage, and strength we can access and embrace as we sense and feel our ways through life's experiences. Therapist Deb Dana states, "The shaping of our nervous system happens not in a flash with one big action, but in little moments that add up. Shaping requires us to be patient, to be persistent, and through the lens of our nervous systems, subtle shifts in our autonomic states and our autonomic patterns translate into new stories about who we are and how we navigate the world."[223]

Don't turn away. Keep your gaze on the bandaged place.
That's where the light enters you.

RUMI

A Personal Narrative Reflecting on the Gift of Our Stories Through Connection

I conclude this chapter with a short narrative that I created after one challenging yet hopeful week in the schools. These six sketches are drawn from the lives of people within the school community: six very different people in six very different roles, united in their daily struggle between exhaustion and hope.

Intersections and Connections

In the dark early morning, Hallway B seemed eerily quiet. He turned the metal knob, and the wooden door led him into his second home. He began scanning the large, barren classroom, observing the empty chairs and cleared-off desks and tables. With a deep, audible breath, he realized that the stories from those scattered, vacant chairs could not stay hidden. This room was anything but empty!

She scrambled around the kitchen table, grabbing ripped, milk-stained folders and a wrecked Chromebook, stashing Takis into the side pockets of each of her siblings' backpacks. Quickly turning toward the front hallway, she saw something familiar. Her book bag lay untouched and zipped as her heart thumped rapidly, screaming the red-hot panic that now felt to be as much a part of her as her skin.

Holding the hot, syrupy coffee with both hands, she walked down the gravel path to Bus 94. She climbed the three deep steps leading up to the torn vinyl driver's seat, and turned to scan the narrow and dark aisle, graffitied seats, and endless memories. The first stop—seven blocks away. This stop... this stop always activated a prayer of desperation. Would he be waiting by the drive kicking rocks, or would she feel the stillness from the unseeing windows of a house whose secrets had finally overcome him—painful secrets she would never learn? She dreaded the stillness most.

The trash was cleared, floors mopped and shining brightly with the morning ceiling lights intensifying the glare. He walked past the lockers, running his fingers along the metal handles and grinning as he anticipated the chaos that breathed life into his aging body each morning when those bells rang.

A small figure exploded like a cannonball from the passenger seat of the red, rusted car in the parent drop-off line, tousled hair like a little bird's plumage. His brown eyes, sad and alert, focused above his ripped and dirt-stained mask, waiting for that smile, always breaking through the growing crowds of students. Her long, purple-polished nails were his checkpoint. He awaited her warm and safe hug, often faking that he didn't care, yet pretending indifference never stopped their predictable and welcomed ritual.

With her eyes cast down counting the tiles on the hallway floor, she felt her untouched book bag begin to slide off her shoulder. Opening the door to her classroom, she lunged toward her desk and dropped to her seat. The green post-it note stared back it her. "It's a new day, and I am just grateful to see you and honored to be your teacher." She took a long deep breath and reached for the small paper. Crumbling it, she slid it into the side pocket of her jacket. Her thundering heartbeat slowed down a bit as he walked over to the corner of her desk and grinned. Two freshly sharpened pencils and a bottle of water fell from his hands, and with a warm gentleness, he knelt. "We will work through this day together. We always do."

To teach and to serve is to be aware and present through it all...acknowledging my challenges, schedules, changing bus routes, mandatory meetings, curriculum, assessments, and protocols. When I resonate with my story, I am able to listen deeply to those stories that are shared.

RESOURCE SECTION

Social and Emotional Competencies for Educators (SEL) Competencies for Educators

Staff and Student Surveys of Regulatory Resources and Anchors

Safety and Connection Survey for Staff and Students

The Six Misunderstandings of Dysregulated Behaviors

The Conflict Cycle for Educators, Students, Therapists and Parents

RECAST 2022

Accommodations Through an ACEs Lens

Polyvagal Chart Simplified for Students

Discipline Ladder

Glossary

Teaching Modules (Polyvagal Theory Modules: Elementary and Middle School Ages)

Social and Emotional (SEL) Competencies for Educators

> **1. Sensorimotor Integration:** the ability to have body awareness and recognize sensations in the body.

Gaining Sensorimotor Integration (also called Sensory-Body Integration) is an important skill for managing transitions, changing routines, increasing alertness for teaching, leading, learning, and improving emotional well-being. Sensorimotor Integration aligns with how we initially experience events and occurrences in our lives. It is the language of the body and lower regions of the brain. When we tune into our bodies and experience the sensations that accompany emotions and thoughts, we create an awareness of how to buffer our stressors and build the capacity for resilience!

Corresponding Collaborative for Academic, Social, and Emotional Learning

(CASEL) Domain: Indiana Specific[224]

Sensorimotor Integration is critically important for educators as they begin to interact with students who will be carrying in pain-based behaviors that often look and feel disruptive, oppositional, and defiant. Our brains and bodies hold implicit fragmented sensory memories which are embodied trauma and adversity experiences from our past. These fragmented and scattered memories are held below conscious awareness. The adversities in our lives often sub-consciously bubble to the surface without our conscious awareness, affecting how we perceive the pain and hurt through negative behaviors that are showing up in a child's or an adolescent's disposition, and therefore brain and body. Meeting ourselves with a gentle understanding of our activated negative brain states (embodied memories of our adversities and trauma) will be foundational for educator emotional, social, and physiological well-being!

Educator Learning Outcome: Educators acknowledge and understand the significance and implication of the science of sensory language and cues through brain and body awareness.

Requirements and Materials: Willingness to take deep repetitive breaths; use of journals, pens; computer or phone access for instructional videos and lectures.

Adult Nervous System Educator	
Indicator/Purpose	**Strategies & Practices**
1. Educators identify and actively participate in sensory practices and strategies for body and brain stress regulation to lessen and mitigate life stressors.	1a. Educators identify troubling sensations in the body by physically placing a hand and holding areas that feel tense, tight, painful, or tired, taking 5-10 slow deep breaths with an extended outbreath. Repeat a few times as needed. Following a repetition of deep breaths, identify two repairing sensory experiences that feel doable, actionable, and helpful in stress-filled moments. Ex.: movement, breath, being outdoors, warmth, pressure, coolness. 1b. Educators identify a bodily sensation and draw or journal what it looks like, using lines, shapes, colors, words, or images to explore how it communicates body and brain awareness. 1c. Educators identify 2-3 experiences where they need to pause, breathe deeply, and contemplate. (What sights, pieces of clothing, postures, sounds, tones of voice, scenarios, tangible felt experiences, etc., consistently push your buttons?) Following a repetition of deep breaths, identify two repairing sensory experiences that feel doable, actionable, and helpful in stress-filled moments. (3 deep breaths, a mint, cup of water, text a friend, write out thoughts, hand massage, short walk or move to another area with some deep breaths.) 1d. Focused Attention Practices: Focusing on a stimulus and extending our breath in a deep exhale engages the parasympathetic nervous system to slow our heart rate and lower our respiration and blood pressure. Our focus can be on a sound, taste, visualization, or movement while we are intentional about our breath and breathing. Some resources: • "30 Meditation Exercises & Activities to Practice Today," Leslie Riopel, https://positivepsychology.com/meditation-exercises-activities/ • "Break the Addiction to Negative Thoughts & Negative Emotions," Joe Dispenza, D.C., https://www.youtube.com/watch?v=AXrdVagSjjg • "Change Your Breath, Change Your Life," Lucas Rockwood, TEDxBarcelona, https://www.youtube.com/watch?v=_QTJOAI0UoU • Tension and Trauma Releasing Exercises: TRE® is an innovative series of exercises that assist the body in releasing deep muscular patterns of stress, tension, and trauma. The exercises safely activate a natural reflex mechanism of shaking or vibrating that releases muscular tension, calming the nervous system. Activating this mechanism in a safe, controlled environment, encourages the body back into a state of balance. Tension & Trauma Releasing Exercises are based on research showing that stress, tension, and trauma are both psychological and physical. TRE®'s reflexive muscle vibrations generally feel pleasant and soothing. After TRE®, many people report feelings of peace and well-being. TRE® has helped many thousands of people globally. https://traumaprevention.com/

Indicator/Purpose	Strategies & Practices
	• Emotional Freedom Technique/ Tapping: The practice consists of tapping with your fingertips on specific meridian points while talking through traumatic memories and a wide range of emotions.
2. Educators identify and befriend the pathways of the nervous system through the Polyvagal Theory with continual attention and awareness of how you experience sensations in your body. • The dorsal vagal system, the oldest pathway of the nervous system, assists us in immobilizing or collapsing when our bodies and brains meet significant threats. This is a reflexive survival response. • The sympathetic system, the second oldest pathway, mobilizes us to fight or run (fight-flight) when we perceive danger. This higher-level survival response on the autonomic hierarchy prompts us to action beyond simply shutting down. • The ventral vagal system, the newest pathway, creates a cohesive, rhythmic partnership between our brains and bodies when activated. It's the neural platform to support social connection and prosocial behaviors creating felt safety in our internal and external environments. The goal is not always regulation, but to recognize when you feel dysregulated. When we experience a regulated nervous system, we are able to move back and forth between pathways throughout our experiences. We begin to notice when we start moving away from the ventral vagal pathway.	2a. Resources supporting Polyvagal Theory and practices: • "Befriending Your Nervous System" is a presentation by trauma therapist Deb Dana on becoming aware of how our nervous system responds to our experiences, and how that can empower and relieve us. https://www.youtube.com/watch?v=TxpxyzZx_rw&t=3409s 2b. Regulatory practices that assist us in regulation and activating the brake on the vagus nerve, or parasympathetic pathways to a sense of calm: • Deep breaths with an extended outbreath • Sighing to regulate the nervous system • Movement to calm the nervous system (taking a walk, yoga, exercise, etc.) • Locating cues of safety for the nervous system in personal and professional environments (images, people, places in our homes or classrooms, a special e-mail or letter written to you, an object you can hold or see that brings some calm to your nervous system)

> **2. Insight:** the ability to be aware of our sensations and emotions and how they affect our thoughts, perceptions, behaviors, and actions.

Acquiring insight and recognizing our own dysregulation are important skills for building self-confidence, self-esteem, and empathy while holding a compassionate presence for others. Insight helps educators begin to identify their activators or triggers from past experiences while identifying strengths and areas of growth.

Corresponding CASEL Domain: Self-Awareness[225]

Educator Learning Outcome: Educators can identify a wide range of sensations and emotions, noting patterns of thoughts through reflective practices each day. These practices activate the parasympathetic response, lowering heart rate and blood pressure.

Adult Nervous System Educator	
Indicator/Purpose	**Strategies & Practices**
1. Educators identify their nervous system states, practicing awareness of self and relationships with others.	1a. Cold showers for 30 seconds, splashing our face with cold water, or an ice pack on a tense area for a few minutes, along with 5-10 deep breaths.
	1b. A 5-10-minute walk or movement exercise of your choice.
	1c. Humming, gargling (with or without water), chanting singing, sighing, or yawning.
	1d. Massaging your feet, providing a relaxing stimulation to the body.
	1e. Massaging the right side of your throat for a few minutes, relaxing and stimulating your carotid sinus.
	1f. Laughing and socializing, even if from a distance.
2. Educators identify personal strengths through reflective practices.	2. According to Learning in Action Technologies[226], there are 8 key daily practices to help in self-reflection:
	a. Practice present moment awareness. (What sounds do you hear? What is a focus at this moment that feels soothing? Is there a taste you could invoke?)
	b. Notice your judgments about yourself and your judgments about others. Do you notice any patterns?

Indicator/Purpose	Strategies & Practices
	c. Practice noticing and naming your experiences and your reactions to them.
	d. Focus on what you want, not on what you don't want.
	e. Recognize that other people could be mirrors of how you are experiencing a condition in that moment.
	f. Practice awareness by noticing the stories you create from your experiences and your interpretation of them.
	g. Take one moment, experience, or condition at a time. Practice unbundling the feelings that you have attached to those experiences (without judgment).
	h. Notice the degree to which your emotions, thoughts, and wants are positive or negative.
3. Educators begin to understand the unintentional ways staff can escalate conflicts and power struggles in the classroom and at school that can affect our relationships with colleagues and students. We explore the values we hold that can trigger negative emotions during a power struggle or conflict.	3. There are 7 reasons that adult staff members can become dysregulated, counteraggressive, and lash out at students.[227]
	a. Counteraggression is a reaction to being caught in the student's conflict cycle.
	b. Counteraggression is a reaction to the violation of our personal and cherished values and beliefs.
	c. Counteraggression is a reaction to our own bad mood. (We are not robots.)
	4. Counteraggression is a reaction to not meeting professional expectations.
	5. Counteraggression is a reaction to feelings of rejection or helplessness.
	6. Counteraggression is a reaction to prejudging a student who is struggling.
	7. Counteraggression is a reaction to exposing our unfinished psychological business.

We hold our values with reverence, and when what we value is challenged through the behaviors of another, we can become triggered or activated, creating conflict and power struggles with our students.[228] The personal button-pushing chart below is a means for us to identify what we value and how we can explore our thoughts and feelings when our values feel compromised. We can also cultivate ways to gradually reduce our traditional reactions.

Personal Plan for Button Pushing			
What am I sensitive about?	What do I think and feel when a student tries to push my buttons?	What do I do when one of my buttons is pushed?	How can I change my typical reaction?

Examples of "What am I sensitive about?"

Cleanliness: When things, people, or experiences feel unclean, I become anxious or irritated.

Neat and organized: I feel very dysregulated when there is disorganization and chaos.

Prompt: I am irritated when people show up late.

Hard-working: Looking unmotivated or lazy triggers negative emotion in me.

Honesty: I am angry when I am lied to.

Polite: When people or students are rude or appear rude, I feel irritation, frustration, and anger.

Precise: I like details, and I feel bothered if plans, projects, or anything feels vague, unclear, or disorganized.

Sexually reserved: Too much skin, open display of affection, or perceived provocative behavior can trigger me.

Emotionally controlled: I am irritated when people are overly emotional.

Happiness: Too much happiness over things or experiences feels ridiculous or inappropriate to me.

> **3. Regulation:** the ability to recognize and become curious about our emotions and perceptions while exploring our belief systems, patterns of thought, and repetitive emotional reactions.

Regulation skills build healthy nervous systems that help us to feel grounded, safe, and flexible while generating feelings of self-efficacy. When we are able to experience a regulated nervous system, we are also able to pause, reflect, and be curious before we react negatively and impact our overall well-being.

Corresponding CASEL Domain: Self-Management[229]

Educator Learning Outcome: Educators will recognize and identify grounding practices that, with increased self-awareness, build emotional fluidity and flexibility of thought and perception throughout daily decisions, interactions, and body regulatory practices. **The goal is to recognize when you are dysregulated.**

Emotional regulation for adults is sometimes a more arduous endeavor because our habits, perceptions, and behaviors have become hardwired circuits in our brains and bodies. These circuits often unintentionally leave out the cortex (the thinking and reflecting part of the brain) where we have accessibility for reasoning, reflecting, reframing, and filtering the emotional reactivity that can live in our words, thoughts, and reactions. The brain and body learn from patterned repetitive experiences, and the more we do, think, feel, or respond to certain events, people, situations, and perceptions, the more difficult it is for us to shift these hard-wired circuits. Neuroplasticity is the good news! We can change how our brains and bodies react with each new encounter, yet this process takes time. Before we delve into practices and strategies, we need to ask ourselves a few questions to strengthen self-awareness as we begin to address our own brain and body states for sustainable well-being. We must be aware of the Adverse Childhood Experiences Study[230] and its high correlation to emotional, mental, cognitive, and physiological health outcomes.

Adult Nervous System
   Educator

Indicator/Purpose	Strategies & Practices
1. Educators recognize life stressors and begin to develop practices to address the dysregulation that accompanies them.	1a. Journaling words, images, reactions, fears, insights, or any thoughts is a powerful activity to employ for a few minutes each day. Below are some topics of reflection to consider as you begin to create that emotional pause in your life. Consider the outcomes, perspectives, and feelings generating old habits of behavior that have not been gently challenged in your relationships. 1b. What is my self-talk (what I say to myself) when things do not go well? How could I begin to replace any negative words that have become my reactive responses? 1c. In a difficult situation today, what are two positive outcomes that I could have recognized? 1d. Am I releasing control of what cannot be controlled, or am I holding onto other people's words and emotions that I cannot control? 1e. Could I journal from the perspective of another person, deeply resonating from their mind, heart, eyes, and words? What do I now sense, experience, and feel from my colleague's or student's perspective that I did not recognize in the moment of conflict?
2. Educators integrate Focused Attention Practices by shifting perspectives and moving inward, listening to our body's communication.	2. Focused Attention Practices: When we take two or three minutes a few times each day to breathe deeply, we are priming the brain for increased attention and focus. These practices might also include a stimulus such as sound, visualization, or the taste of food. Focusing our attention increases oxygenated blood and glucose flow to the frontal lobes of the brain where emotional regulation, attention, and problem-solving occur. These practices also activate our parasympathetic pathway in the nervous system, lowering our blood pressure, heart rate, and respiration. There are many apps that can create a schedule, rhythm, and plan to help us to consistently implement these practices for a few minutes each day. Below is an example of a simple Focused Attention Practice that we can begin to employ. (Read more in Chapter 4.) a. Sit with a relaxed, uplifted posture (you can sit in a chair). Bring your full attention to your breath. When your attention strays, as it surely will, come back to the breath. b. The hardest part is being distracted, yet that is part of the process. You learn by trying to focus on your breath without getting caught up with what went wrong at work yesterday, what you are having for dinner later tonight, or why that student was so damn disrespectful.

Indicator/Purpose	Strategies & Practices
	c. As you slowly and deeply inhale, try to hold your breath for a few seconds before the exhale, extending your exhale by a few seconds. You want to pull the oxygenated flow all the way down to your belly, inflating it like a balloon. Begin slowly and for a short period of time. For example, on Monday, take five deep breaths in the morning and evening. On Tuesday, take ten. Gradually add a minute or two each day as you focus on the sensation of the air coming in and out of your nose each time.
	If you think you are too inattentive, antsy, or fidgety for a Focused Attention Practice, think again. Asking the mind to turn off is like asking the heart to stop beating. It is impossible, and it is not going to happen! Returning to the breath, again and again, trains the mind to be rooted in the present, not the past (work), the future (dinner), or a grievance (that disrespectful student). Our brains are organs that act like muscles, and the more we train certain areas, the stronger they become. Every time you take a few minutes to quiet your thoughts, it is like a set of bicep curls for the brain. In this way, a Focused Attention Practice is a little like being more awake; there is less anxiety and more action.

4. Connection and Collaboration: the ability to work well with others through strong social awareness and empathy processing.

Connection and collaboration work to build touchpoints (moments of connection through deep listening, validation, noticing, and reflective practices) while recognizing how contagious emotions are between human beings. Connection and collaboration call us to become aware of how we begin to create a compassionate presence before, during, and after conflicts and challenging interactions with others.

Corresponding CASEL Domain: Social Awareness[231]

Educator Learning Outcome: Educators become aware of their nervous system states before addressing a challenging relationship, condition, or experience. Connection is about the magic of resonance, as we listen deeply to one another, searching for the possibility of interconnection. This social and emotional competency is a process that requires learning to practice self-reflection and insight before we begin to connect and collaborate with colleagues and students.

Adult Nervous System Educator	
Indicator/Purpose	**Strategies & Practices**
1. Educators will recognize the power of relational contagion and how our nonverbal communication affects the vast majority of all our communication.	1. Hand signals, facial expressions, tone, and gestures cue safety and danger to other human beings. • Resource: "You Are Contagious" is a TEDxLondon presentation by Vanessa Van Edwards about how our behavior signals our level of confidence to others: https://www.youtube.com/watch?v=cef35Fk7YD8&t=555s.
2. Educators will design collaborative nervous system-aligned restorative circles to discuss the cultural and racial inequities that we encounter in our schools, and how these overt inequities can traumatize students. Educators will address their tones of voice, postures, gestures, and facial expressions through learning the supportive research.	2. Nervous System-Aligned Restorative Gatherings bring us together, focusing on solution-oriented decisions and responses.[232]

> **5. Mindset:** the ability to demonstrate cognitive flexibility and a willingness to learn through everyday experiences.

Developing a growth mindset is a critical learning skill for building perseverance, adaptability, self-discovery, resilience, and the ability to receive and give constructive feedback. Much like we see in our students, our adult mindsets are often unconsciously activated when we feel unsafe, disconnected, or threatened. Our early embodied and developmental experiences can trigger present-moment conditions that negatively impact our perspectives. An open, receptive mindset is one that acknowledges cultural diversities and social inequities as we explore our implicit and cognitive biases, and the plasticity to change our thoughts, perceptions, and feelings. A growth mindset *is* neuroplasticity: our brain's ability to change structurally and functionally based on our moment-to-moment experiences. Neuroplasticity is the nervous system's ability to adapt and rewire itself so that we can survive and thrive in life. Our thoughts, feelings, sensations, and behaviors are intimately connected to the functioning of our brain and body architecture and the bi-directional communication between them. The more patterned repetitive experiences that we provide our brains and bodies, the more neural agility they will develop.

Corresponding CASEL Domain: Self-Awareness[233]

Adult Nervous System Educator	
Indicator/Purpose	**Strategies & Practices**
1. Educators will begin to understand how our brain and body systems change structurally and functionally in moment-to-moment experiences.	1a. For 1-2 weeks, choose a habit of thought and journal the reoccurring thoughts that tend to follow this specific experience. During this time, question those thoughts (as science has proven that we tend to think that every thought is true). Questions to Ponder: A. Am I able to plan my behavior for the day? B. What is the greatest expression of myself I can present to the world today? C. Who do I want to be when I open my eyes? D. Can you focus on one aspect of your routine that you could change each morning and evening for 30 days?

Indicator/Purpose	Strategies & Practices
	1b. Through a week or selected period of time of journaling and becoming aware of your thoughts, notice the feelings and sensations that accompany those thoughts. Write those feelings and sensations in your journal or draw images of the body languages that accompany those thoughts. This exercise helps us to see our thought patterns and the connections between thoughts, feelings, and sensations.
	1c. Some reseources about neuroplasticity: · "Discover How to Rewire Your Brain With Neuroplasticity," Quantum University, https://www.youtube.com/watch?v=bbLP-aslABk. · "How mindfulness changes the emotional life of our brains," Dr. Richard J. Davidson, TEDxSanFrancisco, https://www.youtube.com/watch?v=7CBfCW67xT8.
2. Educators begin to identify the "gift" of a mistake, perceived failure, or negative bias that has lodged itself into thinking and feeling patterns in our bodies and brains.	2a. The Gift: This group exercise is a co-regulatory practice in which we work with a partner or small group for a specific amount of time, sharing our mistakes, negative thought patterns, or biases through another person's perceptual lens. Our partner's role is to listen deeply, validate, and help us to reframe or reappraise a challenging situation. This exercise requires trust and a willingness to be vulnerable with one another. It is important to set up group guidelines with this practice. We lean into each other for support and clarity. As you share this scenario or condition and the accompanying thoughts and feelings that you experienced, your partner will begin to generate a variety of angles and perceptions for you to explore. It is important to begin with smaller grievances and not traumatizing experiences. 2b. For resources about guided meditation as related to neuroplasticity, visit Joe Dispenza's website: drjoedispenza.com.

Nervous System-Aligned Restorative Practices and Circles

Restorative Practices and Circles have been implemented for a significant amount of time inside schools. There are hundreds of articles and resources sharing this framework and its purposes for building community and responding to challenging behavior through authentic dialogue. After three solid years of pandemic teaching, we are already seeing dysregulated behaviors from many students as they struggle with anxiety, depression, and a deep mistrust of relationships and experiences. We have been living in chronic unpredictable times with changing schedules and altered routines that have felt overwhelming. Traditionally, Restorative Practices and Circles attempt to shift the conversation between teachers and students to be less punitive, offering an opportunity for all persons affected by an altercation or infraction to have meaningful dialogue, repairing the ruptures, and restoring the classroom community. Restorative Practices and Circles have also been implemented in maintaining cultures of community during neutral times.

In this time of unprecedented trauma, adversity, and cultural and racial tensions, staff and students are carrying in an overwhelming amount of fragmented and unprocessed sensory information and emotions that are highly contagious. These emotions can be activated below the waterline of consciousness and can be triggered in emotional outbursts, impulsive behaviors, or a shutting down and immobilized response. We are not excusing disruptive behaviors, but we need to understand that all implicit embodied memories, when activated, have the sensation and quality of happening right now—likened to visitors from our eternally present past.

One of the challenges with traditional Restorative Practices and Circles is that these are "talking" circles, and are only effective when group members are intentional about working on themselves and finding a balanced, grounded autonomic state from which interpersonal discussions can take place. When the cognitive parts of the brain (the prefrontal cortex) switch off in times of frustration, irritation, anger, anxiety, and worry, talking or reciprocal circles are not always possible. When we feel and sense unsafe environments, when we feel isolated and misunderstood, we are unable to problem solve, emotionally regulate, listen deeply, and attune to others. There are neurobiological reasons that traditional Restorative Practices and Circles may work in the moment or for brief amounts of time, but they are not producing sustainable changes in behaviors and collaboration within school cultures!

In a Nervous System-Aligned Restorative Circle and Practice, we prepare our brains and bodies for co-regulation by providing a bottle of water, a pen, a blank canvas or board, or a small notebook before there is any conversation. We explain that when we draw or journal to name or reappraise our emotions and sensations, they lessen. Our goal is to create a sensory repairing environment before words are spoken. As we prepare our nervous systems for learning, we might begin the restorative time with music, deep breaths, or journaling or drawing. We explain to the members of the circle why we are initiating these regulatory practices, sharing that our nervous systems process survival and safety and that our feelings are highly contagious. When we are in a survival state, our hearts speed up and our blood pressure increases, prohibiting us from thinking clearly, reasoning, pausing, and paying attention to the moment. This is why we should prepare ourselves to reflect our thoughts and feelings back into the circle. In the following suggestions for cultivating Restorative Practices and Circles, we begin with the adult nervous systems.

1. Educators Only

What if schools begin creating Nervous System-Aligned Restorative Practices and Circles with staff modeling these discussions and resolutions within an inner circle, while students in the outer circle listen, critique, give feedback, and reflect on the staff dialogue? This fish tank circle could be recorded and shared at various times with a variety of grade levels, so that all students are exposed to these restorative conversations. When we model our conflicts, sensations, and feelings with a variety of possible resolutions, we are empowering our students with the ability to share freely, without judgment, and to experience how a crisis can lead to connection. Following are possible suggestions for questions.

A. When we speak about how trauma and adversity affect us each uniquely, what sensations (tight jaw, pressure, shaking, shortness of breath, tiredness, rapid heart, etc.) do you experience in your body or brain? How has the pandemic affected your teaching or leading?

B. When you have a difficult conversation and are met with resistance, how do you typically handle your sensations and emotions? What would you like to change? How do you access your cortex so you can find some peace and calm?

C. How is cultural diversity explored and addressed in this school? How is systemic racism connected to our discipline practices? Where do we begin when addressing these inequities in education?

D. When you think of an experience in which you felt afraid, threatened, or growing anger, was it difficult to think clearly and remember that challenging time? How did you respond? What was the outcome?

E. What are your greatest challenges at school right now? How are you handling these? Do you have a plan? How are you caring for your nervous system?

F. What are your greatest strengths? Do your strengths show up when you begin to feel regulated, calm, safe, connected, and capable of clear thinking? If not, what can you do?

2. Talking Pieces and Circle Agreements

Talking pieces and agreements should be created by both students and adults. They are created ahead of time and are subject to change based on the needs of the circles, chosen by everyone as the best way to address specific conflicts or challenges. A talking piece is a physical item that anyone in the circle can hold when it is their turn to speak, representing the time and agency to share their words and feelings with others. In some Native American cultures, this piece is known as a talking stick, but it can be any object that the group recognizes as a symbol of connection and repair: a stuffed animal, a stone, or an item created specifically for this purpose. Grade levels and classes can start constructing their talking pieces at the beginning of the academic year. Creating these pieces can be an ongoing process, reflecting student and educator interests, passions, and purposes.

3. Embodied Lived Experiences

We might ask educators and students to bring and share a memory or favorite photo to the circle. As we pass the photos around, our facilitator reminds us that we all share infancy, childhood, and early experiences of environments, relationships, and events when we felt hurt and when that hurt was misunderstood. This is an important time to remind our circle that brains and bodies develop from experiences, and that patterned repetitive experiences become our values, beliefs, identities, histories, and perceptions. If we do not already have connections with people who can help us integrate, make sense of, and begin to reframe our developing perceptions, we need to cultivate these conditions in our schools. We remind one another that our brains are historical, social, and experience-dependent organs that act like muscles, always predicting the outcomes of present or future experiences based on past experiences.

4. How Are We Similar? How Are We Different?

As we share our baby or childhood photos at the beginning of our restorative gathering, noticing similarities instead of differences, we share other similarities that we notice in the present moment of the circle.

A. What are three ways that we are similar to one another in this circle?

B. What are three ways that we are different from one another in this circle? Do these differences create challenges for us? How?

C. How can we respect our differences and still come together during challenging times?

D. Do we feel important to someone in this school?

E. Can we share our strengths and gifts in this school or class?

5. Nervous System-Aligned Questions for Resolving Conflict in Restorative Practices and Circles
- What is our challenge?
- What led up to this challenge?
- How did we handle this together and/or apart?
- Could we have prevented this challenge?
- What are two adjustments we will make the next time?
- How will we activate the adjustments that we have committed to making? Are we ready to cultivate a plan?

"To understand the suffering of others,
we must first touch our own suffering and listen to it."
THICH NHAT HANH

Staff and Student Surveys of Regulatory Resources and Anchors

In this first survey, we want to address sensory practices that can create a sense of calm and safety within your nervous system. For a better sense of how this might work, ask yourself:

- What would happen if I checked in with my nervous system to decipher what I need or what feels calming?

- What if I began the school year with integrated, periodic check-ins with staff and students using these surveys of regulatory resources that anchored felt safety?

The following survey questions are intended as a resource for staff to identify the experiences that can bring them a sense of grounded calm for those few seconds or minutes when they may not have the luxury of time for going deeper. Being able to sit beside each other sharing ideas for practices and providing feedback is a significant foundation for our collective well-being.

TEACHER SURVEY

When I am feeling dysregulated and there has been a disruption, what regulatory resources and anchors do I need?

1. I need time and space.

      Yes   **No**   **Other:**____ **(optional explanation)**

2. I need to talk to someone I trust.

      Yes   **No**   **Other:**____ **(optional explanation)**

3. I need to take deep breaths.

      Yes   **No**   **Other:**____ **(optional explanation)**

4. I need to move my body.

      Yes   **No**   **Other:**____ **(optional explanation)**

5. I need music, soothing sounds, calming rhythms.

      Yes   **No**   **Other:**____ **(optional explanation)**

6. I need to write out my thoughts.

      Yes   **No**   **Other:**____ **(optional explanation)**

7. I need to express myself through a form of art.

       Yes   **No**   **Other:____ (optional explanation)**

8. I need rhythm (pacing, cooking, walking, rocking, driving in a car, knitting, building, crafting, drumming).

       Yes   **No**   **Other:____ (optional explanation)**

9. I need warmth (hold something warm, wrap up, etc.).

       Yes   **No**   **Other:____ (optional explanation)**

10. I need coldness (chewing on ice, ice pack, cold water).

       Yes   **No**   **Other:____ (optional explanation)**

11. I need to chew or crunch on something.

       Yes   **No**   **Other:____ (optional explanation)**

12. I need to talk to myself out loud.

       Yes   **No**   **Other:____ (optional explanation)**

13. I need to vocalize (singing, humming, sighing, yawning).

       Yes   **No**   **Other:____ (optional explanation)**

14. I need a prayer or a spiritual affirmation.

       Yes   **No**   **Other:____ (optional explanation)**

15. I need my own space with a personal ritual (being with animals, your favorite mug, your favorite place to sit, your favorite view).

       Yes   **No**   **Other:____ (optional explanation)**

16. I need pressure or touch (self-hug, friend-hug, ear/head/hand massage).

       Yes   **No**   **Other:____ (optional explanation)**

17. I need softness (an object or condition that feels warm, pliable, and soothing).

       Yes   **No**   **Other:____ (optional explanation)**

18. I need to be outdoors.

       Yes   **No**   **Other:____ (optional explanation)**

19. I need to cry.

       Yes   **No**   **Other:____ (optional explanation)**

20. I need to laugh.

       Yes   **No**   **Other:____ (optional explanation)**

21. I need this regulatory sensory practice:_____.

       Yes   **No**   **Other:____ (optional explanation)**

STUDENT SURVEY

Predictability feels safe to the developing nervous system. The following questions identify safe, comforting practices for students to use before there is an eruption, conflict, or dysregulation. These questions serve as a resource for students to identify the experiences that bring about a sense of grounded calm for a few seconds or minutes when they feel growing agitation, worry, or anxiety that threatens to overwhelm them. Being able to sit beside each other sharing ideas for practices and providing feedback is a significant foundation for our collective well-being. When we equip our students with the tools that they can access when needed, we help them develop the agency and autonomy that contributes to social and emotional well-being.

1. I need time and space.

    Yes   **No**   **Other:____ (optional explanation)**

2. I need to talk to a teacher, friend, or someone I trust.

    Yes   **No**   **Other:____ (optional explanation)**

3. I need to take deep breaths.

    Yes   **No**   **Other:____ (optional explanation)**

4. I need to move my body (my favorite activity, sports, running, jumping jacks, stretching, etc.).

    Yes   **No**   **Other:____ (optional explanation)**

5. I need music, soothing sounds, calming rhythms.

    Yes   **No**   **Other:____ (optional explanation)**

6. I need to write out my thoughts.

    Yes   **No**   **Other:____ (optional explanation)**

7. I need to express myself through a form of art.

    Yes   **No**   **Other:____ (optional explanation)**

8. I need rhythm (pacing, walking, rocking, building, crafting, drumming).

    Yes   **No**   **Other:____ (optional explanation)**

9. I need warmth (hold something warm, wrap up, etc.).

    Yes   **No**   **Other:____ (optional explanation)**

10. I need coldness (chewing on ice, ice pack, cold water).

    Yes   **No**   **Other:____ (optional explanation)**

11. I need to chew or crunch on something.

    Yes   **No**   **Other:____ (optional explanation)**

12. I need to talk to myself out loud.

    Yes   **No**   **Other:____ (optional explanation)**

13. I need to vocalize (singing, humming, sighing, yawning).

      Yes   **No**   **Other:**_____ **(optional explanation)**

14. I need a prayer or a spiritual affirmation.

      Yes   **No**   **Other:**_____ **(optional explanation)**

15. I need my own space with something special to me (being with animals, your favorite toy, your favorite smell, your favorite view).

      Yes   **No**   **Other:**_____ **(optional explanation)**

16. I need to sit in a place that calms me (in my classroom or school).

      Yes   **No**   **Other:**_____ **(optional explanation)**

17. I need pressure or touch (self-hug, friend-hug, ear/head/hand massage).

      Yes   **No**   **Other:**_____ **(optional explanation)**

18. I need softness (an object or condition that feels warm, pliable, and soothing).

      Yes   **No**   **Other:**_____ **(optional explanation)**

19. I need to be outdoors.

      Yes   **No**   **Other:**_____ **(optional explanation)**

20. I need to cry.

      Yes   **No**   **Other:**_____ **(optional explanation)**

21. I need to laugh.

      Yes   **No**   **Other:**_____ **(optional explanation)**

Safety and Connection Survey for Staff and Students

STAFF SURVEY FOR SAFETY AND CONNECTION

1. This school/organization is emphasizing adult emotional, mental, and physiological well-being.
   Yes No   **Not Sure**   **Explain if you feel comfortable.**

2. Do you feel that you get enough sleep most nights?
   Yes No   **Not Sure**   **Explain if you feel comfortable.**

3. Are you getting some exercise each day or a few times a week?
   Yes No   **Not Sure**   **Explain if you feel comfortable.**

4. Do you feel you drink plenty of water each day (4-6 glasses)?
   Yes No   **Not Sure**   **Explain if you feel comfortable.**

5. Do you spend time outdoors?
   Yes No   **Not Sure**   **Explain if you feel comfortable.**

6. This school/organization supports connection and feels safe to me, my colleagues, and students.
   Yes No   **Not Sure**   **Explain if you feel comfortable.**

7. This school/organization intentionally connects each young person to an adult who serves as a source of support.
   Yes No   **Not Sure**   **Explain if you feel comfortable.**

8. Most of the time, the adults in this school/organization seem relaxed yet alert. **Yes No**   **Not Sure**   **Explain if you feel comfortable.**

9. Most of the time, this school's/organization's staff works together supporting one another even if we have differences.
   Yes No   **Not Sure**   **Explain if you feel comfortable.**

10. This school/organization is focusing on relationships with students through co-regulation and de-escalation practices.
    Yes No   **Not Sure**   **Explain if you feel comfortable.**

11. This school/organization intentionally avoids the use of coercion to motivate and discipline students.
    Yes No   **Not Sure**   **Explain if you feel comfortable.**

12. Are you using strategies this year to help keep your emotions calm?
Yes No   Not Sure   Explain if you feel comfortable.

13. Do you feel that you resolve conflicts peacefully?
Yes No   Not Sure   Explain if you feel comfortable.

14. Do you feel that the staff members in your school/organization know how to resolve conflicts peacefully?
Yes No   Not Sure   Explain if you feel comfortable.

15. Do you feel that you stand up for yourself when you need to?
Yes No   Not Sure   Explain if you feel comfortable.

16. This school/organization intentionally prepares staff to avoid humiliation, shaming, sarcasm, ridicule, or other forms of attack with regard to students' personalities, race, ethnicity, achievements, or behaviors.
Yes No   Not Sure   Explain if you feel comfortable.

17. Throughout the year, this school/organization intentionally gathers perceptual data about its programs and services from all staff and students.
Yes No   Not Sure   Explain if you feel comfortable.

18. Do some or all of these interfere with your teaching and how you feel each day?

__ anger toward students or colleagues   __ students fighting
__ student drug/alcohol/vaping issues   __ worries about my family
__ sadness about the loss of a family member or friend
__ resistance from colleagues   __ stress_
__ feeling sad most of the time   __ my ability to get along with colleagues
__ meeting my personal and professional needs
__ reluctance about coming to school   __ fear of making mistakes
__ fear of being emotionally hurt __ fear of being physically hurt

19. What are two or three things or conditions you feel would help you feel successful in your school/organization?
_____
_____

20. What are two or three changes you would like to see in your school/organization?
_____
_____

21. What is something that you wish your colleagues and students knew or understood about you?

_____

_____

STUDENT SURVEY FOR SAFETY AND CONNECTION

1. Do you feel you get enough sleep most nights?
   Yes No   **Not Sure**   **Explain if you feel comfortable.**

2. Are you getting some exercise each day or a few times a week?
   Yes No   **Not Sure**   **Explain if you feel comfortable.**

3. Do you feel you drink plenty of water each day (4-6 glasses)?
   Yes No   **Not Sure**   **Explain if you feel comfortable.**

4. Do you spend time outdoors?
   Yes No   **Not Sure**   **Explain if you feel comfortable.**

5. This year, have you created relationships with adults that you trust?
   Yes No   **Not Sure**   **Explain if you feel comfortable.**

6. This year, have you created good relationships with other students?
   Yes No   **Not Sure**   **Explain if you feel comfortable.**

7. This school is a safe and secure place.
   Yes No   **Not Sure**   **Explain if you feel comfortable.**

8. Do you feel connected to a few of the teachers in the building?
   Yes No   **Not Sure**   **Explain if you feel comfortable.**

9. Do you feel that everyone is treated with respect, even though we all make mistakes and have off days?
   Yes No   **Not Sure**   **Explain if you feel comfortable.**

10. Do you feel that everyone in the classroom seems relaxed and that your class is learning?
   Yes No   **Not Sure**   **Explain if you feel comfortable.**

11. Are you using strategies this year to help keep your emotions calm?
   Yes No   **Not Sure**   **Explain if you feel comfortable.**

12. Do you have someone in your family that you can go to when you are upset?
   Yes No   **Not Sure**   **Explain if you feel comfortable.**

13. Do you feel that you resolve conflicts peacefully?
    Yes No   Not Sure   Explain if you feel comfortable.

14. Do you feel that the adults in the school know how to resolve conflicts peacefully?
    Yes No   Not Sure   Explain if you feel comfortable.

15. Do you feel that you stand up for yourself when you need to?
    Yes No   Not Sure   Explain if you feel comfortable.

16. Do you know how to care for yourself when people are picking on you?
    Yes No   Not Sure   Explain if you feel comfortable.

17. Do some or all of these interfere with your learning and how you feel each day?

__ anger   __ fighting   __ drugs/alcohol/vaping
__ worries about my family/parents   __ people bullying me
__ sadness about the loss of a family member or friend
__ not getting along with others   __ stress
__ feeling sad most of the time   __ not having enough to eat
__ my ability to get along with my teachers __ fear of coming to school
__ fear of making mistakes   __ fear of being emotionally hurt
__ fear of being physically hurt

18. Do your teacher and the other adults at school make sure that you feel successful, and do they help you when you are not succeeding?
    Yes No   Not Sure   Explain if you feel comfortable.

19. Do teachers emphasize students' strengths and pay attention to their interests? Do they want to know what you like and what you are good at?
    Yes No   Not Sure   Explain if you feel comfortable.

20. Do your teachers and other adults in the building pay attention to your feelings and make sure that you feel safe and connected to others at school?
    Yes No   Not Sure   Explain if you feel comfortable.

21. Do you feel that learning about your brain and nervous system has been or would be helpful?
    Yes No   Not Sure   Explain if you feel comfortable.

22. What are two or three things that you feel would help you feel successful at school?

_____

_____

23. What are two or three changes that you would like to see in your school?

_____

_____

24. What is something that you wish your teachers knew or understood about you?

_____

_____

Download these surveys here:

The Six Misunderstandings of Dysregulated Behaviors

Misunderstanding #1:
Listen, I have had lots of trauma in my life, and I made it!
I am not putting up with this kind of disrespect!

The social and developmental neurosciences are now informing the field of education with research that we did not know or have a few decades ago. Our chronic behavioral challenges with students are actually signals of a dysregulated nervous system. Children and youth who grow up with significant adversity and trauma can carry toxic levels of stress in their nervous systems, which alters their stress response systems and changes how they sense, feel, behave, and learn. Children in a survival brain and body state are *only* paying attention to anything that feels threatening, unsafe, or unfamiliar. There is a critical dose-response relationship between the number of adversities that students carry into school and their emotional, mental, and physiological health outcomes.[234] Trauma is not just an event; it is what happens inside of us and what is carried in autonomic pathways. Trauma can live in the body for years and can be passed on to future generations! While our discipline protocols have traditionally focused on student behaviors, the discipline that we should be practicing begins with adult behavior and awareness of the adult nervous system. Simply put, behavior management is about the adult brain and body state. Trauma responses are not light switches that we can turn on and off. These fast survival reactions take time and patience to shift as we learn to feel safe and trust others.

Misunderstanding #2:
This isn't teaching anyone a lesson; you are rewarding negative behavior! She just said "F**k you" and ran out of the room!
Now you are giving her a fidget and a bottle of water?

A child who grows up without kindness will not develop the circuits in the brain for kindness. The same is true for empathy and regulation! We need to teach our students the science behind their behaviors. When you understand what is happening in your nervous system, you feel validated, empowered, and relieved. Much like kindness, emotional regulation is a learned executive function skill and circuit in the brain; it takes time to develop. During the first thousand days of life, the brain is the most impressionable, and attachment to an emotionally available, predictable, and consistent caregiver is critical for brain organization and integration. Children and youth who continually fail to self-regulate require the practices they would have learned from missed experiences of co-regulation earlier in life. Just because you are 9, 12, 15, or 20 years old does not mean that chronological development aligns with emotional development. Our nervous systems require a safe, emotionally regulated adult who can consistently provide co-regulatory experiences and the opportunities to repair conflicts following ruptures. A new lens for discipline begins first with an adult's awareness of their own nervous system state, and then with being able to share a calm, grounded presence with a student.

Misunderstanding #3:
Rules are rules. When kids know the rules, they make the choices. I have told this student "It's your choice" 30 times today, and I am done!

When students become rough and dysregulated, their nervous system state-dependent functioning has changed rapidly. In fight-flight or collapsed states, children and youth cannot process the usual classroom system of stickers, rewards, time, consequences—or even logic. Our discipline protocols need to begin at the front end of every day through the spaces of safety and connection with adults. Continually repeating a non-working strategy begins to resemble the classic definition of insanity, which is doing something over and over, expecting a different result. In a neutral time, we need to share with our students how our brains and bodies are wired to protect and defend, and to eventually shut down if our needs are not met. We need to create routines and procedures that teach our expectations ahead of a crisis or conflict, because our nervous systems in a state of dysregulation do not hear words. Neuroplasticity takes repetition, time, and an intentional focus on what is going well. If you hear "f**k off" 14 times on Monday and only 13 times by Friday, be hopeful!

Misunderstanding #4:
**For the past few weeks, I have given this student the time and space you suggested, and there is no change.
Their behavior is getting worse!**

When we are addressing children and youth who carry in pain-based behavior, their nervous systems are generally activated to protect, and their stress responses are sensitized to their environments. The circuits in the brain require patterned, repetitive experiences to begin recognizing safety, and providing experiences that feel safe takes time. This can become an endurance event for everyone. Therefore, we need to assess the process and not the end result. As much as we would like to believe that programs and specific strategies can stop unwanted behaviors, this is false. There are no strategies and programs that can "fix" a child or adolescent. We need to create safety and connection through relationships and experiences of regulation that develop through small micro-moments over time. We must teach our children the science beneath their behaviors and how their nervous systems are always trying to protect them—even when that protection isn't needed. We talk about the science of all this in neutral times such as morning meetings, transitions, bell work, and end-of-the-day gatherings. These are micro-moments of a preventative relational and nervous system-aligned discipline protocol that occurs slowly and therefore sustainably.

Misunderstanding #5:
Now everyone in my room wants a water bottle, a fidget, permission to shoot baskets, and time in the Amygdala Reset Area! Now no one is working!

When we plan our procedures and class guidelines at the beginning of the year, we need to constantly revisit these and talk about the challenges we face as a class. We want student input as we share that everyone has different needs. As a "class family," we will support each other in those needs. We traditionally do not think of these practices as discipline, but this is the time to be intentional about accommodations for all students when it comes to social and emotional learning. These are Tier One practices and interventions. Just as we do not hesitate to create adjustments for our academic gaps, we need to change the conversation from "learning loss" as we attune to the social losses. When we meet students in nervous system development, we are preparing them for deep learning as well as emotional connection and safety.

Misunderstanding #6
When this student leaves the room to co-regulate, they are missing significant academic time. This is not fair! They are falling further and further behind!

Students who need to leave the room to co-regulate are taught how this practice will work ahead of a conflict or crisis. This is only a challenge when we have not set up the procedures for when a child or adolescent leaves the room. Pre-planning for this event is critical, along with adult mindset in the moment when it happens. The procedures need to be clear for the students, and in order for them to happen smoothly, we need to be aware of our nonverbal communication: our tone of voice and facial expressions. Students will agree in advance, during a neutral time, that if they need to find calm and safety in a moment of dysregulation, we will co-create a plan to repair and take care of our responsibilities. Our goal is to help the student access their cortex (the thinking region of their brain) so that they are able to think logically and rationally, emotionally regulating and asking for help if they need another person. If there is a conflict or rupture, we need to repair with others when everyone's nervous system is calm and feel safe. We want to model the behaviors we want to see! We also need to think about the work missed and how we can "chunk" the assignments so that our students understand the content and do not feel overwhelmed by the amount. We need to pick and choose our battles, because emotional stamina may be low as we begin the transition into the new school year following a pandemic and all the challenges facing our communities.

The Conflict Cycle for Educators, Students, Therapists, and Parents

Moving From Nervous System States of Protection to the Nervous System States of Growth

In 1988, Dr. Nicholas Long founded Life Space Crisis Intervention Institute[235] (LSCI) in order to train educational practitioners, therapists, and clinicians in effective, strength-based approaches to working with seriously emotionally disturbed children and youth. The Conflict Cycle is a part of this creation and has assisted clinicians, educators, and parents in understanding emotional contagion and the co-regulation practices that, when integrated well, become **embodied shared experiences**. The awareness of our embodied experiences interrupts cycles of conflict inside the nervous system stories of trauma. These stories are infected with maladaptive learned beliefs that began with survival patterns held in the stress response systems.

I am introducing an augmentation of the Conflict Cycle because of recent findings in the evolving research in trauma-responsive practices. Neuroscientists are studying the nervous system, brain development, and the effects of adversity and trauma, along with the potential for repairing relationships as a critical step toward positive identity development and resiliency. These advances in research have occurred since the original creation of the Conflict Cycle in the late 1980s. I believe this augmented revision of LSCI's Conflict Cycle will be mutually beneficial for students, educators, therapists, and parents. During this time, mental and emotional health challenges for our youth and children are growing rapidly across the country and world during a global pandemic and the economic and emotional disparities and challenges that our communities face.

What we now understand is that most of the children and youth labeled emotionally disturbed or behavior disordered are carrying significant trauma and adversity in their nervous systems, creating pain-based behaviors. Trauma therapist Dr. Peter Levine describes trauma in this way: "Trauma happens when any experience stuns us like a bolt out of the blue: it overwhelms us, leaving us altered and disconnected from our bodies. Any coping mechanisms we may have had are undermined, and we feel utterly helpless and hopeless."[236]

Developmental trauma occurs when there is chronic unpredictability in the life of a child or adolescent, and the caregivers may be unavailable or inconsistent. It can disrupt our ability and capacity to form and maintain relationships. Developmental trauma may impair brain pathways and the neural chemistry in the developing nervous system, and young children are the most at risk from stress and trauma due to their under-developed nervous, immune, cardiovascular, digestive, motor, perceptual, and almost every other system in the body. As Dr. Bruce Perry states, "Belonging is biology."[237] When the people who are supposed to love and protect us are the ones who hurt us, this weakens the basic sense of self and trust in our own gut, self-perception, and authenticity, and therefore a child or adolescent's sense of safety and stability erodes, and unexpressed energy becomes trapped in the tissues of the body.

When we are born, we need instruction and direction from our caregivers to build healthy brain architecture. We require connection, as attachment is the carrier of all nervous system development. When our basic needs are chronically neglected, our bodies cue threat and danger, and survival becomes a priority. We do not know how and are unable to release the survival responses that live in our nervous systems, where they create sensations of constriction, tightness, sweating, rapid heartbeat, and restriction. It is as if our legs are knocked out from under us at all moments. Trauma is not the event itself, but rather the aftereffects that may continue living in the nervous system for days, months, or years after the chronic adversity and traumatic events have passed! Our present-moment perceptions become distorted and murky, impacting our everyday experiences even when the traumatic event itself is over. As we continue to react to the trauma that we carry, *our behaviors are misunderstood*. Behaviors communicate the state of our nervous systems, and this is why the conflict cycle needs to address the physiological states of children and youth that we label as emotionally disturbed, behavior disordered, troubled, or dysfunctional in some way.

New research in relational, social, and developmental neurosciences reveals that our bodies hold rage, frustration, anxiety, abandonment and so many other feelings through the millions of bits of sensory information from past experiences, with little to no narrative or cognitive and cohesive understanding of why we carry these feelings. Through chronic conditions of adversity and trauma, we may often lose connection with ourselves, along with the deep attachment to others that assists in healthy brain and body development. Our brains process information in a sequential way, and the lower brain regions may interpret sensory information inaccurately. Neuroscientist and psychiatrist Dr. Bruce Perry explains that if any of the input is a match to a stored memory from past experiences, the lower brain regions react as if the past experience is the one happening in the present moment. Discharging these sensations with a trusted other can help a child or adolescent re-experience and reframe present-moment events independently of past survival patterns that are no longer necessary.

As humans, we create perceptual maps of the world based on our embodied experiences. We gather and digest feelings and thoughts, and when we practice those thoughts with enough repetition, they become our belief systems. These belief systems form our nervous system maps of what feels safe and what feels dangerous. Brains and nervous systems predict future experiences based on past experiences. Trauma can cause our nervous systems to have trouble telling the difference between our unsafe pasts and our now-safe present.

A growing body of research suggests that trauma from extreme stress, among many other factors, can be passed from one generation to the next. Transgenerational Epigenetic Inheritance tells us that what we pass down to the next generation is more than just our genes. It is the influences that express or suppress the gene's readability or expression as well.[238] Without knowledge of what the generations before us experienced, we run the risk of those patterns and cycles repeating and expressing themselves in our lives with feelings of lost control and hopelessness. For educators and parents, it is important to understand how our *lived experiences, perceptions, and beliefs* can become activated or triggered when there is a conflict with a student or one of our own children. Inside this awareness, we can begin to break the cycle of conflict as we look beneath one another's behavior with the understanding that our nervous systems are running the show! As we explore the conflict cycle, I will explain each of the passages through which we move, the opportunities to break this cycle, and the role of co-regulation in post-traumatic growth. To help us in this exploration, I've created a cycle in which adults and students share the magic of resonance in the in-between space where relationships can strengthen.

1. Perceptual and learned beliefs become irrational beliefs when we continue to recycle past experiences that resemble the trauma and adversity from our pasts. In other words, when we continue to live inside past experiences in the present moment, our beliefs keep us in a state of protection and therefore survival.

2. Intergenerational trauma is carried in our nervous systems. The experiences of our ancestors can impact our own lived experiences without awareness, reflection, and the ability to discharge those trapped emotional experiences. With one another, we can begin to explore our sensations, feelings, and thoughts inside an environment and relationship of felt safety.

3. Our social-cultural, physical, and economic environments may create communities in chaos, dysregulated systems where individuals, families, and neighborhood populations are living in protection and survival states. These environments may carry collective trauma and dysregulated nervous system states, affecting our young people and their developing brains and bodies through the instability and unpredictability of these living systems.

4. Embodied lived experiences shape our thoughts and feelings, and therefore our belief systems. Trauma and adversity land in our bodies, possibly creating fragmented sensory information that leads to felt rigidity or chaos from our lived experiences, as different patterns of stress can lead to either sensitization of our stress response systems or strengthening our stress response systems by cultivating resiliency. Dr. Perry states, "Epigenetic changes are involved in altering the sensitivity of our regulatory networks in lower brain regions, and this is another remarkable flexibility of the body to make changes to keep us in balance."[239]

5. Neuroception is our reflexive, automatic intuition that scans our environments in all moments for safety or danger, a continual process of scanning that eventually leads to our perceptions of the world. Our neuroception becomes our perception, which leads to our most dominant autonomic states, followed by feelings that preserve our perceptions and thoughts that can activate similar feelings that can reinforce our thoughts.

6. Our behaviors are signals. They are indicators of our autonomic state

functioning and provide a quick and often superficial and misunderstood glimpse into our nervous systems that are always trying to protect us, searching for a healthy neurological balance. When we address only those signals, we miss the fundamental needs of our children and youth. By focusing on a behavior rather than its deeper cause, we may find compliance for a few minutes, a day, or a week, but eventually, we may return to the toxicity of the conflict cycle once again!

It is my hope that the augmentation of the LSCI Conflict Cycle will address how the student and adult cycles can be activated, but also how our awareness of them will promulgate a dynamic rupture and repair, allowing co-regulation and shared emotional availability while dampening down our young people's stress response systems. When we break these conflict cycles with our children and youth, we are also creating pathways to the cortex, enabling us to access the learning that produces social, emotional, and cognitive well-being. We must realize that these cycles of conflict take time, patience, and repetitive intention as we embrace the co-regulatory experiences that can assist our children and youth to move from states of protection to states of growth.

Download the Conflict Cycle template here:

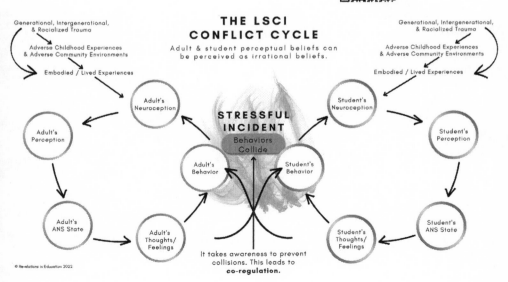

RECAST 2022

Relationships, Emotion, Culture, Attention, Sensation, Tasks

What Is It?

RECAST is a tool designed for all students who may be struggling with behavioral challenges that are regulation issues due to an over- or under-responsive sensory and nervous system, possibly compromised by acute, chronic, or developmental adversities and trauma. Although I have adapted this tool for students who are struggling emotionally and socially in our classrooms and schools, RECAST can be integrated into any organization or home where caregivers, parents, and adults collaborate to discover children's sensory needs beneath their behaviors.

How Is It Used?

RECAST is a template that provides an opportunity for staff, and eventually students, to come together and explore a multitude of options and experiences that support students' emotional, social, and cognitive needs. This template allows us to adjust, modify, and accommodate each student's needs to ensure feelings of safety and connection. As you begin to use this tool, it is important to keep a small notebook of experiences, environments, persons, and times throughout the day that can activate and unintentionally dysregulate a behavior.

Why Do We Need This Tool?

The RECAST template, used in collaboration with all the adults who serve the student, will help us to deeply understand how trauma and adversities are held in our bodies, not just in our thoughts and feelings. Adverse experiences affect our physiological and unconscious need for felt safety, a need that can manifest with increased sensitivity to everyday experiences reprograming our stress response systems so that a student's reactions may look explosive, aggressive, fearful, defiant, anxious, irritated, or shut down. These responses, and the trauma that causes them, can affect our relationships, tasks, attention, emotional temperature, feelings, and thoughts. All behavior can be seen as communication from the student's nervous system.

RECAST and the Adult Nervous System

It is critical that the adults who work together serving our children are able to reflect upon their own nervous system state, checking in with what they themselves are carrying into our classrooms, organizations, and schools. Are we aware of our biases and the diverse cultures that we have brought, along with our autonomic state functioning? In other words, are we asking ourselves:

- What part of my brain is activated right now?
- Can I share a compassionate lens through our work together?
- If not, am I able to reflect and notice what activates negative emotions in my nervous system?
- How can I provide cues of safety, and what signals am I unconsciously sending that may cue danger or threat?

We know that a regulated adult can regulate a child or adolescent. When collaborating to serve our young people, there may be additional meeting times when adults will bring students and their parents or caregivers into the conversation for feedback about what needs, tasks, and relationships feel missing and are desired.

The following questions can be added to what we have:

Relationships:

Who connects and cares for this person deeply? Who provides cues of safety for this person? Who is able to co-regulate and meet this individual where they are in their nervous system state? When this person is feeling anxious, who helps them reconnect with the felt safety or awareness of dysregulation in their life? Does this person need time alone (with a co-regulator available nearby)?

Emotions:

Do I have the capacity to see this person through a compassionate lens? Anger and aggression are often the tips of the pain-based iceberg. Some possible underlying emotions might be sadness, fear, frustration, loneliness, feeling unseen or not heard, rejection, feeling misunderstood, shame, abandonment, confusion, failure, and feeling overwhelmed. Do I have the capacity to see this person through a compassionate lens and look for what's beneath the big emotions? Co-regulating and sitting beside this person may help them to better understand what's beneath their anger and/or painful sensations or feelings.

Culture:

Am I able to understand what this person's activators are? Is this student in a state of sensory overwhelm? Are cues of safety being provided consistently for this student? Are there culturally responsive resources that meet this student in their nervous system state? Are there intentional predictability and rituals that feel available and positively repetitive in our classrooms and school? Do the people supporting this student have the capacity to stay connected through the conflict? Are we aware of the diverse culture and lived experiences of this student? What environment or experience helps this person to feel safe and regulated (quiet room, outside, playground, predictable routines or rituals, watching YouTube, listening to Spotify playlist, another trusted adult)? What environment or experience brings purpose and joy to this student? Does this student have a bit of felt control over their environment or experiences? If not, what can we do to support their autonomy, sense of agency, and efficacy?

Attention:

What type of attention (or a need for solitude) will help this student feel better? How can I provide cues of safety and be a source of co-regulatory support? What activates pleasure, joy, or grounding and peacefulness in this student?

Sensation:

Is this person in hypo-arousal state (shut down) or hyper-arousal state? What sensory input or resources would help this person to feel safe, connected, and regulated (earplugs or noise-canceling headphones, a cold or warm drink, swinging on a swing, deep pressure, drumming, going for a walk, etc.)? Does this person need an adult to share some calm or energy, or both?

Tasks:

What part of the brain is this person able to access? Can they access their prefrontal cortex, or do they need a brain-aligned task that meets them in the midbrain and lower brain regions where there is an emotional override? What tasks feel peaceful or energizing? What tasks bring some sense of agency or identity? Is this person able to advocate for themselves when tasks feel overwhelming? Do the tasks that are given have purpose, relevance, and meaning in this person's life during this time? Do we need to chunk the tasks into smaller assignments and shorter instruction times? Do we need to check in with this person more frequently? What do those check-ins look like? Does this student need more choice? What choices can we agree upon that would ease the level of frustration or anxiety with this task? Are we using a variety of images, colors, audio, and other supports to help these students feel successful in their personal styles of learning? Are we prioritizing the social and emotional well-being of this student, knowing that we cannot access the cortex (where learning occurs) unless we feel safe and connected?

Download the RECAST template here:

Accommodations Through an ACEs Lens

Strengthening Connections and Regulations

What do you need?
What can we do to make it better?
How can I help?

What do you need?

Many of our students who need sensory and emotional support and resources do not have an IEP, 504, or a team of educators and staff available to consistently attune to their sensory and regulatory needs. This absence of support is impacting felt safety each day. Our students often come to school with their nervous systems in a survival state. They are plagued by the adversities that have accumulated throughout the days, weeks, months, or years.

The following template of Adverse and Positive Community Environments is created collaboratively (originally inspired by Dr. Wendy Ellis[240]) to support all students who carry significant adversities or trauma and therefore elevated stress response systems into our schools. These supports and resources address pain-based behaviors. Sometimes students will need accommodations and possible modifications during the school day regarding their environmental, relational, and sensory needs that impact learning and cognition. These supports will address the critical needs of attachment and regulation through a culturally sensitive lens. Often, as students move to different classrooms and environments, the adults are not consistent in providing a routine of two or three practices that can be implemented to find accumulating moments of felt safety.

Download the ACEs template here:

Adverse Childhood Experiences

- Parental divorce, separation, illness, or death
- Deportation or immigration
- Caregiver in jail or prison
- Caregiver depression, mental illness, suicide attempt
- Domestic violence or threats
- Emotional abuse or exposure
- Food, clothing, or housing insecurities
- Physical abuse, hitting or slapping
- Caregiver problem with drugs or alcohol
- Felt unsupported, unloved and unwanted
- Placement in Foster Care
- Mental or emotional illness

- Bullying, harassment, or violence at school
- Intrauterine, birth, or neonatal trauma, or early accidents or illnesses
- Treated badly because of race, sexual orientation, place of birth, disability or religion
- Discipline of our black and brown and special education students in our schools and the disproportionality and overidentification of these groups.
- Traumatizing school experiences
- Social media and technology overuse or unsupervised
- Frequent school or neighborhood violence

Adverse Community Environments

- Poor housing quality and affordability
- Discrimination
- Intergenerational poverty
- Lack of affordable and available mental and emotional therapy and counseling
- Lack of access to safe and clean environments including parks, playgrounds, and athletic facilities needs of children
- Lack of affordable and quality transportation that is accessible, reliable and safe
- Lack of available social supports within the community that are able to nurture the emotional, social and cognitive needs of children and youth

- Opportunity for employment through vocational experiences, mentoring, and apprenticeships in areas of interest, strengths, and passions of youth and young adults
- Childcare support that is affordable and reliable addressing the developmental needs of children
- Lack of supportive and nurturing environments for pregnant women that meets the social, emotional, and physiological needs pre-birth, during birth experiences, and the complexities of aftercare within family systems
- Low sense of collective political and social efficacy

Inspired by https://publichealth.gwu.edu/sites/default/files/downloads/Redstone-Center/Pair%20of%20ACEs%20Tree.png.

Resiliency Building Experiences

- Feeling safe and connected by caregivers, family, neighbors and friends
- Extended family support and nurturance
- Educators, pastors, and coaches provide spaces of felt safety and are relationally available and predictable
- Consistent communication and support of child or youth's school experience (especially when the school environment is a stressor)
- Predictable, consistent and nurturing routines and transitions at home
- Network of trusting and reliable adults within the child or youth's social milieu

- Validation and consistent noticings of a child or youth's mental and emotional well-being by those adults who are in contact with the child or youth
- Adults provide strong support for identity development and autonomy so the child or youth can share authentically and openly even through pain and adversity
- Family/Caregivers are supportive of school experiences and extracurricular activities that are consistently shared and communicated
- Rule, structure, and expectations in household
- Positive outlook on life

Positive Community Environments

- Available and affordable housing
- Access to affordable and healthy food
- Access to affordable and available healthcare
- Access to affordable and available mental and emotional therapy and counseling
- Racism and discrimination is banned and extinguished
- Access to safe and clean environments such as parks, playgrounds, and athletic facilities needs of children and youth
- Affordable and quality transportation that is accessible, reliable and safe

- Available social supports within the community that are able to nurture the emotional, social and cognitive needs of children and youth
- Lots of opportunity for employment through vocational experiences and mentoring and apprenticeships in areas of interest, strengths and passions of youth and young adults
- Childcare support that is affordable and reliable addressing the developmental needs of children
- Supportive and nurturing environments for pregnant women and that meets the social and emotional and physiological needs pre-birth, during birth experiences and the complexities of aftercare within family systems

What can we do to make it better?

We are not adding more work to what we are already doing. These relational and sensory accommodations are intentionally and transparently built into our procedures and routines. **Behaviors are only indicators of a nervous system that is dysregulated; and when dysregulation is ongoing, our children and youth cannot access the cortex where learning occurs.** Pain-based behaviors can show up in disrespectful, defiant, or shut-down ways. Therefore, reaching for the root of the presented behavior can occur when we address nervous system needs through these accommodations. Brain-aligned bell work and Focused Attention Practices can occur naturally through our procedures, routine, transitions, morning bell work, and meetings!

How can I help?

We know that many of our students carrying adversity and trauma into schools do not have the accommodations with accompanying accountability and trusted adults that are able to provide mutual feedback. **As a district, school, department, classroom, or grade level, we need to create these accommodations so they are consistently dispersed, discussed, and implemented each day.**

Are you ready to tackle this with me?

Because our students spend more than 13,000 hours in school during their K-12 span, educators have the opportunity and the obligation to address the social and emotional skills and competencies through creating the accomodations and adjustments needed for emotional, social, and cognitive well-being. In order to address these experiences at school, we need to cultivate a safe, connected space and presence for our students.

Why?

If our social and emotional learning outcomes, programs, and competencies are to accurately reflect the current brain research addressing the impact of severe life disruptions and adversities and trauma that are accumulating in our student populations across the country, we need to address specific areas of brain development with regard to acquiring these competencies. Brain and nervous system development is complex. Even today, we know very little about how individual regions of the brain work collectively through neuronal connections and projections. **However, we do know that human brains are not complete at birth but, by design, continue to develop throughout a person's life.** This development is intimately impacted by experiences.

How Traditional Accommodations and Accommodations for Adversity (ACEs) Support One Another

Our physiological states are inherently social, affecting everything we feel, sense, and do, as young people's brain and body development is constantly being shaped by experiences with others and the perceptions of environments. The chronic behavioral challenges that we face in our schools are often communicating nervous system states of threat and protection. The evolving research from the social and relational neurosciences tells us that education requires *state regulation* so we can access and integrate the cognitive and emotional tasks we need to succeed in school and to navigate our life experiences. For these developmental reasons, accommodations for supporting our children's felt adversity and trauma are critical for social, emotional, and therefore cognitive well-being.

Traditional accommodations and accommodations for adversity and trauma work well together. We do not hesitate to give more time for an assignment, integrate assistive technology, or provide quiet and non-distracting spaces for academic work. We need to generate the same type of accommodations for children and youth that may be experiencing acute, chronic, or developmental adversity and trauma. **These accommodations do not replace an IEP or 504, but they provide the resources and support for our students that need felt safety and predictability in our classrooms and schools.** Below are examples of how accommodations for academic, social, and emotional support with an available, safe adult can provide students with safety and connection. Predictable adults are better able to share their calm, regulated nervous system. This is discipline. This is co-regulation. This is the bio-social and emotional environment that provides the nurturing *nests* that are foundational for our students' overall well-being.

Note: The two columns in the following tables are not intended to show a direct correlation between traditional and ACEs-informed accommodations. Instead, we are illustrating two very different ways of thinking about which accommodations we offer. Traditional accommodations are those adjustments that we make to academic workloads. When the schoolwork feels overwhelming, we provide resources that break down or provide assistance in how students can access the content and show their learning. Accommodations through an Adverse Childhood Experience lens, however, provide adjustments through resourcing the ways in which our children and youth can locate safety and connection.

Classroom Accommodations	
Traditional Accommodations	**Accommodations Using an ACEs Lens**
Seating at the front of the class	I need a seat where I feel safe and secure. *Dr. Stephen Porges suggests that a classroom would be best as a circle of learners where all students have their backs against the wall.*
Graph paper to line up math problems	Two adults in the building who I can trust, and a place to walk when I begin to feel triggered
Multiplication table or use of a calculator	A personalized routine of 3 interventions that I can implement when I begin to feel anxious, angry, or negative in any way (getting a sip of water, 5 deep breaths, drawing for a few moments)
Repetition and explanation of directions when needed	Access to sensory area or table in our classroom for patterned repetitive activities used to calm me down
Pre-printed classroom notes from the teacher	A personalized set of my accommodations given to all who work with me to allow me to de-escalate, calm down, and become ready to learn

School Accommodations	
Traditional Accommodations	**Accommodations Using an ACEs Lens**
Occupational therapy every Wednesday	Meeting with my resiliency team each week (two or three individuals at school who I trust)
Math one-on-one tutoring twice a week during study hall	One-on-one scheduled check-ins with my pre-arranged mentor, whom I can also go see to help me co-regulate as needed

Test Accommodations	
Traditional Accommodations	**Accommodations Using an ACEs Lens**
Extended time on tests and quizzes	Extended time to regulate if I need this, and academic modifications of my assignments when I am dysregulated
Quiet testing room with small group setting	Quiet area for me to use when I need to regulate my nervous system: a practiced routine of 2-3 regulatory strategies (such as deep breaths, hand message, or taking a walk)

My Goals	
Traditional Goals	**ACEs Lens Goals:**
Improve my mental math skills	Learn to regulate with an adult before I reach the tipping point
Get better at asking for help when needed	Use the resiliency team and the Amygdala Reset Area
Join a school club or activity	Create a journal of my ups and downs to track my progress

Determining Goals

What are this student's strengths?

What are this student's areas of interest and expertise?

Who are the adults in the building that can support and uncondi-tionally co-regulate with this student through conflicts and celebrations?

Key mentors assigned to this student:

What are the experiences, events, sights, sounds, smells, relation-ships, and people who can unexpectedly activate or trigger this student resulting in anxiety or negative emotion? How can we mitigate those activators?

Download the entire template:

> *"Education discipline protocols must begin to prioritize*
> *nervous system regulation."*
>
> DR. LORI DESAUTELS

Polyvagal Chart Simplified for Students

Download the Simplified Polyvagal Chart here:
https://supportablesolutions.com/teaching-resources/

Persike, C. (2022). Polyvagal theory: Autonomic nervous system states (Infographic).
Supportable Solutions, LLC. https://supportablesolutions.com/teaching-resources/.
Used with permission.

267

Discipline Ladder

Brain Aligned Classroom Discipline and Leadership

Large Back-Up Systems.
Office is involved.
Create a plan upon return.

"+"   "–"

Omission Practices for the Group.
1. A focus on target challenges that are troublesome for the group.
2. Together, we select the challenges we will practice and work through and eliminate through a gradual process.
3. Reduce the number of time behavior occurs.
4. Preparation focused on process. Begin with an attainable benchmark and number.

Medium Back Up System.
What experiences does this student need to be successful?
- Where is the space?
- What adults are available in this space?
- The goal of the medium back up system is to regulate in this space. When the student and adult are regulated, we then create a plan for re-entry into the classroom.

Omission Process for Individual.
1. What is one behavioral challenge we want to see less of?
2. Students track and record their behaviors with our feedback.

Small Back Up Systems.
1. Routines and sanctions that are taught, modeled, and practiced ahead of time.
2. Establish three regulatory practices that can occur in the moment. (Secondary)
3. Individual Amygdala Reset Bags. (Elementary)
4. Areas are neutral; do not equate to "time out" areas.
5. Use amygdala area to model when you are feeling anxious/overwhelmed. "What do you need when you return to work?"
6. Work missed is made up when there is regulation, and this is discussed ahead of time

Incentive Systems.
- How do I structure the first hour or morning?
- What is our class challenge?
- Incentivizing is not rewarding as we are cultivating "time" to prime the brain and body for emotional, social and cognitive well-being.

Individual Incentive Systems.
1. Individualized – What accommodations can we create for this student?
2. Chunking assignments, time on task, and nervous system regulation (Building in an individualized student plan around specific repetitive behavioral challenges
3. Frequent touch points/ check-ins.
4. Love Language of Student.

Co-Regulation.
Co-regulation is sitting beside one another as we help to digest, integrate, calm and experience the accumulating events that feel overwhelming. Each moment with a child or youth is a therapeutic moment as we deepen our connection and presence with another.

Co-regulation is not:
- Rewarding negative behavior but creates a nervous system state in both adult and student that can process what went awry and possible solutions.
- Enabling negative behavior but to create connections and buy time so the nervous system can find some balance and stability.

Touch Points.
Moments, minutes and periods of time building relationships with students and colleagues. It is in this safe, emotionally available space, we can tap into a student's culture, environments, experiences, passions, interests, and strengths.

Set the Temperature and Build the Nest.
When we prepare a nest for our students, we are planning, constructing and cultivating an environment that meets the bio-social and emotional needs of our students! Nests are created by many materials that hold it together for strength and endurance. How can we prepare a nest for our students?

Educator Nervous System States.
Classroom and school procedures, routines, and structures create predictability.

Download the Ladder here:

Brain-Aligned Classroom Discipline and Leadership Foundational

a. Awareness of Educator Nervous System States

b. Relational, Preventative, and Brain-Aligned Tier 1 and Discipline Practices Are Built Into Our Procedures, Routines, and Rituals, Shifting When Needed

c. Adults' Current Ideology About Discipline Protocols

d. A Review and Reflection of Current Discipline Policies

a. Awareness of Educator Nervous System States

Adult nervous system states lie at the root of student discipline challenges. As educators, we are called to check in with our own nervous systems. This is where we can sense our degree of safety, connection, and awareness of how we are experiencing a situation or condition. We begin by asking ourselves:

1. Do I have three regulatory practices for in-the-moment activators or push buttons?

2. Am I sensing how experiences, settings, specific individuals, and anything from my internal, external, or inter-relational environments are affecting how I feel in my body and mind?

3. Do I have trusting connections with colleagues and school administrators in this district, building, department, or grade level?

4. Guiding questions for deeper exploration:

- Do I feel safe and connected with my colleagues and administrators?

- Are there conflicts around me that are not being repaired or discussed?

- Are there days of the week, times of day, or places where I feel more dysregulated?

- Are there days of the week, times of day, or places where I feel safer and connected?

- Am I able to share my concerns in an authentic way?

- How are we caring for each other in our buildings and districts?

- Do our staff, PLC, and department meetings begin with brain-aligned practices (such as breath, rhythm, journaling, art, and other sensory rituals)?

- Do certain students trigger me more than others?

- Are my responses to each student's behavior the same?

- Which students do I redirect most often?

- What behaviors do they show?

- What behaviors do I expect to see?

- What emotion do I feel when certain students do not follow my directions?

- Which behaviors push my buttons most?

- What time in the day do I feel the calmest and happiest with my students?

- Under what classroom condition do I interact best with my students (silence, chatter, students listening to me speak, students speaking to each other, etc.)?

- To which students do I feel the closest in my class?

- Why do I feel connected to them?

- Which students are my "favorites?" Why?

- Do I understand the cultural identity of my students? If not, what can I do to learn more?

- Do I attempt to make connections to my students' culture and backgrounds in an authentic way?

- Do my students feel safe to be their authentic selves?

- Am I creating a community of inclusion and equitable access? Does everyone get what they need (which may not be the same thing for everyone)?

- Do we have to make people feel bad to change their behavior?

- How would you define consequences?

- What are the purposes of consequences?

- Are consequences intended or implemented to push students away or to strengthen relationships during conflicts?

- How does vocal tonality and timing of a consequence impact a child or adolescent?

- What are three recent consequences that you have experienced in your life? How were they helpful or not helpful?

b. Relational, Preventative, and Brain-Aligned Tier 1 Practices

Consider how our discipline practices are built into our procedures, routines, and rituals, and how they can shift as needed.

- Are we intentional about how we begin and end classes, the school day, and during transitions, allowing ourselves to sit beside our students and help them to feel safe, connected, and heard?

- What do the first 10-20 minutes of the school day look and feel like in this classroom and in this building?

- Is there a coherent rhythm to the collective student body and staff, or is there collective dysregulation?

- How can we create routines and procedures that meet students where they are developmentally in their nervous system?

- Do students experience agency, choices, and autonomy as we set the temperature for the day or class period during these brain-aligned mornings, transitioning, and afternoon rituals or routines?

- How do my guidelines meet students where they are and hold high expectations for their emotional and cognitive well-being?

- Are we checking in with the language of the nervous system (brain and body states), using the language of science to examine our sensations, emotions, and thought processes that we generate, practice, and reflect with others?

- Are students given opportunities and experiences to reflect?

- Is this school or district intentional about providing Focused Attention Practices or nervous system-aligned bell work as we move into academic content and transition throughout the day?

- Are students experiencing the consistency of procedures as they move from class to class, grade level to grade level, and building to building?

- Is there predictability in our classes, schools, and districts?

- Rather than continually discussing behaviors, are we integrating the language of science as we discuss what lies beneath behaviors?

c. Adults' Current Ideology About Discipline Protocols

In the words of Parker Palmer, "We teach who we are." The following questions (from Chapter Five) can help us reflect on our own belief systems, perceptions, nervous system stories, and patterned reactions and behaviors.

1. How were you disciplined as a child?

2. For what behaviors were you typically disciplined?

3. Who disciplined you most often?

4. When you remember your own childhood discipline, what three sensations, feelings, or words come to mind?

5. How did you feel after you were disciplined?

6. What did you usually say, feel, or do to yourself after you were disciplined?

7. How did you repair with the adults (or did you repair with them) after you were disciplined?

8. Did you feel safe when you were disciplined?

9. Through moments of discipline, did you feel connected to the adult?

10. What stories, beliefs, thoughts, and perceptions from these past experiences are activated today?

Applied Educational Neuroscience addresses a new lens for "discipline" through educator brain and body state, co-regulation, touch points, and teaching our staff and students about their neuroanatomy. Educator brain and body state is critical, as discipline is founded upon adult self-exploration of perceptions, strings of thoughts, and belief systems from embodied experiences. It requires courage and transparency to look within.

Why? Because to sit beside a child in distress requires us in all moments to know ourselves through the history of past experiences. Our experiences become perceptions, beliefs, and practiced thoughts that are held in our brains and bodies. These practiced thoughts are encoded with emotion and become hard-wired habits of thought that are challenging to change. When we are unaware of how our past experiences seep into the present moment, we often do not question or wonder if there could be a different way. How we view discipline is personal and often is intimately connected to our values that have formed from the practiced thoughts we have activated repeatedly!

The previous questions help us to explore how our beliefs, values, and perceptions of discipline have formed as we discipline our own children and students. It is an initial step in understanding where and why we feel obstacles and challenges.

d. A Review and Reflection of Current Discipline Policies

- How many of these practices are reactive?

- How many of these practices require student obedience?

- When looking at your consequences, create a list of current practices and consequences.

- Is there a current assessment or mechanism that shows whether these current practices are working?

- What current strategies or practices does your district use to reward or incentivize student behaviors?

- How many of your current practices and strategies are preventative? In other words, are there any current discipline practices you would define as Tier One practices?

- What are your current school and classroom rules?

- In reviewing student discipline handbooks and codes, what are two or three sentences that would describe your current discipline protocols?

- Do you have behavior data for:

    - Classroom kick-outs?

    - Office referrals (parental contacts)?

    - Detentions?

    - Suspensions (in school and out of school)?

    - Other punitive practices, strategies, or rules?

- Are there correlations for specific classrooms with higher numbers of discipline referrals?

- What are the infractions for most of these referrals?

- Is there a repairing protocol (time, effort, discussion, and reflection) for staff and students to amend the rupture together following an incident?

1. Touch Points: Touch points are moments, minutes, and conversations that are intentionally centered inside cultivating relationships with students and colleagues. Touch points occur in an emotionally available interpersonal space where the "magic of resonance" can happen. In this space, we can tap into a student's identity, culture, environment, experiences, passions, interests, and strengths. This is the resonance of connection. These touch points occur all day long. Examples might be greetings, check-ins, morning meetings, bell work, transitions, and end-of-the-day rituals.

- What people or experiences impacted your day today? This week?

- What were the best parts of learning or being in school this week?

- What were the hardest or the most challenging events or situations that occurred this week or over the past few days?

- What people are your touch points? What is it about these people that feels safe to you?

- What experiences have felt unsafe this week or today?

- What has been painful?

- What has made you happy?

- What do you hope for this year?

- If you could choose a book, movie, or song that most resembles your life right now, what would that be?

- Can you think of candy or snacks that describe your autonomic nervous system (ANS) in different autonomic states?

  ◦ When my ANS is calm, happy, and safe, the candy or snack I am most like is _____.

  ◦ When my ANS is irritated or angry, the candy or snack I most like is _____.

  ◦ When I feel sad, alone, or numb, the candy or snack I most like is _____.

  ◦ We can repeat this autonomic check-in with choices of music, drinks, TV shows, books, and colors. When we recognize our brain and body states, we are learning the language of our nervous systems, and this awareness incrementally helps us to feel safe and connected to others.

a. **Validation:** When we listen for the sensations and feelings beneath the words of an experience, problem, celebration, or challenge, mirroring those feelings back, we are helping one another to feel seen, heard, and felt. Examples of validating statements might be:

- I cannot imagine how you must feel.

- This must feel so unfair.

- I cannot imagine how exhausting this is for you.

- What a difficult position you are in.

- I am so sorry that this has happened.

- It must feel so lonely.

- It must make your entire head hurt!

- You must feel unsafe right now!
- Wow! I cannot imagine how relieved you must feel!
- When I hear you share this, I can feel your joy inside of me!

b. **Checking in with Nonverbal Communication:** What are my facial expressions, postures, and gestures? What does my vocal tone share about the way I am experiencing the environment, another person, or a specific encounter or event?

c. **Questions for De-escalation**
- Is there anything you need right now that would ease your mind and your feelings?
- Is there another way you would like to "talk" about this without using words?
- Do you want to draw how your body feels and looks?
- I have paper, pens, crayons, and clay, or you could paint a picture.
- If you could list three or four people who you need right now, who would they be?
- What character, book, or movie best describes you right now? Would you like to write about this or create an image?
- What do you need?
- How can I help?
- What can we do to make this better?

2. **Build the Nest**: When a bird constructs a nest, it builds a structure or place for laying eggs and sheltering its young. When we prepare a nest for our students, we are planning, constructing, and cultivating an environment that meets the bio-social and emotional needs of our students! Nests are created from materials that hold them together for strength, endurance, and adaptability. How can we prepare a nest for our students? As administrators, how are we preparing the nests for our staff?
- Flexible and developmental rules or guidelines that change throughout the year based on the students' developmental, emotional, and social needs.

- Are we providing opportunities (autonomic state check-ins) for our students and staff to emotionally check in throughout the day? What does this look like? Are we asking for periodic feedback (a few times each semester) from staff and students?

- Are we emphasizing nervous system states when we discuss behaviors? In other words, are we delving beneath the behaviors to understand the cultural, social, and neurodivergent needs of our staff and students?

- Are we providing frequent feedback for each other? How is this cultivated and shared? Are we addressing behavioral challenges inside non-public conversations and with our nonverbal communication (such as signals, post-its, messages, and affirmations)?

- Are we continually repairing or augmenting the nest when the structure weakens and loses its sustainability?

3. What Co-Regulation Is: Co-regulation is sitting beside one another as we help a student or an adult to digest, integrate, and discharge toxic emotions that can increase a sense of balance and grounding when we feel overwhelmed and disconnected. Each moment with a child or youth can be a therapeutic moment as we deepen our connection and felt presence with another. The goal of co-regulation is assisting another person to access the cortex of the brain to facilitate clarity of thought and emotional awareness, which leads to regulation through resonance among individuals. Co-regulation is about the setting or space inside a classroom or school that feels safe and emotionally trusted.

- Co-regulation is a practice that is taught ahead of a crisis. It is one of the procedures and routines we teach every day.

- Co-regulation is necessary for strengthening connections with students.

- Co-regulation is a touch point.

- Co-regulation occurs when there has been a rupture in the classroom, with another person, or within any experience where a student has shifted into a survival drive. In this fight-flight or collapsed survival state, children and youth are unable to process redirection, words, logic, and consequences, or look forward to rewards.

- Co-regulation addresses the nervous system state as we focus on "getting to the cortex." When we are conversing, learning, teaching, and processing from the cortex, we can repair a relationship or condition, and reflect upon an experience.

- Co-regulation leads to repairing a relationship, experience or setting, as well as re-engaging with learning missed and finding opportunities to begin again.

The following questions are powerful for all students as we begin to understand how our questions can become a part of the co-regulatory process following our safe presence and validation. We begin by asking ourselves:

- Where is the co-regulation occurring, and with whom?

- Does this setting feel safe?

- Have students had a voice in deciding which adults they trust when feeling dysregulated?

Then we ask our students these questions:

- What do you need me to understand?

- What am I not hearing or understanding? What am I missing?

- How can I help you feel safer?

- What feels unfair or unjust about this situation?

- Can you share an image or a symbol that describes how you are experiencing your feelings or sensations?

- If you could give me the power to be in your head and heart, what would I understand or know that feels confusing to me right now?

4. What Co-Regulation Is Not:

- Rewarding negative behavior. Instead, co-regulation creates nervous system states in both adults and students that can process what went awry, along with recognizing possible solutions.

- Leaving the room, eating cookies, and returning without consequences. Instead, co-regulation creates experiences that support a shift and an understanding of behaviors.

- Enabling negative behavior. Instead, co-regulation creates connections and buys time so that the nervous system can find some balanced calm, safety, and connection.

- Returning to the classroom or school without accommodations, repairing, joint planning, and modifications. Instead, co-regulation is an experience that helps the nervous system find peace and balance by creating an emotionally available space and presence for both students and adults to repair together and create a new plan.

So what *is* co-regulation? Simply put, co-regulation is a means of restoring balance to the teacher-student relationship. It requires that the students and the adults repair together following ruptures while another adult takes over the classroom.

5. Simple Incentive Systems: Incentive systems are a part of the nests that we construct for our classrooms and schools. The following questions can help you cultivate the practices and emotional environments that are conducive to felt safety. Simple incentive systems do not reward negative behavior. They focus on the process of incremental shifts while validating and inviting students to be an active part of this process. These systems provide the time needed for reparation and reflection.

- How do I structure the first hour or morning?
- What is the feel of the collective nervous system state in my classroom or building?
- Am I intentionally meeting students in their brain and body state with check-ins, brain-aligned bell work, novelty, and touch points?
- When the entire class is struggling and the class's collective nervous system is in a state of dysregulation, do I openly question, discuss, and problem solve as I speak to our challenges from the morning, afternoon, day, or week? What is our class challenge at this moment? How can we support one another?
- Are students provided opportunities for reflection, reframing, and sharing challenges through journaling, art, or discussion groups?
- Are we incorporating breath and movement to regulate at the beginning of the day or class period?

6. Tier Two and Tier Three Supports for Students Needing Additional Connection and Co-Regulation: In this section of the discipline ladder, we observe and attend to our students who are carrying in significant pain (and therefore dysregulation) and will benefit from adding accommodations to their procedures and routines. It is critical that we teach these supports ahead of a crisis, and that students clearly understand that everyone in this class and school gets what they need. We plan ahead, practice, and create opportunities for student agency and autonomy through our questions, surveys, and feedback from students and staff.

- What connective and regulatory accommodations can we create for this student to provide consistency as they move from classroom to classroom?

- Our students may feel overwhelmed by the academic content when they are functioning in survival states, so we may need to chunk assignments, add frequent check-ins, and offer additional time on tasks, but the RECAST template gives teams of teachers a protocol for individualized accommodations.

7. Omission Process for Individuals: These questions address the process of gradually lessening the behaviors, while also teaching our students that behaviors are only the signals of how we are experiencing a comment, activity, relationship, or event inside our nervous systems. We can provide students with this autonomic nervous system tracker to begin associating how we sense and feel with an understanding of how that manifests in our behaviors.

Download the PARASYMPATHETIC PATHWAY chart here:

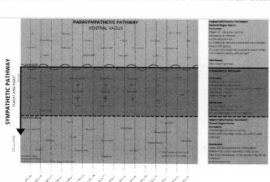

a. What is one behavioral challenge that we want to see less?

b. Students track and record their nervous system states that align with their behavioral responses as we review and reflect with feedback.

c. Guiding questions:

- What did you feel and sense in your body? (hot, see red, numb, fuzzy, etc.)
- What thought or feeling did you have before and/or after the experience?
- Is there a person, place, sound, sight, or thought that you felt may have activated you?
- What options could we explore if something similar occurs tomorrow?

8. Small Backup Systems: These are routines and procedures that teach the sanctions for disruptive behaviors ahead of time. These routines and procedures are discussed, practiced, repeatedly modeled, and rehearsed. We will need to periodically adjust them based on the developmental and changing needs of our students. Students are provided menus of regulatory practices that feel grounding and calming ahead of disruptions. We can offer a space for these practices, or students can choose a space that feels regulative. The new menus for our students and staff can be found on my website. If students spend ten minutes with these practices, they will need to make up any missed work once they are feeling safe and connected again. These areas for regulation are neutral and do not equate to "time out or tabbing out" areas. In a small backup system, students can implement one of their practices for celebratory purposes as well. Examples of celebratory purposes are completing work, talking through a challenge, preparing for an assessment or specific event, and following through with an agreement. We want to normalize these areas and practices as ways we attune and attend to our nervous systems when we feel dysregulated or when we feel a sense of agency or accomplishment.

9. Omission Practices for the Group: This is very similar to the omission practices for individuals except that we are collaborating as a "classroom family." Because we are learning about one another's needs, cultures, and identities, this process is a part of our school or classroom nest. Below are the targeted components of the group omission process.

a. There is an agreed-upon focus of a class challenge that is troublesome for everyone.

b. We discuss in a morning or afternoon meeting what is going well as students provide their thoughts and experiences.

c. Together, we select the challenges (procedures or class rules) on which we will focus and begin tracking as a class. An example of this process would be the time it takes to get seated with our Chromebooks open and tabs ready. Other examples for younger students are the length of restroom breaks, procedures coming in from related arts, or talking over people when someone is sharing. Together, we begin a gradual process of tracking collectively through a process of elimination as we encourage each other with class-driven incentives. What could those look like in your middle-school classroom? What could they look like in a third-grade classroom? If it took us 15 minutes on Monday to break and return to the classroom, we might agree to 13.5 minutes by Friday. We always begin with an attainable benchmark agreed upon by the class.

d. Guiding questions

   • How long does it take for us to return to work mode?

   • How did we support each other?

   • What were our obstacles?

   • How can we mitigate those obstacles?

   • What role or responsibility could each person be assigned in this collective effort?

   • What does leadership look like in this class?

10. Interpersonal Space of Felt Safety/Medium Backup System: This system represents a fundamental change in our discipline protocols. Traditionally, when children become dysregulated and are not able to stay in the classroom to find some calm, most students are sent to the large backup system also known as the school's office. A medium backup system, rather than being the office, is a safe place in the building with a trusted adult. For a medium backup system to succeed, leadership and relationships are a priority. This system can look different in every school, but the common goal is always modeling and teaching the behaviors that you want to see through strengthening relationships. Co-regulation requires an adult that the student trusts and is accessible as needed throughout the day. It requires procedures and structures that are prepared ahead of time by building administrators, and was introduced in my previous book, *Connections Over Compliance*[241].

The following are questions to explore before we integrate the interpersonal in-between space of the medium backup system:

a. Is there a growing and mutual understanding that regulated adults are able to regulate students?

b. Are we providing our staff with the scientific literature on how our autonomic nervous systems drive our feelings, thoughts, and behaviors?

c. Are we providing opportunities for staff to authentically share their nervous system states throughout the days and weeks? What does this look like in our buildings?

d. Can we partner with our students' parents to share how our nervous system states impact thoughts, feelings, and behaviors?

e. Are we creating collaborative discussions where resistance and skepticism are heard, seen, and felt?

f. Have we explored and studied the discipline data in our schools?

g. Are staff making connections and strengthening relationships with those adults who are carrying in nervous system states of survival?

h. Have we explored and discussed the Conflict Cycle with our staff?

i. Are we able to identify staff members who are willing and able to co-regulate students in moments of heightened disruptive behaviors?

j. Do we hold each other accountable for modeling the behaviors that we want to shift, understanding that these behaviors are only the cues of a struggling nervous system?

k. Do we have predetermined spaces in our buildings that are conducive for co-regulation?

l. Are we understanding and willing to provide the needed time it will take for the reparation of conflicts or breaking the Conflict Cycle?

m. Are we teaching our students about the nervous system states and how our brains and bodies prioritize states of protection and disconnection when we feel dysregulated and rough?

n. When both student and adult find calm and can access the cortex, these questions can be answered independently, and then shared with each other.

11. Nervous System Repair and Restoration: Questions create a collaborative experience by cultivating a sense of safety and autonomy once students and teachers have had time and space to prepare for restoration and repair after a conflict.

a. What was our challenge? In other words, was there something that activated or triggered us that we were not aware of?

b. During this challenge, what were we feeling in our body? (hot, sweaty, headache, seeing red, hearing black-out, tight chest or muscle tension, rapid heart rate, etc.)

c. Do we recall any thoughts that we were thinking?

d. What do we think or feel led up to our challenge?

e. How did we handle it? Can we think of one strength we implemented or wish we would have implemented?

f. If we both get a do-over, how could we handle this more peacefully?

g. What are two adjustments in our nervous systems, thoughts, and actions that we will try the next time?

h. How? Let's map out a plan.

12. Large Back-Up Systems: Our "repeat offender" students are often, if not always, living in toxic levels of stress, which sensitize their stress response systems to even ordinary experiences. We cannot always know what adversities they have carried in, but we are learning that these students need daily touch points and check-ins. They may require procedures filled with connections and regulatory practices that provide the nurturing and presence to set them up for emotional-social and cognitive well-being. If these students have been suspended, frequent check-ins with a caring adult will be foundational when they return to school. In a large backup system, the administration and the office are involved and will need to share with parents or caregivers, as restorative practices will be a priority.

Guiding questions:

a. What are the conditions (setting, days, times of day, triggers, people) that activate these suspensions, kick-outs, or referrals?

b. What are the patterned behaviors?

c. What have we in the school created in the past to interrupt these behaviors?

d. Have we tried to replace the behavior that is not acceptable with other options?

e. What has worked well with this student?

f. What have we learned from this string of discipline referrals?

g. What is occurring, or how is the student experiencing the school environment when these referrals occur?

h. What is our plan?

i. How will we collectively move forward?

GLOSSARY

amygdala - These two almond-shaped structures lie deep in the limbic system, where they function as the brain's "smoke detector" to identify whether incoming input is relevant for our survival.

anchors - These are conditions in our lives that cultivate felt safety. Anchors could be safe places, people, or objects.

Applied Educational Neuroscience (AEN) - This framework supports emotional, social, and cognitive well-being. It consists of four pillars that blend together and include: adult brain and body state; co-regulation; touch points; and teaching our staff and students about their neuroanatomy.

brainstem - The most primitive part of the brain (also referred to as the "reptilian brain") is responsible for all the autonomic functions such as breathing, respiration, and body temperature. It is also where we feel temperature changes, coldness, wetness, hunger, and pain. It is the region of the brain that attends to survival.

broken belongings - When we grow up without a predictable, consistent, and emotionally available caregiver, our attachment dynamics become broken, and it is challenging to trust other adults when these broken attachments have been a part of our lived experiences.

co-regulation - This process is our biological priority, as human beings are social creatures who need one another to find feelings of safety and connection.

cortex - This is the outer layer of the brain. The frontal lobes, which make up the bulk of our neocortex begin to develop at a rapid pace in the second year of life. The cortex is the seat of our executive functions which include, among other functions, problem solving, emotional regulation, sustained attention, empathy, planning, and prediction.

crisis teaching - This is teaching when we, our students, or our school are functioning from survival states in the nervous system. In this state, we are sometimes not thinking clearly or emotionally regulating, and may often be reacting rather than acting intentionally.

death feigning - This is a state function of the nervous system when we have moved to a collapsed and immobilized state in which our sensory systems are so overwhelmed that we disconnect from everything around us while our nervous systems prepare for danger.

distorted belongings - Because attachment is our greatest developmental need, we will attach to any group that provides felt safety, even if it is a group or gathering that is harmful, toxic, and could create emotional pain (such as a gang).

downregulating - This is the movement of lessening or diminishing a behavior or emotion. Example: "We want to downregulate the anxiety she is experiencing while upregulating positive emotion from visualization, deep breathing, or moments of gratitude."

embodied shared experiences - We also call these "felt shared experiences." An example would be goose bumps when we experience a loving moment with another.

hippocampus - This seahorse-shaped structure found deep in the temporal lobes of the brain is responsible for learning and memory.

interoceptive - Interoception is the awareness of sensations felt within the body.

myelination - This anatomical term refers to the process of forming a fatty protein coat known as a myelin sheath around a nerve, allowing nerve impulses to move more quickly and efficiently.

Nervous System-Aligned Trauma-Responsive Teaching - This is a collective term for the practices and conditions that we integrate into our classrooms and schools to prepare our nervous systems for feeling and experiencing felt safety through deepening connections and co-regulatory processes attending to our senses. Examples: breath, movement, warmth, pressure, and art.

neuro-rigidity - Joe Dispenza, D.C. coined this term for the hard-wired habits and conditions that we acquire (thoughts, feelings, and behaviors) and that are difficult to change.

neuroception - Dr. Stephen Porges coined this term for our nervous system's autonomic intuition. Neuroception operates below consciousness and attends to everything in our outer and inner environments that feels safe, unfamiliar, or threatening.

neuroplasticity by default - This concept refers to the habits of thoughts, feelings, and behaviors that we embody without intentional thought and that arise from patterned repetition.

neurotransmitters - These can be likened to chemical messengers that carry chemical signals between neurons.

noncoding DNA - This type of DNA does not code for proteins and was once considered "junk DNA," but now we are recognizing that it has important functions such as gene regulation.

prosody - This linguistic term refers to the vocal tonality (or tone of voice) through which we can signal safety or cue threat or danger to our listeners.

relational safety - This is feeling secure and cared for within a human relationship.

relational window of tolerance - Collectively, as a school, department, grade level, or district, we are emphasizing the importance of relationships as we check into our individual and collective nervous system states and the windows of relational tolerance that we activate.

reticular activating system (RAS) - The RAS is a network of neurons located in the brainstem that is responsible for regulating wakefulness and sleep-wake transitions. It is also a central node for most of our senses as we process the world around us, filtering stimuli and connecting them to our conscious thoughts, feelings, and sensations.

Sensorimotor Integration - This complex process in the central nervous system produces task-specific motor output based on the rapid and selective integration and organization of sensory information from our internal, external, and relational environments.

social loss - Educators use this term to describe the deficit of social skills that our children and youth have and are experiencing based on the isolating and unpredictable hardships of the global pandemic.

state regulation - This is the activation of our autonomic functioning at any given moment.

synapses - These are connections between neurons in the brain that begin to form pathways and circuits producing feelings, thoughts, and behaviors.

touch points - These micro-moments of personal connection help the nervous system to feel safe, secure, and connected.

Teaching Modules

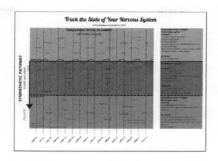

BONUS

Download the "Polyvagal Theory Modules: Elementary and Middle School Ages" here:

EPILOGUE

It is critical to begin deeply understanding that our bodies are the social and emotional organs that we often attribute to the brain. Our bodies lead our brains as there are many more nerve fibers that travel from our bodies to the brain than from the brain to the body, which I discussed in this book. When adverse and traumatic experiences occur in our lives, we can unconsciously embody these experiences, cultivating our own unique set of associations, patterns, and defense strategies that emerge out of our cultures, relationships, and environments.[242]

In early childhood, our nervous systems are adapting to our environments through our sensory and emotional systems to help us to survive. We sense and feel our way through the world as our capacity for sensation and motion develops and comes online prior to speech and language. Author and therapist Amanda Blake writes, "As children, we adopt emotional and relational patterns not as an abstraction, but primarily through what we sense and feel."[243]

Because we do not have access to language and conceptual thinking in the early years, we hold our memories through a felt body-based and unconscious memory as these implicit emotional memories are first to develop and this occurs through images, sensations, and feelings. These implicit memories are fickle and can be confusing. Implicit memory is not experienced as a memory that you recall and verbally share. When an implicit memory occurs, we often feel it through contraction, tightness, tears, goose bumps, cringing, squinting our eyes, shortened or shallow breathing, feeling sweaty, or a reaction that feels as if we are on autopilot. Physical contraction referred to as "armoring" can occur when we have a physical reaction to implicit memories and our bodies hold this reaction with tension as if we are holding our breath until the danger passes.[244]

If we tighten and tense up repetitively, our bodies develop a neuromuscular pattern that can impact our physiological, emotional, and cognitive health. Our bodies begin to take on the shape of our repeated sensory and emotional experiences.[245]

On the other side of armoring, is a hierarchical state I shared throughout the book that occurs when we disconnect from our bodies and the world around us. When human beings face a terrifying or overwhelming experience, they may mentally and emotionally escape or retreat in the only way that is accessible or available to them. They may move into a quiet and possibly imaginative world, shutting down the overwhelming external environments and experiences.[246]

Intentional Neuroplasticity: Moving Our Nervous Systems and Educational System Toward Post-Traumatic Growth is about meeting our children, youth, families, and colleagues in their nervous system states. It is in the present moment, where we can address the sensations and feelings that can begin to repair emotional pain, by integrating experiences and relationships that provide and nourish felt safety. Our bodies are both our lens of perception and our instruments of action.[247] Our biology is perception as we see the world as we are.

ACKNOWLEDGMENTS

These pages are filled with stories, questions, applied research, and practices that have been germinating in my mind and heart for a lifetime, but this book has manifested in this time because of the brilliant and courageous educators and students whom I have had the privilege to sit beside and learn from each day as we move through the challenges and shifts that our schools, families, and communities have recently encountered and are encountering yet again as another school year is born. I am learning that growth and healing occur in the present time. We are learning how trauma impacts the developing brain and body as we now address how connection, resiliency, and growth are significant players in our healing and wholeness. Post-traumatic growth is present-time work.

I want to thank my graduate students, colleagues, and exceptional educators Sarah Guest, Jenn Haak, Dr. Dustin Springer, and Pennie Gregory for enthusiastically sharing their personal narratives at the end of each chapter with extraordinary authenticity and passion. I am forever grateful for these contributions. Educator, colleague, and friend Kathryn Parthun was my brilliant contributor and co-author of the Polyvagal Theory-informed educational content and practices for educators and students; this material is shared throughout the book. I want to give educator Connie Persike a huge thank you for working through many of the practices and resources with her eye for detail and precision of content. A huge thank you to the Metropolitan School District of Lawrence Township (Indianapolis) for allowing me to be an integral, daily part of co-teaching at Harrison Hill Elementary and Belzer Middle School during the past two years of a global pandemic. These schools are where so many of the practices shared in this book came to life each week in our second-, third-, fourth-, sixth-, and seventh-grade classrooms. These past two years were filled with chronic unpredictability in our schools, and I am forever grateful for the educators who invited me in each week to co-teach during this unprecedented time.

This book would not be complete if I had not had the input, feedback, and encouragement of my graduate students from Cohort Six and Cohort Seven in Butler University's Applied Educational

Neuroscience Certificate program. The exquisite illustrations for each chapter and the book's cover were collectively created by my youngest daughter Regan Desautels and her fiancé and best friend Alexis Gomez, astonishing artists who worked tirelessly and passionately for months bringing each chapter to life through the intricate images, colors, and graphic stories originating from their selected quotes in each chapter and the introduction. I am struggling to find the words to thank my editor and friend Alan Lipton, whose genius in capturing my mind and heart in every word and sentence is a gift of language for which I will be forever grateful in this book, as well as my previous book, *Connections Over Compliance*. Alan, thank you for the opportunity to work beside you for so many years and for dedicating this past year to the stories, research, and the applied practices that you have so eloquently and linguistically helped me express. Nancy, it is because of you and Wyatt-MacKenzie Publishing that this book will take flight in the world, and I am eternally grateful and so in awe of how you and your team have crafted and cultivated each book that I have authored and co-authored on this educational journey: *Unwritten, The Story of a Living System: A Pathway to Enlivening and Transforming Education*; *Eyes Are Never Quiet: Listening Beneath the Behaviors of Our Most Troubled Students*; *Connections Over Compliance: Rewiring Our Perceptions of Discipline*; and now *Intentional Neuroplasticity: Moving Our Nervous Systems and Educational System Toward Post Traumatic Growth*.

Thank you to my friends and family who always support this on-going work that drives my deep passion and presence with students, colleagues, and school communities around the world. Andrew, Sarah, and Regan, it is an honor to be your momma in this lifetime, as you teach me each day about co-regulation, connection, repairing together and the importance of presence. Michael Desautels, I love how you love and understand me in all moments, but especially those times when I am tucked away nearly every weekend in my office researching, writing, and preparing for a much different and hope-filled future for our educators, parents, and students across the world.

To my readers: May you begin to challenge, become curious, and question old ways of thinking, feeling, and believing as you lean into the miraculous superpower of our nervous systems!

END NOTES

1. Oprah Winfrey and Bruce Perry, *What Happened to You?: Conversations on Trauma, Resilience, and Healing* (New York, NY: Flatiron Books, 2021), 49-50.

2. Moheb Costandi, *Neuroplasticity* (Cambridge, MA: The MIT Press, 2016).

3. Norman Doidge, *The Brain's Way of Healing: Remarkable Discoveries and Recoveries from the Frontiers of Neuroplasticity* (New York, NY: Penguin Books, 2016), xiii.

4. Ibid., xiv.

5. Ibid., xviii.

6. Ibid., xx.

7. Lara Boyd, "Neuroplasticity Gives You The Power To Shape The Brain You Want," New World Artificial Intelligence, last modified November 4, 2020, https://www.newworldai.com/neuroplasticity-gives-you-the-power-to-shape-the-brain-you-want-dr-lara-boyd/.

8. Costandi, *Neuroplasticity*, 1-2.

9. Costandi, *Neuroplasticity*, 2.

10. Doidge, *The Brain's Way of Healing*, xix.

11. Bessel Van Der Kolk, *The Body Keeps the Score: Brain, Mind, and Body in the Healing of Trauma* (New York, NY: Penguin Books, 2015), 54.

12. Rebecca T. Leeb, Rebecca H. Bitsko, Lakshmi Radhakrishnan, Pedro Martinez, Rashid Njai, and Kristin M. Holland, "Mental Health-Related Emergency Department Visits Among Children Aged <18 Years During the COVID-19 Pandemic—United States, January 1-October 17, 2020," *Centers for Disease Control and Prevention's Morbidity and Mortality Weekly Report,* November 13, 2020, no. 69(45); 1675-1680. Available at: https://www.cdc.gov/mmwr/volumes/69/wr/mm6945a3.htm.

13. "Protecting Youth Mental Health: The U.S. Surgeon General's Advisory" (2021). Available at: https://www.hhs.gov/sites/default/files/surgeon-general-youth-mental-health-advisory.pdf.

14. Suniya S. Luthar, ed., *Resilience and vulnerability: adaptation in the context of childhood adversities* (Cambridge, U.K.: Cambridge University Press, 2003).

15. Arielle Schwartz, *The Post-Traumatic Growth Guidebook: Practical Mind-Body Tools to Heal Trauma, Foster Resilience and Awaken Your Potential* (Eau Claire, WI: PESI Publishing, Inc., 2020), 7.

16. Nicholas J. Long, Frank A. Fecser, William C. Morse, Ruth G. Newman, and Jody E. Long, *Conflict in the Classroom: Successful Behavior Management Using the Psychoeducational Model* (Austin, TX: PRO-ED Publishing, 2014), 52-53.

17. Ibid., 31-32.

18. Ibid., 35.

19. Costandi, *Neuroplasticity*, 2.

20. Zaretta L. Hammond, *Culturally Responsive Teaching and the Brain: Promoting Authentic Engagement and Rigor Among Culturally and Linguistically Diverse Students* (Thousand Oaks, CA: Corwin Press Inc., 2015), 34-36.

21. Ibid., 36.

22. Ibid., 48.

23. Winfrey and Perry, *What Happened to You?,* 29.

24. Ibid., 29-30.

25. Center on the Developing Child, Harvard University, "Brain Architecture," https://developingchild.harvard.edu/science/key-concepts/brain-architecture/#neuron.

26. Long, et al., *Conflict in the Classroom,* 52.

27. Ibid., 52.

28. Ibid., 55.

29. Vince Gowmon, "Sacrificing Authenticity for Attachment: The Adaptive Survival Responses of Children and Their Influence on Future Relationships," https://www.vincegowmon.com/sacrificing-authenticity-for-attachment/.

30. Martha B. Straus, *Treating Trauma in Adolescents* (New York, NY: Guilford Press, 2017), 44.

31. Ibid., 44.

32. Ibid., 45.

33. "PV Podcasts & Videos," Polyvagal Institute, https://www.polyvagalinstitute.org/copy-of-pv-pod-casts-videos.

34. Beth Tolley, "The problem with behaviorism," Alliance Against Seclusion & Restraint, https://endseclusion.org/research/the-problem-with-behaviorism/.

35. Lori L. Desautels, "Connections Over Compliance: Rewiring Our Perceptions of Discipline," Revelations in Education, http://revelationsineducation.com/the-book/connections-over-compliance-rewiring-our-perceptions-of-discipline/.

36. Nancy A. Heitzeg, "Education Or Incarceration: Zero Tolerance Policies And The School To Prison Pipeline" (Urbana, IL: The Forum On Public Policy, 2009). Available at: https://files.eric.ed.gov/fulltext/EJ870076.pdf.

37. Christina Caron, "In 19 States, It's Still Legal to Spank Children in Public Schools," *The New York Times,* December 13, 2018, https://www.nytimes.com/2018/12/13/us/corporal-punishment-school-tennessee.html.

38. Children's Defense Fund, *The State of America's Children, 2020: Child Poverty* (Washington, DC: The Children's Defense Fund, 2020). Available at: https://www.childrensdefense.org/policy/re-sources/soac-2020-child-poverty/.

39. Kirsten Weir, "Safeguarding student mental health: COVID-19 and its repercussions are shining a light on the critical need for school-based mental health services," *Monitor on Psychology,* no. 51(6) (September 1, 2020); 46. Available at: https://www.apa.org/monitor/2020/09/safeguarding-mental-health#:~:text=%E2%80%9CIf%20you%20look%20at%20the,at%20Chicago%20and%20chief%20k nowledge.

40. Bianna Golodryga and Yon Pomrenze, "Teachers and social workers search for students who are 'missing' in the pandemic," CNN, last updated October 19, 2020, https://www.cnn.com/2020/10/19/us/students-missing-class-pandemic-wellness/index.html.

41. Stephen W. Porges, "Neuroception: A Subconscious System for Detecting Threats and Safety" (Washington, DC: Zero to Three, May 2004). Available at: https://static1.squarespace.com/static/5c1d025fb27e390a78569537/t/5ccdff181905f41dbcb689e3/155 7004058168/Neuroception.pdf.

42. Polyvagal Institute, https://www.polyvagalinstitute.org/.

43. Nicholas J. Long, "Why adults strike back: learned behavior or genetic code?" *Reclaiming Children and Youth: Journal of Emotional and Behavioral Problems,* no. 4(1), (1995): 11-15. Available at: https://cyc-net.org/cyc-online/cycol-0104-long.html.

44. Deb Dana, *Polyvagal Exercises for Safety and Connection: 50 Client-Centered Practices* (New York, NY: W.W. Norton & Co., 2020), 6.

45. Ibid., 8.

46. Winfrey and Perry, *What Happened to You?,* 73.

47. Ibid.

48. Joe Dispenza, *Breaking the Habit of Being Yourself: How to Lose Your Mind and Create a New One* (Carlsbad, CA: Hay House Publishing, 2012), 45.

49. Joe Dispenza, *Evolve Your Brain: The Science of Changing Your Mind* (Deerfield Beach, FL: Health Communications Inc., 2007), 302, 315.

50. Dana, *Polyvagal Exercises for Safety and Connection,* 110-112.

51. Bruce D. Perry, "Video Series 1 & 2: Understanding Traumatized and Maltreated Children: The Core Concepts" (Houston, TX: ChildTrauma Academy), 58. Available at: https://www.slps.org/site/handlers/filedownload.ashx?moduleinstanceid=53801&dataid=47987&File-Name=The%20Brain%20AA%202020%20Info%20Sheet.pdf, p.58.

52. Dan Seigel, *The Developing Mind (2nd edition)* (New York, NY: Guilford Press, 2012), 39.

53. Dispenza, *Evolve Your Brain,* 212-214.

54. Straus, *Treating Trauma in Adolescents,* 58.

55. Bonnie Badenoch, *The Heart of Trauma: Healing the Embodied Pain in the Context of Relationships* (New York, NY: W.W. Norton and Co., 2018), 233.

56. Schwartz, *The Post Traumatic Growth Guidebook*, 15.

57. Dispenza, *Evolve Your Brain*, 43.

58. Dispenza, *Breaking the Habit of Being Yourself*, 58-59.

59. Ibid., 59.

60. Boyd, "Neuroplasticity Gives You The Power To Shape The Brain You Want."

61. Joe Dispenza, *You Are the Placebo: Making Your Mind Matter*, (Carlsbad, CA: Hay House Publishing, 2014), 60-61.

62. Ibid.

63. Ibid., 65.

64. Phillippa Lally, Cornelia H.M. van Jaarsveld, Henry W.W. Potts, and Jane Wardle, "How habits are formed: Modeling habit formation in the real world," *European Journal of Social Psychology* no. 40(6) (2010); cited by Dana, *Polyvagal Exercises for Safety and Connection*, xxv.

65. Badenoch, *The Heart of Trauma*, 113.

66. Schwartz, *The Post Traumatic Growth Guidebook*, 99.

67. Richard Brown and Patricia Gerbarg, *The Healing Power of the Breath: Simple Techniques to Reduce Stress and Anxiety, Enhance Concentration, and Balance Your Emotions*, (Boston, MA: Shambhala Publications, 2012), 2.

68. Ibid.

69. Jack P. Shonkoff, "How Racism in Early Life Can Affect Long-Term Health," *Knowable Magazine,* January 3, 2022. Available at: https://www.scientificamerican.com/article/how-racism-in-early-life-can-affect-long-term-health1/.

70. Ibid.

71. Ibid.

72. Ibid.

73. Ibid.

74. Ibid.

75. Ibid.

76. Ivan A. Hernandez, "Experiences Are Assets: Teachers Can Help Marginalized Students Recognize Their Strengths," *Education Week,* December 8, 2021, https://www.edweek.org/leadership/opinion-experiences-are-assets-teachers-can-help-minority-students-recognize-their-strengths/2021/12.

77. Ibid.

78. Connie Persike, "Teaching Through Trauma With the Applied Educational Neuroscience Framework," Alliance Against Seclusion and Restraint, December 5, 2021, https://endseclusion.org/2021/12/05/teaching-through-trauma-with-the-applied-educational-neuroscience-framework/.

79. The Understood Team, "3 Tiers of RTI Support," Understood for All, Inc., https://www.understood.org/articles/en/3-tiers-of-rti-support.

80. Rachel Naomi Remen, *Kitchen Table Wisdom: Stories that Heal* (New York, NY: Penguin Random House, 1996), 52.

81. "About" page for Calm mobile app (2022), https://www.calm.com/blog/about.

82. Brené Brown, *Atlas of the Heart: Mapping Meaningful Connection and the Language of Human Experience* (New York, NY: Random House, 2021), 215.

83. Lori Desautels, "Huge Emotions and the Adolescent Brain," Edutopia, June 30, 2022, https://www.edutopia.org/article/huge-emotions-and-the-adolescent-brain.

84. Bruce Perry and Maia Szalavitz, *The Boy Who Was Raised as a Dog: And Other Stories from a Child Psychiatrist's Notebook—What Traumatized Children Can Teach Us About Loss, Love, and Healing* (New York, NY: Basic Books, 2017).

85. Michele Coulombe and Kate Lafferty Márquez, "Supporting Multilingual Students in the Early Grades," Edutopia, December 2, 2020, https://www.edutopia.org/article/supporting-multilingual-students-early-grades.

86. Van Der Kolk, *The Body Keeps the Score*, 21.

87. Ibid., 64.

88. Stephen Porges, *Polyvagal Safety: Attachment, Communication, Self-Regulation* (New York, NY: W.W. Norton and Co., 2021), 91.

89. Dispenza, *Breaking the Habit of Being Yourself*, 43.

90. Ibid., 45-46.

91. Ibid., 57.

92. Perry and Szalavitz, *The Boy Who Was Raised as a Dog,* 85.

93. Winfrey and Perry, *What Happened to You?,* 26.

94. Ibid., 29.

95. "Understanding the Effects of Maltreatment on Early Brain Development," Child Welfare Information Gateway, October 2001. Available at: https://www.childwelfare.gov/pubPDFs/earlybrain.pdf.

96. Perry, *What Happened to You?,* 29-30.

97. Lori Desautels, *Connections Over Compliance: Rewiring Our Perceptions of Discipline* (Deadwood, OR: Wyatt-MacKenzie Publishing, Inc., 2020), 65.

98. Long, et al., *Conflict in the Classroom,* 32.

99. "Excessive Stress Disrupts the Architecture of the Developing Brain," National Scientific Council on the Developing Child, Working Paper 3 (Cambridge, MA: Center on the Developing Child Harvard University, updated 2014). Available at: https://46y5eh11fhgw3ve3ytpwxt9r-wpengine.netdna-ssl.com/wp-content/uploads/2005/05/Stress_Disrupts_Architecture_Developing_Brain-1.pdf.

100. Ibid.

101. Winfrey and Perry, *What Happened to You?,* 108.

102. Peter Levine and Maggie Kline, *Trauma Through a Child's Eyes: Awakening the Ordinary Miracle of Healing* (Berkeley, CA: North Atlantic Books, 2007), 4.

103. Dispenza, *Breaking the Habit of Being Yourself,* 61.

104. Ibid., 62-63.

105. Porges, *Polyvagal Safety,* 25-26.

106. Van Der Kolk, *The Body Keeps the Score,* 80.

107. Deb Dana, *Anchored: How to Befriend Your Nervous System Using Polyvagal Theory* (Louisville, CO: Sounds True Publishing, 2021), 7.

108. Ibid., 57.

109. Ibid., 56.

110. Porges, *Polyvagal Safety,* 26-27.

111. Ibid., 177.

112. Ibid.

113. Dana, *Anchored,* 7.

114. Marilyn R. Sanders and George S. Thompson, *Polyvagal Theory and the Developing Child* (New York, NY: W.W. Norton and Co., 2022), 5-6.

115. Dana, *Anchored,* 4.

116. Dana, *Anchored,* 124.

117. Maria Shriver, "I've Been Thinking..." The Sunday Paper (Los Angeles, CA: Shriver Media, 2022). Available at: https://shrivermedia.cmail19.com/t/ViewEmail/t/721EA0F08B9337752540EF23F30FEDED/FDFDF856FB3EE9B76A4D3D471B02C3D7?alternativeLink=False.

118. Porges, *Polyvagal Safety,* 145.

119. Van Der Kolk, *The Body Keeps the Score,* 113.

120. Resmaa Menakem, *My Grandmother's Hands: Racialized Trauma and the Pathway to Mending Our Hearts and Bodies* (Las Vegas, NV: Central Recovery Press, 2017), 54.

121. Dana, *Polyvagal Exercises for Safety and Connection,* 28.

122. Matthew Lieberman, *Social: Why Our Brains Are Wired to Connect* (New York, NY: Broadway Books, 2013), 43.

123. Ibid.

124. Ibid., 45.

125. Porges, *Polyvagal Safety,* 68.

126. Ibid.

127. Ibid.

128. Ibid.

129. Ibid., 263.

130. Lou Cozolino, "Interpersonal Neurobiology: Integrating Science and the Human Experience," https://www.drloucozolino.com/.

131. Louis Cozolino, *Attachment-Based Teaching: Creating a Tribal Classroom* (New York, NY: W.W. Norton and Co., 2014), 50-52.

132. Porges, *Polyvagal Safety,* 75.

133. Cozolino, *Attachment-Based Teaching,* 105-106.

134. Lou Cozolino, "The Core Elements of Social-Emotional Learning," https://www.drloucozolino.com/education/the-core-elements-of-social-emotional-learning.

135. Amy Novotney, "The risks of social isolation," *Monitor on Psychology,* no. 50(5) (May 2019); 32. Available at: https://www.apa.org/monitor/2019/05/ce-corner-isolation.

136. Lieberman, *Social*, 4.

137. Porges, *Polyvagal Safety,* 160.

138. Yasmin Anwar, "Gasp! First audio map of oohs, aahs and uh-ohs spans 24 emotions," Berkeley News, February 4, 2019, https://news.berkeley.edu/2019/02/04/audio-map-of-exclamations/.

139. Ibid.

140. Porges, *Polyvagal Safety,* 147-148.

141. Ibid., 149.

142. Ibid., 79.

143. Ibid., 26.

144. Ibid., 27.

145. Ibid., 76-77.

146. "Dr. Stephen Porges: How Social Connection Combats Stress," Finding Mastery, Episode 290, August 18, 2021, https://findingmastery.net/stephen-porges/.

147. Sarah McKibben, "The Two-Minute Relationship Builder," ASCD, https://www.ascd.org/el/articles/the-two-minute-relationship-builder.

148. Schwartz, *The Post-Traumatic Growth Guidebook,* 28.

149. Lori Desautels, "Our Nervous Systems and Trauma-Informed Teaching," Crisis Prevention Institute, July 13, 2021, https://www.crisisprevention.com/Blog/Our-Nervous-Systems-and-Trauma-Informed-Teaching.

150. Porges, *Polyvagal Safety,* 65.

151. Ibid.

152. Kalyn Belsha, Melanie Asmar, and Lori Higgins, "'I still just worry': 3 Teachers on Covid's Long Shadow Over American Schools," *The New York Times*, March 19, 2022, https://www.nytimes.com/2022/03/19/sunday-review/pandemic-school-education.html?campaign_id=9&emc=edit_nn_20220320&instance_id=56236&nl=the-morning&regi_id=116373801&segment_id=86039&te=1&user_id=7231d518f3e27011b90c89b021ff1dce&fbclid=IwAR0-x4ql7e5RdM3TGiMmb5oPsEOG-gM7VSj_9o7X13a3iIfuV933kG1EzJw.

153. Carolyn Thompson, Heather Hollingsworth, and Kalyn Belsha, "With COVID relief money, schools across U.S. take on a bigger role in student mental health," Chalkbeat, November 11, 2021, https://www.chalkbeat.org/2021/11/11/22772037/student-mental-health-covid-relief-money.

154. Kalyn Belsha, "Cardona to educators: 'I know you're stretched'," Chalkbeat, January 27, 2022, https://www.chalkbeat.org/2022/1/27/22904563/cardona-speech-educators-exhaustion-tutoring.

155. Lori Desautels and Michael McKnight, *Unwritten, The Story of a Living System: A Pathway to Enlivening and Transforming Education* (Deadwood, OR: Wyatt-MacKenzie Publishing, Inc., 2016).

156. Thema Bryant, Ruth Buczynski, Howard Stevenson, Beverly Greene, Daryl Rowe, Usha Tummala-Narra, Kevin Nadal, Anneliese Singh, Raymond Rodriguez, Shena Young, Adriana Alejandre, and Jeffrey Ring, "The Psychological Toll of Racism (and How to Work with It)," Module 1 of *The Trauma of Racism: Expert Strategies to Help Clients Heal*, National Institute for the Clinical Application of Behavioral Medicine. Available at: https://www.nicabm.com/program/trauma-racism/?itl=store.

157. Van Der Kolk, *The Body Keeps the Score*, 209.

158. Ibid, P 274.

159. "15 Most Amazing Animal Nests in the World!" The Finest, https://www.youtube.com/watch?v=Dk0IKCHhT-4.

160. "What Are Some Common Traits Between Birds and Humans?" Amazing Life.Bio, https://www.amazinglife.bio/common-traits-birds-and-humans.

161. Nel Noddings, "Schools Face "Crisis in Caring,'" *Education Week* (December 1988): 32. Available at: https://www.edweek.org/education/opinion-schools-face-crisis-in-caring/1988/12.

162. Desautels and McKnight, *Unwritten, The Story of a Living System.*

163. Lisa D. Delpit, *Other People's Children: Cultural Conflict in the Classroom* (New York, NY: The New Press, 1996), 199.

164. Stephen R. Covey, *The 7 habits of Highly Effective People: Powerful Lessons in Personal Change*, (New York, NY: Simon and Schuster, 1989), 241.

165. Brown and Patricia Gerbarg, *The Healing Power of the Breath*, 2.

166. Ibid., 3.

167. Ibid.

168. W. Timothy Gallwey, *The Inner Game of Tennis: The Classic Guide to the Mental Side of Peak Performance*, (New York, NY: Random House, 1974), 31.

169. Ibid.

170. Ibid.

171. Jill Bolte Taylor, "My stroke of insight," TED, February 2008, https://www.ted.com/talks/jill_bolte_taylor_my_stroke_of_insight.

172. Brown and Patricia Gerbarg, *The Healing Power of the Breath*, 10-11.

173. Adapted from Dana, *Polyvagal Exercises for Safety and Connection*, 87.

174. Judy Willis and Gina Mitchell, *The Neuroscience of Learning: Principles and Applications for Educators* (Chandler, AZ: Zovio, 2014), 3.

175. Ibid., 39.

176. Ibid.

177. Ibid., 51.

178. Ibid., 41.

179. Ibid., 49.

180. Dana, *Anchored*, 40.

181. Menakem, *My Grandmother's Hands*, 10.

182. Ibid., 14.

183. Albert Wong, "The Magic of Resonance," Somatopia, https://www.somatopia.com/trauma-therapy-core-skills-masterclass-day-2.

184. Cozolino, *Attachment-Based Teaching*, 177.

185. Ibid., 183.

186. Ibid.

187. https://www.somatopia.com/products/somatic-approaches-to-healing-trauma/categories/759870/posts/2485541.

188. Cozolino, *Attachment-Based Teaching*, 182.

189. Ibid., 180.

190. Mark Wolynn, *It Didn't Start With You: How Inherited Family Trauma Shapes Who We Are and How to End the Cycle* (New York, NY: Penguin Press, 2016), 24.

191. Ibid., 56.

192. Ibid., 17.

193. Ibid., 29.

194. Alice Park, "Junk DNA—Not So Useless After All," *Time*, September 6, 2012. Available at: https://healthland.time.com/2012/09/06/junk-dna-not-so-useless-after-all/.

195. Danny Vendramini, "Noncoding DNA and the teem theory of inheritance, emotions and innate behaviour," Medical Hypothesis 64 (2005): 512-19, esp. 513, doi:10.1016/j.mehy.2004.08.022.

196. Danny Vendramini, "Paper 5 of 5: The Teem Theory of NonMendelian Inheritance," 23, 25, https://www.thesecondevolution.com/paper5dna.pdf.

197. Tori Rodriguez, "Descendants of Holocaust Survivors Have Altered Stress Hormones," Scientific American Mind 26(2) (March 1, 2015), https://www.scientificamerican.com/article/descendants-of-holocaust-survivors-have-altered-stress-hormones/.

198. Alisha Rouse, "Holocaust survivors pass the genetic damage of their trauma onto their children, researchers find," The Daily Mail, August 21, 2015. Available at: https://www.dailymail.co.uk/sciencetech/article-3206702/Holocaust-survivors-pass-genetic-damage-trauma-children-researchers-find.html.

199. Tracy L. Bale, "Epigenetic and transgenerational reprogramming of brain development," Nat Rev Neurosci 16, 332–344 (April 29, 2015). https://doi.org/10.1038/nrn3818.

200. David Samuels, "Do Jews Carry Trauma in Our Genes? A Conversation With Rachel Yehuda," Tablet Magazine, December 11, 2014, https://www.tabletmag.com/sections/arts-letters/articles/trauma-genes-q-a-rachel-yehuda.

201. Menakem, My Grandmother's Hands, 43.

202. Monte Syrie, "My Room: A Realm of Possibility," http://www.letschangeeducation.com/.

203. Cozolino, Attachment-Based Teaching, 89.

204. Menakem, My Grandmother's Hands, 152.

205. Ibid., 258.

206. Ibid., 246.

207. Dana, Anchored, 38.

208. Ibid., 6.

209. Dana, Polyvagal Exercises for Safety and Connection, 75.

210. Ibid.

211. Ibid.

212. "The Shadow—Carl Jung's Warning to The World," Eternalised, October 1, 2021, https://eternalised-official.com/2021/10/01/the-shadow-carl-jung-warning/.

213. Cozolino, Attachment-Based Teaching, 189.

214. Bryant, Buczynski, et al., The Trauma of Racism.

215. Cozolino, Attachment-Based Teaching, 215.

216. Brown, Atlas of the Heart, 48.

217. Ibid., 62.

218. Porges, Polyvagal Safety, 105.

219. Desautels, Connections Over Compliance, 116-117.

220. Menakem, My Grandmother's Hands, 50-51.

221. Schwartz, The Post Traumatic Growth Guidebook, 175.

222. Parker Palmer, The Courage to Teach: Exploring the Inner Landscape of a Teacher's Life (San Francisco, CA: Wiley Publishing, 1998), 30.

223. Dana, Anchored, 123.

224. Brandie M. Oliver, "Indiana Department of Education Social-Emotional Learning Toolkit: Built Upon A Neurodevelopmental Culturally Responsive Framework" (2018). Scholarship and Professional Work – Education. 161. https://digitalcommons.butler.edu/coe_papers/161.

225. "What Is the CASEL Framework?" CASEL, https://casel.org/fundamentals-of-sel/what-is-the-casel-framework/.

226. Jan Johnson and Dave Erb, "Emotional Intelligence In the Workplace," Learning in Action (2013), https://learninginaction.com/wp-content/uploaded-files/2013/01/EQ_in_the_Workplace.pdf.

227. Long, "Why adults strike back: learned behavior or genetic code?"

228. Ibid.

229. "What Is the CASEL Framework?" CASEL.

230. https://www.cdc.gov/violenceprevention/acestudy/index.html

231. "What Is the CASEL Framework?" CASEL.

232. Brandie M. Oliver, "Indiana Department of Education Social-Emotional Learning Toolkit."

233. "What Is the CASEL Framework?" CASEL.

234. "Adverse Childhood Experiences (ACEs)," Centers for Disease Control and Prevention, last reviewed April 2, 2021, https://www.cdc.gov/violenceprevention/aces/index.html.

235. "Online Resources," Life Space Crisis Intervention, https://www.lsci.org/professionals/online-courses/.

236. Levine and Kline, *Trauma Through a Child's Eyes,* 4.

237. Winfrey and Perry, *What Happened to You?,* 108-109.

238. Ali Jawaid, Martin Roszkowski, and Isabelle M. Mansury, "Chapter Twelve—Transgenerational Epigenetics of Traumatic Stress," *Progress in Molecular Biology and Translational Science*, volume 258, 2018, 273-298. Available at: https://www.sciencedirect.com/science/article/abs/pii/S187711731830053X.

239. Winfrey and Perry, *What Happened to You?,* 61.

240. "Wendy Ellis, Director, Center for Community Resilience," https://redstone.publichealth.gwu.edu/staff/wendy-ellis.

241. Desautels, *Connections Over Compliance,* 142.

242. Amanda Blake, Your Body is Your Brain (Trokay Press, An imprint of Embright, LLC, 2018), 19.

243. Amanda Blake, Your Body is Your Brain (Trokay Press, An imprint of Embright, LLC, 2018), 20.

244. Fogal, Alan (2009). The Psychophysiology of self-awareness: Rediscovering the lost art of body sense (1st ed.). New York, NY. W.W. Norton. 100.

245. Amanda Blake, Your Body is Your Brain (Trokay Press, An imprint of Embright, LLC, 2018), 32.

246 Fogal, Alan (2009). The Psychophysiology of self-awareness: Rediscovering the lost art of body sense (1st ed.). New York, NY. W.W. Norton. 100.

247. Ibid., 100.

THE AUTHOR

Dr. Lori Desautels has been an Assistant Professor at Butler University since 2016 where she teaches both undergraduate and graduate programs in the College of Education. Lori was also an Assistant Professor at Marian University in Indianapolis for eight years where she founded the Educational Neuroscience Symposium that has now reached thousands of educators and is in its 10th year. Lori's passion is engaging her students through the social and relational neurosciences as it applies to education by integrating the Applied Educational Neuroscience framework, and its learning principles and practices into her coursework at Butler.

The Applied Educational Neuroscience Certification, created by Lori in 2016, is specifically designed to meet the needs of educators, counselors, clinicians and administrators who work beside children and adolescents who have, and are, experiencing adversity and trauma. The certification is now global and has reached hundreds of educators.

Lori's articles are published in Edutopia, Brain Bulletin, and Mind Body Spirit international magazine. She was also published in the Brain Research Journal for her work in the fifth-grade classrooms during a course release position with Washington Township Schools.

Lori continues her work co-teaching in the K-12 schools integrating her applied research into classroom procedures and transitions preparing the nervous system for learning and felt safety. Her third book, *Connections Over Compliance: Rewiring our Perceptions of Discipline,* was released in late 2020, and *Intentional Neuroplasticity: Moving Our Nervous Systems and Educational System Toward Post-Traumatic Growth*, her fourth book, was released in January 2023.

Lori has met with well over 100 school districts across the country, in Canada, Costa Rica, Australia, Scotland, England and Dubai equating to more than 100,000 educators with much more work to be done!

Made in United States
Troutdale, OR
08/07/2024